IT LOOKED LIKE FOREVER

A Ukrainian Girl's
Journey Into an
American Life
Embracing God,
Family, and
Country

Nastya Ryan

IT LOOKED LIKE FOREVER

E.B.C.K.M.E.B. Publishing Group

ISBN: 979-8-9887428-0-7 (hardcover)

First edition

Printed in the United States of America

Interior design/formatting by Vickie Swisher, Studio 20|20

This memoir is a work of non-fiction. The various experiences, places, people, and institutions mentioned are true according to my best recollection. However, some of the names of the characters and institutions have been changed to protect their identity. Also, I do not represent any companies, brands, or institutions mentioned in this memoir. The opinions...my own.

Dedication

In loving memory of my parents, Justyna and Josyf,
and all the other Ukrainian immigrants
who proudly embraced American life.

Also, with a heavy heart, I am dedicating this book
to all the brave men, women, and children
who sacrificed their lives defending their sovereign nation
after it was invaded without provocation
and then brutally attacked by Russian troops
on February 24, 2022!
Our thoughts and prayers go out to all the
courageous and freedom-loving Ukrainians.

God bless Ukraine. Slava Ukraini!

Contents

Acknowledgments vii

Chapter 1 1

Chapter 2 17

Chapter 3 29

Chapter 4 41

Chapter 5 51

Chapter 6 57

Chapter 7 63

Chapter 8 69

Chapter 9 73

Chapter 10 83

Chapter 11 89

Chapter 12 93

Chapter 13 99

Chapter 14 103

Chapter 15 111

Chapter 16 117

Chapter 17 125

Chapter 18 131

Chapter 19 137

Chapter 20 145

Chapter 21 153

Chapter 22 159

Chapter 23 165

Chapter 24 175

Chapter 25 187

Chapter 26 193

Chapter 27 199

Chapter 28 205

Chapter 29 211

Chapter 30 217

Chapter 31 223

Chapter 32 233

Chapter 33 239

Chapter 34 243

Chapter 35 251

Chapter 36 257

Chapter 37 265

Chapter 38 273

Chapter 39 283

Chapter 40 289

Chapter 41 299

Chapter 42 307

Bibliography 311

Acknowledgments

It is my privilege and honor to thank Mr. Michael Baransky, a proud American patriot and fellow Ukrainian immigrant for his valuable insights into the early days of my family's acclimation to American life. In addition, I would like to thank my sister, Katyrina Brandys, for her unwavering support and encouragement from "day one" of my endeavor. And extend my sincere appreciation to my two fine editors: my husband, Dennis Ryan, and Sue Baugh for their professional comments and suggestions as well as my outstanding formatter, Vickie Swisher.

Chapter

1

As the rain beat ferociously against the window pane, a loud boom reverberated throughout the already soaked atmosphere. Flashes of light zoomed across the sky followed by peals of thunder. For a spring day, this was not unusual, but it was almost December, and the temperature was in the sixties. The warmer weather had inspired many of our neighbors to put up their outdoor Christmas decorations.

I was sitting in our bedroom looking at an album filled with old black-and-white photographs. Suddenly, a snapshot of my young mother and father caught my eye. I wondered how they had survived a time when the world was at war, life was fragile, and the future looked bleak. Survival was a daily struggle, and freedom seemed merely a fool's dream. I realized that it was because of my parents' faith and courage that I now lived in America, the land of the free. My mind wandered back in time – trying to remember how it all began.

I was a passenger onboard the USS *General R. M. Blatchford* when it departed from Bremerhaven, Germany, on September 14, 1949. I was only three-and-a-half years old, but I can vividly recall the fury of the North Atlantic Ocean as its huge waves began pounding the decks of our vessel.

Mama and I were huddled below the deck in a small cabin with the other women and girls. I was already nauseated when the ocean's wrath descended upon our vessel. It frightened me so much that I was certain our ship was going to sink. Mama tried to reassure me that everything would be all right, but I could sense fear in her voice.

I couldn't understand why my father was not with us. Mama explained that he was on the other side of the ship. Tato, or father, was working in the kitchen. During the arduous voyage to America, the immigrants had a lot of time on their hands, so they were often assigned various duties on the large troopship. Generally, single women and young girls were in crowded quarters on the forward side of the ship, while mothers with small children occupied small designated cabins. The men were stationed at the rear of the ship, separated from the women and children.

I did not know or care about the ship's regulations. I just wanted to see my Tato and tell him how scared I was and how much I missed him. As much as Mama tried to comfort me, I knew she was just as worried as I was. When the waves finally began to subside, my mother and I, along with other seasick women and children, were grateful to be alive.

Mama, Tato, and I were refugees immigrating to the United States of America after it had opened its doors to displaced persons living in Europe. My parents were born in different villages in western Ukraine: Tato in Borynychi and

Mama in Stanislaw. I was born in Bad Reichenhall, Germany, after the war. My German birth certificate identified me as Anastazya; however, my parents always called me Nastya, a shortened derivative of that Christian name. I was named after my father's mother.

Many of the immigrants on board the USS *General R. M. Blatchford* were Slavic people who had been abducted from their homes and transported to live in forced-labor camps. Hitler's Third Reich needed young, able-bodied men and women to help run its war machine. I had heard the story of how my parents were abducted.

For Mama, it began on a cold winter afternoon, on January 18, 1943, when three German soldiers arrived in Stanislaw, the Ukrainian village where Mama lived with her family. She would never forget that day because it was one of the saddest days of her life. Ironically, it had started out joyously as the family prepared to celebrate the feast of Epiphany, or the "Second Christmas Eve." The religious feast day, which the family had celebrated for generations, was integral to Mama's life. She had just completed preparing a traditional Ukrainian dinner of *holubtsi*, or stuffed cabbage rolls, for her father, Michajlo, and her five siblings.

Everyone had been looking forward to the meal when a loud pounding and shouting in German "Öffne die tür" (open the door) shattered the silence. Michajlo tried to calm his children as he walked to the door and cautiously opened it. Three German soldiers, dressed in long weather-beaten coats and dirty boots, pushed their way past him into the modest home. The tallest one asked Michajlo how many women were there. Michajlo replied that he was the head of his family and the father of six children, four young girls and two boys

3

who were living with him. (Two of his children had died.) He nervously added that his wife had recently passed away and that Justyna, his oldest, was taking care of her younger siblings.

The German soldiers ignored Michajlo's comments and barked that they were there to take one young woman to Germany to help the Third Reich. One of the soldiers harshly grabbed Nastia and yelled that she was going with them. She screamed and tried to push the soldier away. Michajlo pleaded with the soldiers to let Nastia, who was only thirteen, remain at home. She and the other children, he said, had already suffered enough. His young wife, Varvara, had passed away at the age of thirty-six after giving birth to their eighth child. The new infant, a baby girl who was never named, had lived only two weeks.

The Germans were not moved by his pleas. Instead, they told him that they were going to leave with Nastia the youngest, and any interference from any of the family members would result in severe consequences. Nastia started to cry and turned to her oldest sister Justyna (my future mother). At that moment, Justyna, a lovely twenty-three-year-old with delicate features, a tremendous memory, and thick, long brown hair confronted the head German, begging him to let her go in Nastia's place.

That fateful day, my Mama, shaking and with a heavy heart, said goodbye to her father and her siblings as the German soldiers escorted her outside to the waiting truck. She was terrified. Mama had never been away from home and was leaving with only the clothes on her back. She had no idea where they were taking her or whether she would live to talk about this time. She could only trust that God would help her cope with her uncertain future. Her father and siblings feared they would never see her again.

The German soldiers took Mama by train to Görlitz, Germany, roughly 550 miles away, to live in a forced-labor camp. She was given a small cubicle in the barracks with a few other women. Like the others, she was given one flannel dress and one pair of underwear for the entire year! The Germans assigned her to the *kofferfabrik* (luggage factory) on February 13, 1943, which assembled military backpacks and luggage. Mama's job was to sew buckles and loops on the backpacks and handles on the luggage. Soon after her arrival at the camp, she wrote a letter to her father, telling him where she was. Upon receiving it, he immediately put together a care package consisting of dried bread, pears, and apples and sent it to her. Even in the forced-labor camps, the Germans allowed inmates to receive letters and packages. On one occasion, her father sent her a piece of bacon hidden inside a bread box. Instead of eating the delicacy, she traded it to a local townswoman for a pair of small shoes. She sent the shoes to her thirteen-year-old sister. Mama believed that her father's packages helped keep her alive.

Life was harsh for Mama and the other young women in the forced-labor camp. They were given only a small bowl of kasha (buckwheat groats), dried bread, and a bowl of watered-down turnip soup for their labors. On Sundays, the women received rations of six red potatoes, which they often hoarded so that they could eat one each day throughout the week. They also received one or two discontinued German Marks, or Reichsbanknotes, which they could redeem only at the labor camp for certain items that the Germans offered their workers. In 1944, Mama received her second pair of underwear and a flannel dress. She worked in that factory until February 17, 1945.

Coincidentally, my future father, Tato, had been living in the same forced-labor camp since 1940 and working in a tank factory. He had swarthy good looks, thick dark hair, piercing hazel eyes, a quick wit, and shrewd street smarts. He was only seven when his mother passed away. To make matters worse, Tato lost his only sibling, a younger brother, to pneumonia. His father remarried a woman with two daughters who epitomized the cruel stepmother in storybooks. She ignored the young boy's cries for acceptance and affection. She even had the audacity to inform the instructor at the local school that she was pulling her stepson out of school because he would never amount to anything anyway and he was needed to help work the fields. That incident generated a love of learning and education that Tato carried with him for the rest of his life.

After Tato was removed from school, he spent most of his days working the land and trying to cope with a stepmother who treated him more like a laborer than a son. Often undernourished, Tato had to find creative ways to obtain food from a stepmother who purposely kept it hidden from him while generously dispensing it to other family members.

One day Tato, now a young man, was hurriedly returning home from working in the fields until dusk. As he entered the house, he was stunned to find two German soldiers talking with his father, Pavlo. One of the Germans told Pavlo that they had orders to take one of the younger men back to Germany. Pavlo, an honorable man, had fought bravely during World War I, but that night he felt helpless.

Nevertheless, he was about to reply to the Germans' demand when his second wife brazenly interrupted. She pointed at Tato and told the two Germans to take him instead of one of the two young men crouching in the corner and trembling with fear. As the German soldiers walked up to Tato, Pavlo tried to stop them but was pushed aside. The soldiers grabbed Tato's arms and forcibly pulled him out the door. That cold, rainy night, he was whisked away at the age of twenty to a German forced-labor camp.

The men and women brought into the labor camps lost their freedom. They were coerced to work for the German government from early morning until late evening for a cause they did not believe in. The men worked twelve-hour days. They were given a short break around noon to eat a small meal consisting of a broth, which was basically colored water, and a slice of bread made of wheat and wood pulp. They were physically and mentally abused and lived in fear for their lives.

Living in cramped, dreadfully unsanitary, and bug-infested barracks with no showers and only a sink, the laborers had to observe strict curfews, which made their lives even more miserable. If sick or injured, they were forbidden to stay inside the barracks to recuperate. In Tato's barracks, if a man claimed that he was too ill to work, German soldiers with huge dogs would forcefully drag him out of his bunk and beat him with sticks. On several occasions, Tato felt weak and feverish with the flu but never once complained or admitted to the German soldiers that he was sick. Instead, he dragged himself out of bed, got dressed, and walked an hour in wooden shoes to the tank factory.

One day, there was an accident at Tato's station on the tank assembly line. German officials accused Tato of purposely sabotaging the production of German tanks. As a result, the production schedule would be delayed for months.

Tato was told that he would be executed the next day as an example to the other workers. That night, Tato wrote a farewell letter to his father, explaining why he would never see him again. In the morning before he was taken out of his detention cell, Tato handed the letter to one of the German soldiers and asked him to mail it. Then he was taken to the German Commander where he pleaded for his life one last time, describing that what had occurred was an accident and that he had never intentionally tried to sabotage the weapons program. The expressionless German official looked up at Tato and then viciously punched him in the face, breaking his jaw and injuring his left inner ear, causing permanent hearing loss. But the execution was called off.

Years later, Tato would say that his life was spared that day only by the grace of God and probably because he was Ukrainian and not Polish or any other nationality that the Germans hated. But even though he lived, he never heard from or saw his father again. Numerous times during the war, when bullets were flying over Tato's head, he managed to stay alive. Tato attributed his good fortune not to chance but to the worn and tattered holy picture he carried with him, an image of the Blessed Virgin Mary.

After the war, Mama and Tato could not return to their homeland. It had been ravaged by war and was now under Russian control. They lived in a refugee or displaced persons camp called Luitpold in Dillingen, Germany. Fortunately, it was under the auspices of American and not Russian forces.

The young men and women in Luitpold were allowed to socialize without fear of reprisals from the Germans, who had forbidden marriage in the forced-labor and concentration camps. Finally, the young people could speak freely, discuss issues, tell jokes, laugh, cry, fall in love, and even get married. In fact, in 1945 and 1946 many couples who wanted to get married had to wait because there weren't enough clergymen to officiate at their nuptials. At some camps, large numbers of couples would gather in front of a clergyman for a single ceremony. The couples also faced the challenge of affording and securing proper wedding attire.

My parents met in 1945 at Luitpold through mutual friends. They fell in love and wanted to be married by a priest in a church followed by a traditional Ukrainian reception for their friends. They also needed a special person whom they admired and respected to serve as their "*starosta*." A starosta is a village elder who oversees a bride and groom's wedding. They chose *Pan* (Mr.) Volodymyr, a good friend who also lived at the camp with his wife and children. He took his responsibility as starosta very seriously. Pan Volodymyr and Tato were able to secure potatoes, sausage, and sauerkraut after seeking advice from previously married couples and several people who had access to food outside the camp. Pan Volodymyr located tables and chairs so that Mama and Tato's guests would be able to sit and celebrate with the bride and groom. Finally, Pan Volodymyr provided some dancing music by asking several guests to bring accordions to the reception. On the day of the wedding, Mama looked beautiful in her veil and long white dress made by a seamstress in the camp, while Tato looked handsome in the dark suit that he had pieced together by bartering. Their guests were enjoying their meal while listening to heartfelt wishes for the bride and groom when a warning alarm blared. Most of the guests instinctively fled to a nearby forest. It was not uncommon for false alarms to go off sporadically.

Camp life was far from easy for the refugees. Approximately, four to six people lived in a single room, slept in bunk beds, and stored their personal belongings in cardboard or wooden suitcases. They cooked and baked in zinc tubs kept near their beds. Their meals consisted of bread, potatoes, beans, and a few vegetables. Meat was served only once a week. There were few toilets, and refugees were allowed to shower only on Saturdays.

Many displaced persons were bored, lonely, and often depressed about their living conditions and uncertain future. They lacked skills and education. Luckily, skilled artisans in the camps volunteered their time to train their fellow refugees as carpenters, butchers, dressmakers, tailors, and woodworkers. The classes also gave the refugees an incentive to improve their minds and living conditions. The U.N.R.R.A (United Nations Relief and Rehabilitation Administration) also offered courses. In 1945, Tato took a course in carpentry (Carpenter and Joiner School of U.N.R.R.A., Team 159, in Traunstein, a United States Zone in Germany).

He trained for four months and was given an examination. After successfully passing it, he was awarded a Certificate by the Members of the Examining Commission. He was now officially a Carpenter Help Workman. Mama also encouraged Tato to enroll in a free woodworking class. Folk art was popular at the time in Europe. Tato and his fellow refugees were grateful for the opportunity to work with fellow displaced persons who generously shared their professional talents in the arts, literature, theater, dancing, athletics, and youth groups.

Mama often told us of two groups who worked with young people in the camps: SUM (*Spilka Ukrainskoi Molodi*), the Ukrainian Youth Association, and PLAST (from *Plastun*, which means "scout"). She was impressed that the young women and men who were members of SUM were well-mannered, poised, and enthusiastic volunteers in camps, schools, and hospitals. SUM members also put their hearts and souls into cultural activities. They learned and performed folk dances, sang ethnic songs, and memorized lines for plays. Mama also praised the PLAST members. They were known for being polite, brave, talented, and disciplined. Their members were involved in scouting, camping, and mastering life-saving skills.

In the refugee camps, barter was one of the keys to survival. Cigarettes (which were like gold), chocolates, and alcohol were valuable commodities. While in Germany, my father secured food, medicine, toiletries, and clothing by trading everything from simple foods to tools he had or made. He also learned how to use grapes and other fruits as well as grains to make homemade wines and whiskey. A natural entrepreneur, Tato set up a small clandestine business, often selling or trading his spirits with people he had met before or after the war.

Pan Slawko, one of Tato's customers, had requested two bottles of wine to celebrate a special occasion. Tato prepared and put the prized two bottles in an inconspicuous bag and headed outside the camp to meet his client. Suddenly, he spotted a German policeman stopping civilians, checking their credentials, and inspecting any items they carried. Tato knew that if the German policeman checked his bag and found the bottles of wine, he would be in serious trouble.

Coincidentally, my mother had taken me out for a buggy ride to the same location. Tato quickly got Mama's attention and handed her the bottles of wine. She promptly hid them inside my buggy and covered them up. The German policeman noticed Tato and ordered him to show some identification. After checking it, he signaled Tato to leave. My father took a deep breath and casually walked back to his wife and child.

Despite the risks, he knew that his wine-making skills were a necessity that helped keep his family afloat. But my father was also a generous person. He would share his homemade wines without charging friends and fellow refugees whenever they celebrated birthdays, weddings, or anniversaries.

All through his time in the refugee camps, Tato often thought about his father, Pavlo, and the rest of his family, wondering if they were still alive. After much hesitancy, he decided to take one last trip to his home in Ukraine while Mama and I stayed behind in Germany.

Tato traveled to Borynychi, the village where he was born. He desperately hoped he would find his family in the house that he had once called home. But when Tato located the wooden structure, he stared in disbelief. It was the same traditional two-room house that his father had built with his own hands, but now barely recognizable. The once bright and welcoming exterior was dark and dingy, the roof damaged, and one window boarded up. "Could this be the home where I experienced happiness when my mother was alive, tragedy when my only younger brother passed away, and terror the night the Germans took me away?" A man who did not easily cry, Tato felt tears streaming down his face.

Tato knocked several times on the door before a stranger cautiously opened it. Tato introduced himself and told the elderly gentleman that he had once lived there. The stranger seemed uneasy at the unexpected revelation. Tato tried to reassure the squatter that he merely wanted to find out where his father was. He was not there to reclaim his family's property. Relieved, the man said that he had never heard of Tato's father or any of his family members. Most of the villagers had been killed during the war. My father thanked him and walked away.

Tato searched around the village for some signs of his previous life but found only desolation and ruin. Ukraine was celebrated as the breadbasket of Europe. Its fertile black earth, or *chornozem*, had been faithfully tilled by farmers who grew life-sustaining wheat, grains, and other crops. However, after the plundering and ravaging of their village, that once rich soil became dry and hard. Even the sun's powerful rays that had once nurtured the golden wheat stalks seemed to have retreated from the blue sky. Weeds now flourished where huge sunflowers, beautiful red poppies, and various fruit trees once grew. Tato, as a boy, had often picked and eaten the fruit before getting caught by a neighbor.

My father looked for the barn that was not only home for the farm animals but often a refuge for himself from his stepmother. He recalled the winter when he caught pneumonia after falling into an icy river near his home. During that long illness, Tato's stepmother continued to chastise him for not completing his chores. Now the barn was gone and the surrounding land barren. The sights of elderly villagers who had survived the war were dismal reminders of how the war had destroyed families and shattered their dreams for a better life. With tears stinging his eyes, Tato looked back one last time at his former home and way of life and then walked away.

Tato returned to the German refugee camp with a heavy heart. He knew that he could never return to his homeland. In the meantime, the President of the United States, Harry

S. Truman, had signed the *Displaced Persons Act* on June 25, 1948. The astounding news trumpeted throughout the refugee camps. America was accepting refugee families with one child. Tato had been patiently biding his time so that his family could immigrate to the "land of the free." He had often refused to join friends and fellow-refugees who had already immigrated to countries such as Argentina, Brazil, Canada, and Venezuela.

My father did whatever was necessary to put us on a waiting list to immigrate to the United States of America. It was a long and arduous process. Every refugee not only filled out many forms but had to pass medical exams and be scrutinized to determine if he or she were ever involved with the Nazis during the war. The World Health Organization (WHO) required the refugees to keep a record of required vaccinations in small booklets called <u>International Certificate of Inoculation and Vaccination</u>.

Refugees also needed sponsors to help them resettle in America. Like most of the refugees in the camp, Tato and Mama had no relatives or friends living in America to sponsor them. Fortunately, an organization founded in 1944 called the United Ukrainian American Relief Committee, Inc., or UUARC, Inc., helped Ukrainian refugees to resettle in America and other countries. (This humanitarian, non-profit organization continues to help Ukrainian individuals and communities throughout the world. It celebrated its 75th Jubilee on October 12, 2019, in Jenkintown, PA.)

The day before we were scheduled to depart for America, I was hot and feverish. Mama was worried that we might be held back. Every person boarding the ship had to be in good physical condition. Tato was anxious: he had been longing for a chance to immigrate with his wife and child to the United States. Mama needed a quick remedy to break my fever. She consulted her good friend, Maria, who had been raised in a Ukrainian village where people used natural and herbal remedies to cure illnesses. Maria told Mama to find a fresh yellow lemon, squeeze out its acidic juice, and let me drink it.

It sounded like such an easy and commonsense solution, but obtaining citrus in those days was a daunting task. That night, Tato went out and searched the town until he found a fresh lemon. Mama promptly prepared and served it to me. The next morning, I was no longer feverish. Mama thanked God and Maria, while Tato breathed a sigh of relief.

On September 14, 1949, we departed from the port of Bremerhaven in Germany. Mama had packed our few possessions in a wooden suitcase. The items included a traditional native Ukrainian blouse with intricate designs that Mama had embroidered for me, a red velvet vest, a white cotton slip, and a skirt with a touch of reddish embroidery by a seamstress in the camp. To complete the ensemble, she put in a headdress made with artificial white flowers attached to a circular headband with long, colorful cascading ribbons.

Mama also packed an art print of a haloed guardian angel in a long beige dress extending her right hand over a little brown-haired girl wearing a blue dress and pantaloons while chasing butterflies in a forest. Blessed by a local priest after I was born, the print was inside a wooden box frame made by my father. Tato had prepared and carved the wood and then painted a complex design of diamond, circular, and square shapes and fine symmetrical lines on the frame. He had spent over a hundred hours working on it. I treasured my print for years.

IT LOOKED LIKE FOREVER

The displaced persons aboard the USS *General R. M. Blatchford* were on a life-changing journey that would take them from the horrors of war to a country known for its freedom and opportunities. They hoped to build a better life for themselves and their families.

Chapter

2

On September 24, 1949, my parents and I, along with the other passengers, reached the United States. We didn't dock at New York's well-known Ellis Island, but at the port of New York, New York. Passengers had mixed feelings of hope and apprehension about the future. Would they be accepted in their new country or treated as outsiders? And what about the language barrier? How would they communicate? The refugees who lived in the camps had had to learn German. Now they would have to learn English. As the passengers picked up their tattered baggage and meager belongings, they wondered what other new challenges were awaiting them.

The United Ukrainian American Relief Committee, Inc., had contacted businessmen, farmers, and landowners all over the United States seeking employment and housing for their sponsored Ukrainian refugees. They had assigned my family to St. Paul, Minnesota, where we would live and work on a farm. However, fate intervened. On the day of our arrival in New York City, government officials announced that refugees assigned to go to Minnesota or Wisconsin instead would board Greyhound buses for Falcon, Mississippi, nearly 1, 200 miles away. There they would work for one of several plantation owners, such as Mr. J. M. Johnson who needed many hands to work his land. However, first the immigrants had to sign a contract stating that they would work for him for one year. Since most of them could not speak English, they chose one volunteer to represent them. That individual signed the contract with Mr. J. M. Johnson, enabling the other refugees to work in Mississippi for one year.

That day, more than two-hundred immigrants boarded five Greyhound buses. I sat near a window and stared at the never-ending wires strung across poles along the dusty roads. At the time, I had no idea what they were, but the sight of those poles and wires would forever stay etched in my mind. During that long journey, I got hungry. Mama would reassure me that we would be eating soon as she pulled out crusty bread and dried fruit that she had kept wrapped up and tucked away in her pocket.

The bus drivers drove many miles before stopping at a local restaurant in Tennessee where Ukrainian men, women, and children could have something to eat, compliments of Mr. Johnson.

The refugees finally arrived in Falcon, Mississippi, tired and hungry but grateful to be there. As they moved around the grounds, an unexpected breeze wafted a mysterious but enticing aroma. "Could there be a hot meal nearby?" asked one of the younger travelers. Smiles and laughter quickly ensued, renewing the refugees' spirits as they waited patiently for further instructions.

As twilight descended, the refugees marched to an open field where large bonfires emitted red-hot flames beneath cooking vats. Black men were stirring the contents and welcoming us with smiles and hand-signals to join in the meal. Meanwhile, other Black men were dispensing old Army ration pans and utensils to the guests so that they could enjoy a hearty meal of beans with pieces of pork smothered in a brown reddish sauce. That evening, my parents, our fellow travelers, and I happily devoured an American dish we found out was called pork and beans. It was so good to be eating something warm and tasty.

The refugees also discovered that only about half of the families would stay and work in Falcon. The rest would board buses again and travel to Gunnison, Mississippi. Tato, Mama, and I were bound for Gunnison, about eight miles east of the Mississippi River.

Upon arriving in Gunnison, we met Mr. J. M. Johnson, a plantation owner. He announced that the men and women in our group would be working for him. Mr. Johnson explained that everyone would be assigned jobs based on their abilities and experiences. An educated and accomplished landowner, Mr. Johnson acknowledged that Eastern Europeans had excellent skills as builders, mechanics, electricians, and carpenters.

Mr. Johnson identified the mechanics in our group and assigned them to repair his tractors and combines. He designated electricians and carpenters to work on electrical and construction projects. Mr. Johnson also expected the refugees to pick a certain daily quota of his cotton crop from early morning to late evening. Finally, everyone would do small chores around his vast grounds, particularly if he, his wife, or another family member requested it.

After traveling hundreds of miles from New York to Mississippi, the refugees yearned to settle down in a place where they could bathe and rest in a comfortable bed. Instead, they were led to a cluster of small crude shacks built off the ground. Looking on in disbelief, they learned that the shanties would be their new homes. Four families could live in one shack and use an outdoor hand-well for their cooking and bathing needs. There was no indoor plumbing, only an outhouse. Once again, the refugees' quest for a better life had turned up empty. They felt as if they were back in Germany huddled in overcrowded rooms with no privacy.

Once the refugees were settled in their shacks, Mr. Johnson summoned his builders, carpenters, electricians, and anyone else with carpentry skills. He announced that apart from performing their daily tasks, they were expected to help construct four-room houses on his property. Tato helped construct one of those dwellings. He had taken carpentry classes in Germany and was adept at working with wood and building materials. Mr. Johnson was pleased with the way his building project was progressing; however, he never revealed why or for whom the refugees were constructing the buildings. They knew only that Mr. Johnson never offered them the option of moving into the newer units. They continued to live in the shacks.

Around that same time, the refugees heard a rumor that Mr. Johnson was planning to subdivide his land and make them his sharecroppers. Yet, for some unknown reason, he never presented that proposal to them. He must have realized that they would never agree to it.

Mr. Johnson did, however, open a grocery store for his workers. He did not want them traveling to and from town to purchase canned goods and other incidentals. That considerate enterprise impressed the refugees, especially when they learned that Mr. Johnson would not charge them for their purchases.

Mr. Johnson needed a trustworthy store clerk who spoke some English to operate the grocery store. After careful consideration, he picked Michajlo, an eighteen-year-old student who had come to America with his parents. Mr. Johnson instructed Michajlo to serve his fellow refugees and keep accurate records of their complimentary purchases. The student performed his tasks in an efficient and organized manner, demonstrating his abilities as a future entrepreneur. Michajlo also used his English skills to help his fellow refugees by translating English words, sentences, correspondence, and documents for them. He readily earned the trust, respect, and admiration of the people he served. Michajlo demonstrated that diligence, benevolence, and cooperation were essential components when dealing with patrons.

In October, the new arrivals faced their most arduous task yet: meeting their daily quotas of picking cotton under the sweltering Mississippi sun. One morning, Tato invited me to join him for a limited time to watch him pick cotton. He also surprised me with a small cotton sack so that I could assist him. I excitedly thanked him as we made our way toward the cotton field. When we arrived, Tato demonstrated how to pick cotton out of the bolls with both hands and rapidly stuff it into a sack about twelve feet long. He commented that sometimes adults had to stoop down to pick the cotton. I followed his directions and carefully filled my small sack with the fluffiest cotton. Coincidentally, a foreman saw me, walked over, and checked my cotton sack. He smiled and complimented me on a job well-done. Then he reached into his pocket, pulled out a shiny nickel, and handed it to me. Tato said that he was very proud of me and then asked if he could save the nickel for me. I dutifully handed it to him. Whenever Mr. Johnson compensated Tato for his repair projects around his spacious residence, Tato would quickly squirrel the money away.

In addition to the refugee workers, Mr. Johnson employed Black caretakers who performed household duties such as cooking and cleaning or outdoor tasks such as picking cotton. I often heard Mama telling Tato that she empathized with the Black workers. She said that they were good, hard-working people who lived in poverty.

Within six weeks of arriving in Gunnison, several disgruntled families decided to leave. They contacted relatives in America to help them relocate to another state. One family left Gunnison after living there for only three weeks. Working for a landowner and living in a shack was not the life that many refugees had envisioned for themselves or their children. Bigger dreams beckoned. Moreover, some refugees were young professionals who had earned degrees in their native countries. They had hoped to take English classes and eventually become accredited in their chosen fields. Conscientious students like Michajlo, the store clerk, were eager to return to school, continue their education, and earn a university degree.

Mama and Tato wanted to leave Mississippi. However, they had no relatives in America, and Tato had not saved enough money to buy out his contract with Mr. Johnson. He asked Mama to be patient. Tato would keep working until an opportunity presented itself to leave the farm for a better life.

My family continued living in our shack. Every day, Mama made dozens of trips to the well-water pump to get water for cooking, cleaning, and bathing. We also used an outhouse. During daylight hours it was tolerable, but at night, especially when it rained, we had to be especially careful to skirt muddy puddles. We shared our living quarters with Pan Ivan and his wife *Pani* (Mrs.) Sofia and their young daughter, Iryna. Fellow Ukrainians, they had come to America with us. Despite the small size of our shack, the six of us lived together amicably. We had more space to move around in than the refugees who shared a shack with four families.

Despite our primitive surroundings, my parents, along with Pan Ivan and his family, tried to make our lives as pleasant as possible. Whenever Tato and Pan Ivan came home after working all day, they were greeted with affection and home-cooked meals. They discussed the day's events, laughed, talked about strategies to create a better life, and made the best of their cramped conditions.

Tato cared about the health, welfare, and safety of his family. He was also keenly aware that Mama was pregnant and that a new family member would soon arrive. So when she requested special foods, toiletries, or medicines, Tato was determined to go into town and find them for her.

But the first time that Tato and Pan Ivan walked to town, they got lost. While they were trying to get their bearings, a local driver stopped and offered them a ride. In those days, it was perfectly acceptable for a Southerner to offer a stranger a ride. Tato and Pan Ivan thanked the driver and in broken English asked him where they could board a bus to take them into town. The driver directed the men with words and hand signals toward the nearest bus stop. There they boarded a bus that took them to their destination. While in town, Tato walked into a food shop and asked the clerk for some *rumyanok*. The clerk looked puzzled until Tato pointed toward some tea leaves and held his stomach. The clerk finally understood that Tato was looking for chamomile herbal tea to soothe an upset stomach.

I found the farm a mix of fear and wonder. One summer afternoon, while strolling through a lovely garden, I spotted something slithering along the path toward me. I screamed and ran as fast as I could to our shack. Mama was taken aback when she saw me crying. She embraced me and tried to calm me down. I told her that I was frightened by a threatening snake in the garden. Mama tried to reassure me that the reptile was probably harmless. She also warned me to stay out of the garden or go there only with an adult.

We didn't just work in the fields. Mama and Pani Sofia were expected to do certain chores for the Johnson family as well. Mama had to plant, prune, and water the flower and vegetable gardens. She never complained because she enjoyed working outdoors with plants and vegetables just as she had in her homeland. Mama even planted a small garden with cabbage, cucumbers, dill, onions, potatoes, radishes, and tomatoes for us. While she and Pani Sofia worked, Iryna and I along with Mr. Johnson's daughter, Amanda, played together.

Despite Mama's constant watering, the harsh Mississippi sun continued to parch the flower and vegetable garden. Then one day, dark clouds and overcast skies replaced the puffy white clouds and bright sunshine. Iryna and I were playing outside our shack when I felt a drop of water on my forehead. I looked up, saw the ominous clouds in the sky, and ran inside to tell Mama the good news. She came out and stared at the steadily falling rain and happily predicted that the dry earth, along with its drooping plants, would soon come back to life.

Around midnight, I was awakened by bursts of thunder. Startled and drowsy, I wondered how a soothing rain shower could turn into a deluge. I looked around the room and saw Tato checking the shack's ceiling for possible water seepage from the timeworn roof. Mama tiptoed over, kissed me on the forehead, and asked me to go back to sleep. She reassured me that the downpour and rumbling would eventually die down, allowing everyone to get a good night's sleep.

The next morning, when I opened the front door, I was surprised to see a usually dry earth look like an enormous mud puddle. I was tempted to splash through the squishy mud as we headed toward the hen house where Mama sometimes gathered eggs. When Mama abruptly stopped me, I looked up and watched in total disbelief as the hen house bobbed up and down like a capsized sailboat. A rush of sadness came over me as I witnessed frightened fowls clucking, scrambling, and frantically flying in different directions.

That evening, when Tato came home, Mama woefully told him about the hens' waterlogged home. She said that it was time to leave the farm. Most of the other refugees had already left or were about to leave for New York, Chicago, or Philadelphia. Tato tried to explain that he, too, wanted to leave Mississippi and go north. Regrettably, he had no specific destination, family member, or trusted friend who could advise him. They would have to continue living in Mississippi.

My father had developed a good rapport with the Johnson family. Mr. Johnson was a good boss, and Tato respected him. Tato decided to continue working, improving his skills, and saving enough money so when the timing was right, he could move his family to another state and a better life.

In the spring of 1950, my mother was close to giving birth. Mr. Johnson and his wife had arranged for Mama to deliver her baby at a hospital in Cleveland, Mississippi. When the joyful day arrived in March of 1950, she gave birth to my brother, the first person in our family to become a United States citizen. Tato had been saving part of his earnings to pay the doctor's fee and Mama's hospital stay. When it came time to pay the bill, he didn't have enough money. He asked Mr. Johnson for a loan. A kind and generous man, Mr. Johnson not only agreed to give Tato the money but told him that he wouldn't have to repay it. Then he jokingly asked Tato not to mention the hospital and the doctor's bill to his wife.

Not long after his birth, my infant brother was baptized Roman George at a Roman Catholic Church in Cleveland, even though we were Ukrainian Byzantine Rite Catholics. My parents had planned on giving my brother only a first name since most Europeans did not give middle names to their children. However, after Mr. Johnson explained that American boys and girls were given middle names, my parents relented. They even agreed to Mr. Johnson's suggestion that they name him George. For that momentous occasion, I stood next to Mama, Tato, Mr. Johnson and his family in my traditional Ukrainian attire in the Catholic Church.

A short time later, my parents received a letter from their good friend, Pan Jaroslaw, in Chicago, Illinois. Mama and Tato had last spoken with him at the labor camp in Germany. Before World War II, Pan Jaroslaw had been a professor in a well-known university. After the war, he had tutored young men and women in the barracks. Tato and Pan Jaroslaw had become close friends and had even made a pact: if either one of them ever immigrated to America, then that person would contact the other. In his letter, Pan Jaroslaw told Tato that he was able to track him down because a fellow refugee who had worked in Mississippi had mentioned Tato's name.

In his letter, Pan Jaroslaw strongly urged my parents to come to Chicago where they would receive food and temporary housing at the local Ukrainian Catholic Church. He also indicated that a huge influx of Ukrainian refugees from Europe had established a Ukrainian community with the Church as their base. Tato immediately wrote back that he was grateful that Pan Jaroslaw had contacted him and pleased to hear that he was doing well. Tato told Mama that her prayers had been answered. They finally had a destination: Chicago, Illinois.

Mr. Johnson and his wife were disappointed when Tato announced that he was planning to leave Gunnison. Pan Ivan, his wife, and daughter, Iryna, also had made plans to leave Mississippi and head to Chicago. Mr. Johnson had hoped the two families would continue to work for him. Tato, who had completed nine months of his contract with Mr. Johnson, bought out the remaining three months to honor his twelve-month commitment. Mama began to pack our meager belongings for the trip to Chicago while Tato bought Greyhound bus tickets for our bus ride. Since my brother was a baby and Mama did not have a carrier for him, she put him in a sturdy box with a small blanket to keep him cozy.

Chapter

3

We arrived in Chicago, Illinois, in July of 1950 wearing light summer attire while some of the residents were wearing long-sleeved clothing and sweaters. I asked Mama why it was so chilly outside when it was summertime. She replied that she had no idea. We had been living in Mississippi where temperatures often soared and were uncomfortably hot, but now we were in a city where it was unseasonably cool. While Mama was trying to keep my baby brother warm, Tato asked the bus driver for directions to the Ukrainian Catholic Church. He pointed to a busy street where we could catch the first of two buses to reach our destination.

Finally, we found our way to a majestic church with thirteen huge onion-shaped golden domes. Mama joyfully said that they represented Jesus and his twelve apostles. Around the same time, three men were walking toward us, speaking Ukrainian. Tato was thrilled. He stopped the men and told them that he and his family were Ukrainian immigrants looking for the lodging facility offered by the Ukrainian Catholic Church. The men looked surprised and quickly informed Tato that St. Nicholas Ukrainian Catholic Church was not taking in any immigrants.

When I heard that remark, I realized we had no place to spend the night even though we were cold, hungry, and tired. Tato was speechless. He couldn't impose on Pan Jaroslaw, who was sharing a small apartment in the city with other single immigrant men. The Ukrainian strangers were about to leave when one of them recalled that a Ukrainian Orthodox Church was providing newly arrived immigrants with food and temporary housing. He told Tato that the church was nearby and gave him directions. My parents gratefully thanked the man for his help and began walking toward the Orthodox Church. While Mama carried my brother, Tato held my hand and our paltry belongings.

Mama sighed with relief when she spotted St. Volodymyr Ukrainian Orthodox Church. A more traditional-looking house of God without the imposing onion-shaped domes, this church symbolized hope for her family. Tato noticed a group of people milling around a brick building when a woman dressed in a traditional Ukrainian blouse walked over and graciously welcomed us. She asked my parents if they were Orthodox. Mama replied that we were Ukrainian Catholics who had just arrived from Mississippi and had no place to stay.

The woman appeared sympathetic but emphasized that she had no authority to admit newly arrived immigrants into the church's parish building. However, she would speak with someone who did. About twenty minutes later, she returned and told my parents that they would not be able to spend the night because the parish building was overcrowded with Orthodox immigrants. Tato urgently told her that we had no place to go. The woman relented and said that she would be back shortly. When she returned, she said we could come into the parish hall.

As we entered the attractive brick building, I felt a sense of relief. We were finally inside a warm place filled with adults and children speaking a language I understood. I followed my parents into a room packed with men and women who were talking, eating, or simply resting on the floor with their children. Mama and Tato spoke with some of the Orthodox immigrants and discovered that they were waiting for their relatives to pick them up. They were also proudly expressing their desire to become members of the parish. Tato reminded Mama that we did not have any relatives to call and could stay only the one night. Therefore, he had to find a job and a place for us to live as soon as possible. Tato excused himself and said that he was hoping to find at least one familiar face among the many immigrants in that building.

Soon, a gentleman who appeared to be the supervisor entered the crowded room. He spoke briefly with the immigrants and then answered their questions. When he spotted Mama, he walked up to her and asked if she was a new Orthodox arrival. She replied that she and her Catholic family were tired, hungry, and needed a place to spend the night. He simply mumbled something under his breath and then assured Mama that he would be right back with some food for us.

A short time later, Tato strolled in. Mama cheerfully informed him that the man in charge of the parish hall had promised to return with food. Tato was relieved to hear that his family was finally going to have a warm meal. He also mentioned that he had run into a fellow immigrant, Pan Toma, living at the parish hall, who was also searching for work. Tato asked him if he could come along. Mama reminded her husband that wandering with limited English skills around an unfamiliar city was not a good idea. Tato reassured her that exploring the neighborhood could possibly lead to a job. And besides, he and Pan Toma would be back before dark.

My baby brother began to stir restlessly. Mama knew that he was getting hungry and that her supply of canned PET milk was getting low. When he started to whimper, Mama tried to rock him back to sleep. She also whispered in my ear that we would be eating soon.

Minutes turned into hours. Mama was becoming visibly upset waiting for the man who had promised to come back with some food. Meanwhile, Tato returned to find his wife and daughter awake in a room filled with slumbering people. Mama was cradling her son in one arm and holding me with the other. Tato tiptoed up to Mama and apologized for being late. He explained that he and Pan Toma had taken a wrong turn when they tried to find their way back to the parish hall. He also had surmised that his wife and children had been fed and were sleeping. Mama tearfully told Tato that the man who had vowed to return with food never showed up. Tato was appalled. He asked Mama to describe the man. Mama said that he was middle-aged, had short dark hair, and wore a white shirt with a tie and dark trousers.

Tato began searching for the elusive man. When he found him, Tato thought that he was hallucinating. It was Pan Ihor, a man Tato had not seen since they had lived in the same German barracks! Pan Ihor had been not only a good friend but a mentor to Tato. The two men embraced and warmly shook hands.

"Pane Ihor, it's so good to see you! The last time we spoke, we were still in Germany."

"Thanks to Almighty God, we are now in America."

"*Tak* (Yes). My wife and I, along with our two children, arrived from Mississippi today. We are still waiting for something to eat after our long journey."

"Pane Josyf, I'm so glad that you are here!"

Then he quickly excused himself and returned with warm soup, milk, and several kanapky, or open-faced sandwiches with lunch meat, cheese, lettuce, cucumber, and tomato. He also brought some pillows and a warm blanket. My family finally had a meal to eat and a place to rest after a long and frustrating day in a city called Chicago.

The next morning, Tato realized that he had to find another place for us to stay. He also needed to find a job, so he sought out his new friend, Pan Toma. While Tato was out looking for work, Mama and I spent the morning visiting with the other immigrants. In the afternoon, she accompanied my brother and me outdoors to get some fresh air. When we returned to our room, Mama experienced a scene right out of a novel. A tall, ruggedly handsome man with a strong jaw loudly shouted, "Justyna! Justyna! Is it really you?"

My mother was stunned when she saw a face from the past staring at her. It was Pan Volodymyr, a loyal friend and the "starosta" at her and Tato's wedding in Dillingen, Germany. The two old friends joyfully embraced.

Pan Volodymyr lifted me up, kissed me on the cheek, and said that I looked so grown-up since he had last seen me at the Luitpold refugee camp. Tragically, his young son had died in

Germany after the war. Pan Volodymyr had immigrated to America with his lovely wife and three daughters looking for a new life.

Pan Volodymyr and his family were registered members of the Ukrainian Orthodox Church. A patriotic and caring Ukrainian, he would regularly visit the parish center to inquire whether any recently arrived immigrants needed his assistance. He understood what it meant to be displaced. He also told Mama that he would wait for Tato to come back, so that the five of us could drive to his home for a cooked meal and a comfortable place to sleep.

Tato couldn't believe his eyes when he returned to find Pan Volodymyr and my mother conversing! When Pan Volodymyr spotted Tato, the two men ran up to each other like long-lost brothers. After that incredible meeting, Pan Volodymyr walked us to his automobile and drove us to his apartment.

When we arrived at Pan Volodymyr's home, his wife and three daughters warmly greeted us. He also handed his oldest daughter, Kateryna, some money to purchase additional food, milk, and sweet cakes at the local grocery store. Within a short time, she returned with a bag filled with groceries including several cans of PET milk for my little brother. My parents were grateful they had friends who were so kind and generous.

Pan Volodymyr's daughters were very friendly, thoughtful, and helpful. They were especially considerate of my little brother and me. Nastya, who had the same name as I, had dark hair and a beauty mark near her lip. Ann, the youngest, was a blond, and Kateryna, the oldest, was tall with brownish hair. She was the one that the other two sisters regarded as a role model. Pan Volodymyr's wife, Pani Olena, a soft-spoken and gentle woman, asked us to stay with them until Tato found a job and a suitable place to live.

During the time we stayed with Pan Volodymyr and his family, Tato went out every single day except on Sundays looking for a job. On Sundays, Pan Volodymyr would take his family to an early morning service at the Ukrainian Orthodox Church. After the Divine Liturgy, he would drop them off at home and then drive us to the Ukrainian Catholic Church. In those days, most of the Ukrainian immigrants joined either the Ukrainian Catholic or the Ukrainian Orthodox Church. I had no idea how many families were registered at the latter church, but at the Ukrainian Catholic Church, every Divine Liturgy was packed with parishioners.

When the last Divine Liturgy was over, parishioners would gather in front of the church and nearby sidewalks to visit with one another. Sooner or later, a parishioner would run into a relative or friend who had once lived in his or her Ukrainian village or had been in a camp in Germany. As the number of immigrant parishioners grew, so did the need for safety in the streets. "Wooden horses" had to be placed in strategic places to protect the churchgoers from oncoming automobiles. The parishioners considered themselves not only Catholics but members of an extended family that cherished freedom, culture, language, and a desire for a better life. We were now part of that family.

During one of those Sunday afternoons, while my father was mingling with his fellow parishioners and asking for leads to find work, he met Pani Anna. Kind and well-liked, Pani Anna told Tato that she worked for the Chicago and North Western Railway and that it was hiring new employees. Tato was eager to apply for a position. Pani Anna told him to arrive early Monday morning so that she could introduce him to the person in charge of hiring. Pani Anna also gave him bus directions to the railroad yard where she had worked for a number of years as a respected employee. The railroad hired Tato soon after.

On Tato's first day as a Chicago and North Western employee, Pani Anna introduced him to her American coworkers and a few Ukrainian immigrants who worked with her. They would become Tato's coworkers and friends.

My father had artistic and construction skills that he hoped to hone at a new job. However, the position that the railroad offered him didn't provide that opportunity. Nevertheless, Tato didn't complain because he was grateful to have a job and earn a paycheck. His duties included keeping the railroad commuter cars clean and clear for all the passengers. Tato discarded newspapers, candy wrappers, and other items that passengers had left behind. He was a responsible man who did his best to keep the trains in pristine condition. With a steady job, Tato could secure an apartment and support his family.

Over the years, Tato would work his way up to become a machinist who maintained the train's engines. His English language skills would greatly improve because he strongly wanted to learn English. However, whenever he came home from work, he spoke in his native tongue. He and Mama didn't want my brother and me to forget or neglect our native Ukrainian language. They insisted that we learn English because we were living in America but continue to nurture our own ethnicity and appreciate our heritage. They also believed that Americans should learn about and appreciate diverse cultures.

Once Tato was employed, he was ready to rent an apartment in an established neighborhood near the Ukrainian Catholic Church. He quickly discovered that apartments in that area were expensive and occupied primarily by tenants who had been in this country for quite some time. After a while, Tato was urged by his friends to check out a section of the city with more affordable units. Unfortunately, they were located near busy streets and intersections with many automobiles, trucks, and buses.

Not wanting to overstay our welcome with Pan Volodymyr and his family, Tato decided to look for a unit in a reasonably priced apartment building. Before long, he informed Mama that he had found an apartment for us. Although hesitant about moving into an apartment that she had never seen before, she knew that we needed a place of our own.

Mama held my hand while Tato carried my brother up a flight of stairs to our new apartment on the second floor. Tato opened the door with the key he had been given by the building's owner. Mama walked in, looked around, and didn't say a word. However, her face revealed her dismay as she saw unfurnished rooms, dirty walls, floors, and window panes. She knew there was a lot of cleaning ahead for her and Tato since the landlord had never bothered to clean the apartment before renting it to them.

It wasn't just dirt we had to face. One night, around midnight, Mama went to the bathroom and saw rats scampering around the toilet and inside the old rusty tub. She was so upset that she roused Tato, asking him to get rid of the rodents at once. She also insisted that he find another place for us to live because she was concerned about her children's health and safety.

Tato wholeheartedly agreed but begged her to be patient because we could not just move out. We had to stay in the apartment until he could find better housing. In the meantime, he would set some traps in the bathroom and try to speak with the landlord about the rodent problem. The landlord, however, rarely came around except to collect the rent.

Another unsettling incident made my mother put her foot down about moving. I was in the apartment with my baby brother when Mama walked downstairs to pick up our mail. She opened the front door, briefly stepped outside, checked the mailbox, and was about to return when the front door slammed shut and locked. Mama started banging frantically on the front door, hoping that someone in the building would hear her. No one responded, and her two children were upstairs alone. Mama was about to continue knocking when she recognized the landlord walking toward the building. She quickly approached him and tried to explain in broken English that she was locked out and that her children were upstairs. The landlord must have understood her because he reached into his pocket, pulled out a metal ring of keys, and asked Mama if she would like to buy the key to the front door. She replied, "No money!"

Mama couldn't believe the landlord's insensitivity and greed. She walked toward the busy street and flagged down a police car. The policeman stopped his vehicle and walked out. Mama ran up to him with tears in her eyes, pointed to the landlord, and tried to explain that he would not open the front door unless she gave him money. "No money," she explained. The policeman ordered the landlord to open the door. Begrudgingly, he pulled out his set of keys and opened the door for Mama. The policeman's quick response convinced Mama that he probably had past run-ins with her landlord. She thanked the policeman in Ukrainian and English. "*Diakuyu*, Diakuyu, thank you, thank you." Then she ran back upstairs to be with her children. That evening, my father vowed to find his family a better place to live.

Chapter

4

The next morning, Tato asked his fellow employees if they knew of anyone who was renting an apartment because his family needed decent housing. One of his Ukrainian coworkers suggested that he contact a Ukrainian lady by the name of Pani Olya. She was an elderly Ukrainian woman who had lived in America for quite some time. Pani Olya was an active member of the Ukrainian community and a parishioner at the Ukrainian Catholic parish. She was considered a successful immigrant who had come to this country as a young woman with little money and few possessions. After a while, she had learned English, found a job, and gotten married. She and her Ukrainian husband owned a two-story building with a basement apartment.

Tato spoke with Pani Olya and explained his urgent need to find a clean and safe place for his family to live. He described his current apartment and added that his family needed to move as soon as possible. Pani Olya had a big heart. She loved children, even though she and her husband were childless. She told Tato that there was a good chance that she would be able to help his family, but first she needed to speak with her husband.

That evening, Tato informed Mama that he was hopeful that Pani Olya would offer them a safer and better place to live. Pani Olya was well-liked and respected in the Ukrainian community. Mama predicted that she would be an ideal landlady.

Before long, we were living in Pani Olya's frame house located on a quiet street in a neighborhood with single-family homes and a smattering of apartment buildings. The building, which was partially sided with cement asbestos and set far away from the sidewalk, had a spacious front yard adorned with large maple trees.

The basement apartment was small but spotless. Pani Olya and her husband had furnished it with a kitchen table, chairs, lamps, beds, and a small sofa. The apartment also had windows. Mama commented that having trees that swayed back and forth on windy days would provide fresh air in our new home. And on windless days, we could appreciate the freshly-cut grass and scented flowers that surrounded the building. That small apartment was a godsend for our family.

The neighbors to the right owned a single-family home, while the neighbors to our left lived in an apartment building. The large dwelling was crowded with fellow Ukrainian immigrants, including a group who had once lived in the same German refugee camp as we had. Mama often invited our friends, Pan Michajlo and Pani Hanya, with their two sons to our home for some good food and conversation. While the adults conversed, I played with their son Slawko, who was close to my age. Pani Hanya once disclosed that their apartment building had too many people in small and cramped quarters. She and her husband craved some privacy. One evening, I overheard Pan Michajlo confide that he was trying to save enough money to afford a larger apartment with a play area for his growing sons.

Since my parents had no relatives in America, their good friends were as close as family members. Whenever they visited us, I was expected to address them as *Vujko* (uncle) or *Teta* (aunt). Over the years, Mama and Tato had formed many friendships with faithful and trustworthy people. Pani Olya and her husband, Pan Dmytro, would eventually become two of their lifelong friends. Mama had great respect and admiration for Pani Olya. She affectionately called her *Babcia* (grandmother) Olya, whenever she spoke about her.

Pani Olya often invited me upstairs in the evenings and introduced me to a wooden piece of furniture with a screen in it. That mesmerizing screen produced sounds and moving pictures that truly delighted me. Even though I did not understand every word spoken by the actors, I was able to follow the story line by watching the various actions and listening to Pani Olya's translations. Watching television with her helped me to learn English. It also introduced me to many popular westerns such as *The Cisco Kid, Hopalong Cassidy, The Gene Autry Show,* and *Roy Rogers. I Love Lucy* was the one comedy show that I never wanted to miss because Lucille Ball, the zany red-haired lady, was so funny. Her husband Desi Arnaz and friends Vivian Vance and William Frawley contributed to the hilarious weekly mayhem.

I had a standing invitation from Pani Olya not only to watch television but to feast on her homemade cookies, cakes, and sandwiches. Her kitchen was always filled with delicious aromas. I began to associate them with her kindness and looked forward to coming over. The two of us ate, laughed, and got excited watching one of our special shows. A gracious lady with curly, short dark hair, roundish glasses that rested on her nose, and a smile that warmed a little kid's heart, Pani Olya was like the sweet grandmother I never had. Her husband, a caring landlord, often told Tato that if he ever needed anything to let him know. Pan Dmytro wanted our stay in his basement apartment to be a happy one.

In the summertime, my brother and I finally had a place to play. The large yard had a spacious park-like setting with trees, birds, and squirrels. I played with the children whose parents were friends of my family. They would come over quite often, so I always had plenty of energetic playmates. We had a lot in common because of our age and nationality. When my friends and I engaged in our imaginative activities, our parents along with their guests would talk endlessly, recalling stories from the past, both serious and hilarious. Many of those tales must have really been funny because during some of our quieter games, loud and hearty bursts of laughter interrupted my friends and me.

I also played with a number of English-speaking children in the neighborhood. We always managed to have a good time despite my limited English vocabulary. They showed me how to make huge bubbles with bubble gum without using my fingers and catch lightning bugs in the evening. I asked Mama for a jar and then gave it to Tato so that he could make holes in the lid. Before long, I was catching and placing lightning bugs in my jar so that I could watch them light it up like a lantern. By the end of the evening, my friends and I would always let them out.

Countless green grasshoppers with short antennae and long mighty hind legs that rubbed against their wings thronged Pani Olya's front yard. I loved watching, chasing, and catching them as they jumped all over the grass. Also ants scampered in groups. I didn't like them. One day, I told Tato that I loved watching and chasing grasshoppers but didn't care for the ants. They were a nuisance, and I asked him if he could get rid of them. Tato looked surprised and saddened by my request. He said that the hardworking ants had every right to be outdoors with the rest of the insects. Then he told me the tale of the ant and the grasshopper. Tato said that the grasshopper played his fiddle all summer long entertaining himself and other bugs while the indefatigable ant spent the entire summer finding and setting aside food for the coming winter. When Tato finished his tale, he stressed that ants deserved the same respect as the grasshoppers, crickets, and cicadas. Years later, I discovered that his tale about the ant and the grasshopper was based on one of Aesop's fables.

Other insects included the crickets and cicadas that leaped through the air and chirped late into the night. Not everyone on our block liked them. Some adults complained that the crickets were too noisy. Tato said that all the insects were God's smallest inhabitants that enjoyed the summer nights along with the rest of us.

Occasionally, when my brother and I were playing with our friends, Mama would venture outdoors, sit on a blanket beneath one of the trees, and embroider pillow covers, doilies, and Ukrainian blouses. Around noontime, she would put down her embroidery, go back inside our apartment, and return with some *obid* (lunch) and milk for everyone. Eating beneath those huge maple trees was almost as good as being at the park.

Meanwhile, my father was working very hard. He would come home in the evening, eat supper, and then return to work. Mama began to worry about his health. He was working too many hours and getting too little sleep. Tato reminded her that his paycheck had to cover the rent, groceries, clothing, and unexpected expenses.

Mama knew that the only way to rectify the situation was for her to find a job. Her son, Roman, was no longer an infant. A year-old toddler, he was walking, talking in phrases, and following his older sister around the apartment. Mama quietly spread the word among her friends and neighbors that she was looking for work. She wanted a job that did not require proficiency in English and would also allow her to stay at home during the day with her children.

A neighbor who shopped downtown gave Mama a lead: a prominent store was hiring housekeepers for its late-night shift. My mother wanted to make a good impression for her interview, so she picked out a pretty long-sleeved cotton dress with a black belt. She also arranged for a lady friend to baby-sit my brother and me while she took a bus downtown.

Mama arrived at the Marshall Field and Company store. When she caught sight of the attractive décor, display cases, shoppers, and sales people, she knew that she wanted to work there. Mama recalled a brief saying that she often used for spiritual guidance: "*Hospody Dopomozhy*" (God help me). She headed toward the elevators run by women in attractive uniforms. One of the young ladies guided her to the employment office where a Polish-speaking Marshall Field manager interviewed her. Mama had no difficulty communicating with the manager since she understood and spoke Polish. The manager hired her on the spot. He told Mama that she would fit in well with the other Ukrainian and Polish night-shift employees. Her salary would be paltry, but a Marshall Field discount card could save her money on most purchases. Mama would be assigned a floor and an area that she would regularly clean for the next business day. She would start at six o'clock in the evening and work late into the night.

That evening, when my father came home from work, Mama happily announced that she had found a job. Tato could officially quit his second shift. Mama would have supper on the table at five o'clock when he came home from work. She would leave for her job and return home before midnight. At first, my father did not like the idea that his wife would be working late. Mama said that she was not concerned about riding buses late at night since Chicago was a safe city. Also, working nights enabled her to stay home during the day with her children, cook, clean, and take care of household chores.

Mostly, Chicagoans enjoyed the hot days of summer. But when the heat became so oppressive that they couldn't get a good night's sleep, something had to be done. On one such night, the air in our apartment was so stifling that Tato announced that we were going to sleep outdoors. I thought he was kidding until he brought four wooden cots outdoors and set them up on the grass beneath the huge maple trees. He probably envisioned the trees as nature's gigantic fans because of their strong branches and multitude of leaves.

When Mama came home from work, she saw four cots on the grass. Three of them were occupied by her sleeping husband, daughter, and son. She didn't want to wake us up, so she went to the apartment, changed out of her work clothes, and returned to sleep in the empty cot. At last the four of us slept through the night despite the heat. The next morning, Tato woke up refreshed and ready for work. He never feared for our safety because at that time in America people knew, trusted, and respected their neighbors. My parents always felt that most Americans were caring individuals who wanted to help and not hurt their fellow human beings.

My American friends had been talking about the Fourth of July for weeks. They even boasted that their parents had been purchasing fireworks to commemorate America's birthday. I wanted to be a part of that celebration, even though I wasn't very familiar with that holiday. I decided to speak with my father and convince him that he should get some fireworks for us. Tato didn't respond the way that I had hoped he would. He said that we could enjoy the Fourth of July without any fireworks.

The adults and children on our block expressed a genuine joy and pride celebrating Independence Day. They had picnics in the backyards, played games, and eventually shot off colorful fireworks. When it was getting dark, I caught sight of my father carrying some candle-like objects. He took them to the curb and set them up in front of Pani Olya's house. My friends and I followed him. He looked up and cautioned us to stand back at a safe distance. One by one, he lit the flares. Yellowish flames shot up high into the air and emitted mighty hissing sounds. That night, our neighbors were pleasantly surprised to learn that their immigrant neighbor not only complemented their fireworks with his flares but celebrated America's birthday with them.

Mama's job at Marshall Field was going well until one night when she boarded a bus that was fairly empty except for a few passengers. Mama sat down since she had been on her feet all day and much of the night. The bus driver stopped to pick up another passenger. The new rider paid his fare and sat down directly across from Mama. She didn't pay much attention to the burly looking stranger until she realized that he was staring at her. At first, Mama thought that it was only her imagination until she looked up and saw the man glaring at her. Mama looked down and tried to ignore him. The stone-faced man continued to watch her. Mama felt uncomfortable. She wanted to say something to the bus driver, but what was she going to tell him? The man sitting across from her was staring at her. What was so terrible about that? Mama decided to ignore the stranger, hoping he would soon get off the bus. He didn't move.

Finally, the bus driver called out her stop. Mama calmly exited the bus, but the stranger followed right behind her. She sensed his presence and started to walk faster than normal. Mama continued to hear his footsteps. Her heart began pounding when she realized that he was still in pursuit. She picked up speed and started running with the stranger closely behind her. Mama ran all the way to the front door of her home. She turned around and saw that the stranger was right behind her. Mama started screaming. Tato, lying on the sofa, heard his wife's screams. He quickly jumped up and ran to the door and opened it. The stranger fled. That morning Tato was so upset that he told Mama to quit her job. She refused but did agree to have him meet her at the bus stop every night at an arranged time.

Over the years, my mother worked diligently at her job and

became a valued employee. She was personable, respected, and eventually learned to speak English quite well. Her bosses recognized Mama's abilities and offered her sales positions, but she always declined them. She preferred to be a stay-at-home mother during the day and work in the evenings with her immigrant coworkers, who had become her dear friends.

Chapter

5

My brother and I were content living in a small apartment without many material possessions. Mama took excellent care of us, kept our home tidy, and always had supper ready before Tato came home from work. I eagerly awaited his arrival because Tato usually came home with comic books for me. Those entertaining books featured the most colorful and amazing characters. Tato's job was to clean up the train's cars and discard any debris, newspapers, and comic books left behind by children and adults. He discarded everything except the comic books, which he saved for me.

Comic books gave me an incentive to learn how to read. I would carefully study every illustration, trying to figure out what the story was about and what the characters were saying. Comic books also offered me an opportunity to venture into the exciting world of superheroes like Superman and Batman. Whenever I felt like laughing at the silly antics of some of my favorite characters, I would pick up a copy of *Little Lulu and Tubby* or *Richie Rich*.

One fall day, after I had just exited our apartment through a side door, I noticed young people walking together in bizarre clothing. Their faces were covered with outlandish makeup. A female with long straggly hair was wearing an outfit that looked nothing like the garments that youngsters in our neighborhood wore. Another girl looked pretty scary. She reminded me of a character right out of one of my comic books. I loudly called for Mama. She asked me, "*Shcho stalosia*" (what happened)? I pointed to the strangely dressed children. Mama laughingly explained that they were just boys and girls dressed up in costumes because it was Halloween. She said that children dress up every year on October thirty-first and go "trick or treating" for candy, apples, and other treats. I felt a sense of relief and fascination at the same time. Halloween would ultimately become one of my favorite holidays.

Autumn leaves in vibrant hues of orange, yellow, brown, and violet graced the city. Tato enjoyed raking brittle leaves and piling them "sky high" so that my brother and I could jump up and down without fear of getting injured. It was especially delightful to hear the crackling and crunching sounds whenever we landed on the leaves. Sometimes, Tato pointed to the squirrels scampering for acorns around the changing trees.

On weekends, Mama would take walks with me around the neighborhood to view the array of autumn leaves. What she didn't like was watching property owners gather up their leaves, light them, and watch them burn. In the 1950s, burning leaves was a legal way to dispose of them. As a result, the neighborhood's fresh air would reek with pungent odors.

She told me that she loved natural scents but not the polluting smoke that marred nature's fall landscape.

Many trees were already bare when November brought numbing winds to Chicago. Thanksgiving Day was also approaching. Though grateful to be in America, Mama and Tato had not yet familiarized themselves with traditional Thanksgiving fare. Instead of turkey, Mama served us chicken with mashed potatoes, *kapusta* (cabbage sauerkraut with bacon bits), vegetables, and a freshly baked loaf of bread purchased at the Polish bakery. Before she served it, she made the sign of the cross on the back of the loaf. That traditional symbolic gesture expressed thanks to the Lord for her daily bread.

The cold continued to penetrate our clothes with brisk winds and rain. The ground began to freeze, and rain turned into snow. During those wintry December days, my brother and I played in the snow with our neighborhood friends. They introduced us to snowballs. I wanted to build a snowman, but none of them knew how to build one. Tato promised to teach me after the next heavy snowfall.

I didn't have to wait long. After the next storm, Tato announced that it was an ideal time to build a snowman in the yard. He showed me how to roll a snowball into an oversized head and body. Then I found a bucket to place on the snowman's head, and Roman found a carrot for the snowman's nose. Tato used lumps of coal for its eyes and mouth. Meanwhile, Mama brought out an old scarf and placed it around the snowy neck. Our snowman was the envy of the neighborhood.

That same winter, Tato surprised my brother and me with our first red Radio Flyer sled. When I first laid eyes on it, I screamed with joy! Before long, I was sitting on the sled ready to go for a ride with my toddler brother sitting in front of me. I held Roman with both arms so he wouldn't fall off the sled. That day, Tato pulled my brother and me on our Radio Flyer up and down the entire block. When we came back home, Tato whisked the snow and dirt off the sled and placed it in the shed. I escorted my brother back into the house where Mama was waiting for us with hot chocolate.

Around that time, one of our neighbors told Mama about a small English-speaking preschool in the area. Mama was pleasantly surprised to hear that there was a place where I could go during the cold winter months to improve my English-speaking skills.

The preschool was located in a medium-sized room, a short distance from where we lived. My fondest memory of that school occurred in December when a rotund man with a white beard and dressed in a red suit walked into the room. In a resounding voice, he introduced himself as Santa Claus. He also said that he had a huge sack of wrapped presents for all of the good boys and girls. Everyone in the room was so excited. I couldn't believe that I would finally meet the rotund man that everyone talked about. When Santa Claus handed me a large package wrapped in bright green and silver paper, I said, *"Duzhe Diakuyu"* (thank you very much). When I realized that I had spoken in Ukrainian, I quickly corrected myself and said "Thank you." Santa Claus smiled, and his large white-gloved hand gently patted my head. That day, I felt so lucky to be holding an unexpected present. When I finally opened it, I found a pretty doll inside. She had dark hair and wore a red velvet dress with white ankle socks and shoes.

Our Ukrainian culture honors a similar gift-giving person, *Sviatyj Mykolaj*, or St. Nicholas. He also has white hair, a thick

54

white beard, and a long mustache; but he carries a crosier and wears a bishop's robe. Ukrainian families traditionally celebrate St. Nicholas Day on December 19th by hanging up stockings the night before in hopes of finding presents inside of them. I would ask Tato if I could borrow one of his socks since his feet were so much bigger than mine. On the night of December 18th, I would hang up a pair of Tato's socks, one for me and one for Roman. The two of us would go to sleep dreaming of candy and toys. On the morning of the 19th, we would find our stockings bulging with an apple, orange, Hershey chocolate, and a special gingerbread cookie that looked just like the gift-giver. Mama said that St. Nicholas visited the best-behaved boys and girls all over the world and sometimes left images of himself. At first, I couldn't bring myself to eat the St. Nicholas gingerbread cookie. After all, St. Nicholas was a saint. But after several delightful whiffs of the soft and delectable treat, I peeled off his picture and devoured the cookie.

St. Nicholas also left me a cash register that I had wanted ever since I discovered it at the toy store. It had red keys, a drawer that opened and closed, and looked like the cash registers that adults used. While I excitedly showed Mama my new present, Roman unwrapped a box that contained a blue carpenter's apron with pockets filled with various tools such as a hammer, wrench, and screwdriver. He proudly donned the carpenter's apron and asked Mama if anything needed to be fixed in our apartment.

Glancing out our apartment window on Saturday afternoon, I noticed one of our neighbors carrying a tall evergreen tree with wide boughs. When Tato walked into the room, I asked him when he was planning on buying our tree.

He said that it was too early to buy a tree since we did not celebrate *Rizdvo* (Christmas) on the twenty-fifth of December. As Ukrainian Byzantine Rite Catholics, we along with the Orthodox Christians observed Jesus' birthday on January seventh according to the Julian calendar. After watching my neighbors carry Christmas trees into their homes, I told my father that the best trees would be picked over by the time he purchased one for us. A short time later, I heard Tato tell Mama that he would have a *yalynka* (Christmas tree) for us after the twenty-sixth when his neighbors would begin tossing out their still fresh, fragrant, and reusable trees.

Searching through the Christmas trees discarded by their owners, Tato picked out the tallest and fullest evergreen tree. He brought it home, made a wooden stand, and filled it with water. Mama purchased peppermint candies, wrapped them in brightly colored crepe paper, and hung them on the branches. She also had found a striking star at Marshall Field and asked Tato to place it on top of the evergreen. Our yalynka had no lights, so Mama decorated the branches with icicles to make them sparkle with silvery lights. My family was ready for our January seventh celebration.

Mama loved the distinctively elegant ornaments that adorned the Marshall Field's Christmas tree in the Walnut Room. She hoped to purchase similar ones for us. When Marshall Field's Christmas decorations went on sale, Mama started her own collection. My brother and I tried to be extra cautious handling those exquisite ornaments. Despite our best efforts, however, we still occasionally brushed against a tree branch a little too vigorously, causing one or more of the beautiful but fragile ornaments to fall and shatter.

Chapter

6

Warmer weather and milder temperatures returned to Chicago. I was preparing to play outside with my friends when Mama told me to stay home. She said that the dark clouds that hung over the entire block looked ominous. Tato walked in after working on some outdoor chores. He told Mama that he still had to go back out to finish when a blazing bolt of lightning and a powerful burst of thunder shook our apartment. Tato ran to the window and shouted that flames were shooting out of our next-door neighbor's house. He left our apartment and headed toward the burning house. Fred, a neighbor who lived nearby, stopped him. He told Tato that firemen were on their way to the burning house. Tato asked Fred about the family who lived there. Fred replied that fortunately they were not at home at the time of the lightning strike. When the fire truck arrived, the firemen bravely fought the blaze and put out the flames. But sadly, the home was badly charred.

The next day, our landlady, Pani Olya, said that our next-door neighbors were devastated by the damage to their home but grateful to be alive. They were temporarily living elsewhere until they could return to their home. My family thanked God that our neighbors were safe and that the flames coming from their house had not spread to ours!

After that close call, things settled down again. During the sultry summer evenings, Tato would put my little brother and me in a stroller and push the two of us until we reached the main thoroughfare. Since we didn't have a television set, my father, brother, and I would regularly visit two air-conditioned movie theaters within blocks of each other. Tato would first take us to the Alvin Theater to see what movies were playing there and then head to the Hub Theater to check its features. If both movie theaters were showing films we had already seen, we'd go back home, disappointed.

In the 1950s, tickets were cheap, and most of the movies were suitable for children. The theaters played coming attractions, two feature films, and a newsreel along with a cartoon or two. Going to the movies became part of our family routine. They were not only entertaining but educational. After I had learned how to read in first grade, Tato would ask me to read the names of the studios and beginning credits. I became familiar with MGM, Warner Brothers, Twentieth Century Fox, and Republic. While watching the features, we would munch on the best-buttered popcorn that a nickel or dime could buy. If my brother or I got hungry, Tato would pull out a couple of sandwiches he had brought from home.

Moviegoers went to see stars such as Kirk Douglas, Dean Martin and Jerry Lewis, Marlon Brando, Gene Kelly, and Marilyn Monroe. Some of my father's favorite actors were John Wayne, Humphrey Bogart, Edward G. Robinson, and Clark Gable. Roman and I loved the cartoons: Mighty Mouse, Woody Woodpecker, Tom and Jerry, Heckle and Jeckle, Bugs Bunny, Elmer Fudd, Porky Pig, and many others.

We loved going out with Mama as well. Whenever she needed to do some shopping, she would put my brother in a stroller, and I would walk beside her to Chicago Avenue where people shopped for groceries, clothing, meats, bakery goods, and many other items. Many stores were family owned. One day, we made our way toward a store that did not have a store front window or signs. When we arrived, I opened the door and heard clucking sounds. I looked around and saw chickens scurrying around the room while some hens poked their heads out of cages in the fowl-smelling store. Mama walked up to a short, dark-haired man wearing a large white apron with red stains. "You speak Ukrainian? Polish? *"Tak, mówię po polsku!"* replied the man. Mama smiled, "I speak Polish." Then she pointed to a chicken and in Polish told the man that she wanted a *kurczak* (chicken). He nodded and then grabbed one of the chickens and showed it to Mama. She looked at the frightened, squirmy creature and nodded in approval. The man walked out of the room holding the bird. When he returned, he handed Mama our dinner, wrapped in white paper. I did not have the heart to tell my brother what was inside that package. He was too busy staring and waving at the clucking chickens.

There were no supermarkets or freezers in our neighborhood that carried processed or cut-up poultry. No mess, no fuss, no culpability for killing a fowl! Mama sensed my disapproval and sadness over the fate of the chicken. She suggested that we walk a few blocks to where a vendor was selling ice cream.

I chose a large square-shaped vanilla wafer filled with Neapolitan ice cream. I peered through a small toy store window crowded with a multitude of dolls, board games, cars, planes, trucks, trains, bouncing balls, and other items. I saw a doll with a pretty hat and coat and asked Mama to buy it for me. She replied that we were not shopping for *zabawky* (toys).

Immigrants like my parents were always looking for places to shop that offered quality and fair prices. They found what they wanted at the Randolph Street Market. With blocks of unpretentious stores, the Market provided customers with the freshest fruits, vegetables, meats, and condiments at reasonable prices. The stores were managed by wholesalers who primarily catered to restaurants and grocery stores. The workers would start at dawn to meet the truck drivers who delivered the freshly picked fruits and vegetables.

During the day, wholesalers would display produce outside in baskets, bushels, and other containers. Through the open doors, customers inhaled the tantalizing aromas of smoked hams and Polish *kielbasa*, or sausage. Mama would stroll from store to store to find the best deals on large quantities of apples, oranges, pomegranates, and other fruits. Once she made her selection, the wholesaler would make arrangements to deliver her items. On a few occasions, when my parents didn't bring enough money, the wholesaler still arranged to deliver the produce.

Once when I was playing outside, a portly and robust man behind the reins of a horse-driven wagon unexpectedly pulled up in front of our home. In a booming Greek accent, he shouted, "Ma a ma, Ma a ma, po ta a to, po ta a to!" My mother came outside and cheerfully greeted the driver and asked him to "please come." With a huge burlap sack of potatoes on his back, the delivery man followed Mama to the coolest spot in the apartment. She thanked him, and he jovially replied, "Goodbye, Mama. See you next time."

Why did my parents buy potatoes in such large quantities? Because we ate them almost every day! They kept us well-fed through the entire winter. Mama made *platsky* (potato pancakes) with sour cream for lunch and prepared whole, baked, or mashed potatoes for supper. On weekends, we had potato dumplings with beef and brown gravy. Potatoes were a staple in my mother's cooking arsenal.

My parents patronized the same Randolph Street stores for many years, even after the original owners retired and their children took over the business. Good service, quality, and trust were hallmarks of this remarkable place.

Chapter

7

One morning, I woke up with a sore throat and fever. At first, Mama wasn't very concerned because her home remedies always helped me get well. However, when my throat continued to hurt, Mama took me to our Ukrainian family physician, *Dochtor* (Doctor) *Stefan*. He examined my inflamed throat and recommended that I have my tonsils removed as soon as possible. In the early 1950s, it was standard procedure for children to have tonsillectomies. Many boys and girls underwent the procedure on the recommendation of their family physicians.

On that miserable day when my father took me to the hospital, I cried as I was wheeled out of the elevator and into the operating room. Before long, I was unconscious. I dreamed that I was standing in front of a large empty Ferris Wheel that just kept turning round and round. There was also a terrible odor in my dream unlike any that I had ever experienced before. I just wanted that Ferris Wheel to stop spinning and the horrible odor to go away.

I finally woke up in a hospital bed and saw my father standing beside me. He kissed me and then handed me a wrapped package. A nurse entered the room with a small container and said that she had a special treat for me. Even though I felt woozy, I recognized vanilla ice cream. For the first time in my life, I was not in the mood to eat my favorite cold dessert. The nurse kept encouraging me to take a bite. I reluctantly did, but when I tried to swallow, my throat hurt. I turned my head away when I was offered another bite.

I wanted only to open my father's wrapped gift. He helped me untie the ribbon, and to my surprise, I found a toy called a View-Master, along with a few circular movie reels. Tato inserted one of the reels into the View-Master and held it up to the light so that I could look through the lenses. Just like at the movies, the figures on the reel came to life when I began to click from one frame to another. Hopalong Cassidy in his full black cowboy gear stood beside his white horse, Topper. I loved my new toy and was so happy that my parents had thought of buying it for me.

That gift helped to relieve some of the unpleasantness of having my tonsils removed. When my brother developed a similar problem with his throat, the doctor suggested that Roman also have a tonsillectomy. Luckily for him, Mama and Tato wisely refused.

As children, we were always thrilled when it snowed. Early in November, soft white flakes drifted from the sky. By evening they turned into a heavy snowstorm that brought the city to a standstill. The thick white flakes continued falling through the night. The next morning, the ground was covered with nine inches of snow. I was at home trying to convince Mama to let me go out to play but she said *ni* (no). I walked to the nearest window, a pane completely encased with sparkling snow. Tato went outside to shovel and quickly discovered that the snow was thick and heavy. He would have to pace himself. It took a while, but eventually, he cleared the main walkways. When he came back into the house, Mama had a large cup of hot coffee and a freshly baked apple strudel waiting for him.

Whenever deep snow covered the ground, I would beg Tato to take me for a sled ride. He always said *tak*, which made me even more eager to get on a sled. Tato would pull it as fast as he could while maneuvering around the sidewalks blocked by the chunky snow. I never saw any other children on my block ever getting a sled ride from their fathers! Thanks to Tato, the snowiest days of winter became some of my fondest memories.

During the cold weather, blustery winds unleashed their fury, penetrating the walls of our frame home. Periodically, Tato had to replenish the coal in our coal-burning stove to keep us warm. One evening, he was struggling to ignite the coal embers and sprinkled starter fluid onto the coals. The flames shot up and singed his face. He screamed in pain.

It was late evening, and no adult was around to help him. Mama was at work, and we had no telephone. Tato needed to apply something quickly to his raw and inflamed face. He ran to the cupboard, grabbed a bottle of fish oil, nervously opened it, and poured the contents into his hand. He applied the fish oil to his face while grimacing in pain.

Tato began to pace the floor. I started to cry because I knew that my father was in terrible pain and I could not help him. My little brother was also upset even though he was too young to understand the seriousness of his father's injury. Tato must have had a high tolerance for pain, because he still managed to get my brother and me ready for bed. I couldn't fall asleep. I just lay in bed worrying about my father, waiting for my mother to come home.

It was late when Mama entered the apartment. She was shocked to see her husband's inflamed face. Mama started crying and urged him to get medical help. Tato told her that he could not afford to take time off to see a doctor. Instead, he would go to work and not tell anyone about the accident. Tato was concerned that his employer might not allow him to work with such a serious burn. He decided to cover his face with a ski mask to protect it from the cold and to keep his employer and fellow workers from learning about his injury. In the meantime, Tato would continue to treat his face every morning and night with fish oil.

As the days went by, his curious co-workers began to ask Tato why he was always wearing a ski mask. Tato would say something about the cold weather and then change the subject. His employers never did find out about his injury. My father's face completely healed without a single scar or mark from the burn. Mama said, "*Bohu diakuvaty*," (thank God) that his face healed without any scarring.

Even though my parents would occasionally try to heal themselves, they did secure medical help for my brother and me. Mama would take us to the local Ukrainian family physician, Dochtor Stefan. He was a tall, strong-looking man with a small mustache slightly curled up around the edges. His wire-rimmed glasses surrounded his kind eyes, and his face lit up when he smiled. He looked like a serious professional with a sense of humor. Dochtor Stefan and other family physicians in America took great care of their patients. Since there was no medical insurance in those days, patients paid merely nominal fees for their physicians' services. It was also common practice for doctors to visit their patients' homes whenever they were too ill to travel for diagnosis and treatment. Remarkably, the doctors never overcharged for home visits. Reasonably priced health care enabled American citizens as well as immigrants to receive timely treatment and medications for their illnesses.

Dochtor Stefan was not only a skilled physician but also a caring person. His office was located on the second floor in a building near a busy intersection. His patients would sit and wait to be called on a first-come, first-served basis. The later they arrived, the longer they had to wait. Dochtor Stefan's office was often crowded with sick patients of all ages.

Dochtor Stefan did not have a receptionist to schedule his appointments. He would simply come out of his office and ask the next person in the waiting room to come in. However, when a mother arrived with one or more sick children, he would ask the other patients to be understanding and allow him to treat the sick child or children first. I liked Dochtor Stefan and never felt uncomfortable around him, even though I did not especially like going to see a doctor.

His personable manner made his patients feel confident that he would help them. Dochtor Stefan communicated with patients in their own native language, making it easier for them to correctly describe their symptoms, ask questions, and discuss treatment options. If an illness were not serious, he would recommend the patient treat it with a home remedy. As a family physician, Dochtor Stefan treated minor colds, took x-rays, delivered babies, and performed surgeries. In those days, there were few specialists in the medical field.

The doctor also kept a supply of free medications in his office that he packaged, labeled, and put in small white boxes before dispensing to his patients. Mama had the greatest respect for Dochtor Stefan. He truly followed the Hippocratic Oath, dedicating his life to healing sick people to the best of his ability even if they could not afford to pay him.

Besides using natural remedies, my mother also learned about preventative measures of modern medicine that would help keep her family healthy. She made sure that my brother and I were vaccinated against childhood diseases. Mama would also get free chest x-rays from a Mobile Chest-X-Ray Unit that offered screenings for tuberculosis to local residents. Medicine was much more of a personal exchange between doctors and patients back then.

Chapter

8

My parents being immigrants often reached out to help other immigrants who were experiencing difficult times. One evening during supper, I heard my parents talking about their good friend Pan Ivan, a bright, gentle, educated man with captivating eyes hidden behind thick glasses. His soft but confident tone calmed and impressed his listeners. Tato had recently spoken with him and learned that Pan Ivan was feeling poorly. He worked long hours and had little time to rest or prepare meals for himself. Pan Ivan laughingly told Tato that as a bachelor, he had to cook for himself but was not very good at it.

Pan Ivan was educated in Europe. Before immigrating to America, he had earned the respect of his professional colleagues as well as his fellow refugees living in the German camp. Mama told my father that Pan Ivan was a wonderful friend who needed someone to cook for him until he could regain his strength and feel well enough to live on his own. She wanted Tato to ask Pan Ivan to live with us. Mama also reminded her husband that Pan Ivan would need a room of his own. Tato mentioned that an extra room in our apartment was being used for storage. He could remove the items and replace them with a bed for Pan Ivan. However, before Tato could invite Pan Ivan to live with us, he would have to seek permission from our landlady, Pani Olya. Mama felt good about their decision and excited about cooking for her dear friend.

Tato discussed the matter with Pani Olya and got her approval. He then told Pan Ivan that he and Mama would be honored to have him move in with our family. Speechless, Pan Ivan smiled and extended his hand in gratitude. He was living in small cramped quarters with other single young men who lacked cooking skills. Tato invited Pan Ivan to our home to discuss the details with Mama, the cook and the lady of the house.

When Pan Ivan arrived at our apartment, he told Mama that he was humbled and appreciative that she and Tato had invited him to share their home. He would gladly accept their offer but only if he could help defray some of the cost of household expenses. Mama and Tato did not want Pan Ivan's money but agreed to his request. They knew it was the only way he would accept their invitation.

My family welcomed a real gentleman into our home. Pan Ivan was reserved, polite, kind, and well-read. He would come home from work, eat Mama's hearty meals, and spend some time chatting with my brother, Roman, and me about our day. After we went to bed, Tato and Pan Ivan would discuss the day's events, topics that ranged from local politics to world happenings.

Chapter 8

On the weekends, our newest family member liked to surprise us with freshly baked coffee cakes and other delectable pastries from the local bakery. I also learned that Pan Ivan had a witty sense of humor. I loved listening to his stories, which he told with enthusiasm and spiced up with vivid details. Living with him was a wonderful learning experience. As the months went by, Mama's cooking did wonders for our guest. He not only gained weight but looked noticeably stronger and healthier.

His help was vital for my brother that spring. Inside our warm apartment, my little brother Roman was coughing. At first, the cough didn't appear serious, but when he developed a high fever, Mama and Tato became very concerned. Tato tried unsuccessfully to contact our family physician, Dochtor Stefan. In the meantime, Mama applied cold compresses to her son's hot body to try to bring down his temperature. Eventually, the fever broke, leaving Roman with a deep chest cold.

My parents were concerned about how to best treat their son who was only a toddler. They discussed the situation with Pan Ivan. He told them that he knew how to stop the constant coughing and clear up his congested chest. Pan Ivan left the apartment and returned with a heating lamp. He told my parents that the heat from the lamp would clear up the congestion in Roman's chest. Pan Ivan stayed up all night with my brother, carefully positioning the heating lamp over his chest area so as to not injure his skin. He reassured my worried parents that he knew what he was doing. Mama and Tato had to trust their friend. Thankfully, the next morning, my brother looked and felt better. His coughing subsided and his appetite returned. Within days, he was running around and playing. My parents were grateful to Pan Ivan and felt that he had saved their son's life.

Pan Ivan continued to live with us for about a year. When he moved out, we were sad but happy for him. Mama said, "Pan Ivan was healthier, had a better job, and had found a new apartment." We would miss him, but over the years he would visit us and continue to be a lifelong friend.

Chapter
9

Our parents were always eager for us to make the most of our abilities and get a good education. My little brother was a typical toddler brimming with energy and curiosity. One day, he scared Mama when she found him on top of a dresser. A very curious boy, he would take apart various gadgets in our home just to see how they worked. One day, he took apart a clock and put it back together. Mama was amazed that her young son could accomplish such a feat. When Tato came home from work, she told him what Roman had done. At first Tato was surprised, but then he predicted that Roman's thinking and motor skills would one day serve him well.

For me school began when I was six years old in 1952. My parents enrolled me as a first grader at St. Nicholas Ukrainian Catholic School. The school had no kindergarten classes until about 1955.

In August, my mother and I visited the local department store to pick out my first school bag. I found a number of leather bags with handles and selected a shiny brown one and then picked out a notebook and pencils. After she paid for my purchases, the two of us headed toward the children's clothing section.

After trying on several different dresses, I chose a pretty yellow cotton dress with ruffles. Mama paid for it, and we made our way to the shoe department where I found a pair of beige shoes with ankle straps along with a new pair of white socks. I was ready for my first day of class! What I didn't know was that my parents still hadn't decided how I was going to get to school. Tato couldn't take me because he left for work very early in the morning. Mama would have to wake my little brother so that he could accompany me to and from school five days a week. After some further discussions, my parents made a decision. Tato would go with me on the bus to the school.

We caught the bus on Chicago Avenue. Along the way, Tato pointed out the street signs and landmarks. When we arrived at our destination, we walked a short distance to the church. My father escorted me inside and helped me to locate my first-grade classroom. When classes were over, Tato walked me to the bus stop and asked me if I would be willing to travel to school by myself. I instantly replied, "*Tak.*" I never hesitated because I knew that I was a big girl who could confidently travel between home and school.

The next day, I knew that I was on my own. I felt independent and proud that my parents trusted me enough to let me travel by myself. I also knew that they were a bit apprehensive. The night before my first solo trip, Mama and Tato lectured me about how I should always be careful and aware of my surroundings. Also, I was never, ever to go anywhere with a stranger.

My route to school was easy and convenient. I walked to Chicago Avenue, boarded a westbound bus, looked for a window seat, and paid attention to street signs and landmarks. After school, I was often joined by other Ukrainian students traveling in my direction. They were always very friendly and helpful, but since I was the youngest, they probably felt that they should watch over me.

The year I started first grade, a massive influx of immigrants settled in the Chicago area. They became members of St. Nicholas Ukrainian Catholic Church and registered their children for the parish grammar school built in 1934. That building could not accommodate all of the incoming students, so plans were made to construct a larger and more modern school building. The land for that new school was blessed and dedicated around the time I was in first grade.

Because of overcrowding, I spent my first year of school in a drafty room beneath the church. Even though the room was cramped, my classmates and I were able to get a good start on our education. Our teacher belonged to the order of the Sisters of St. Basil the Great. She wore a long black dress, or habit, with a matching head piece that was black on the outside but white around her face and neck. Sister was a strict disciplinarian. Parents expected their children to respect and obey her because, like the other nuns in the school, she was a special woman who had dedicated her life to God.

Sister introduced us to the English alphabet and the three R's: reading, 'riting, and 'rithmetic. For reading, we used the *Dick and Jane* series. Every one of my classmates had to read aloud and pronounce every word correctly before proceeding to the next story or book. One day, I mispronounced a few words, so Sister asked me to stay after class. Sister told me to inform my parents that one of them had to come and speak with her.

I gave Tato the message, and the following afternoon, he met with Sister. She told him that I had to take my reading book home and practice correctly pronouncing every word in the story. Tato promised her that he would work with me. I was surprised to hear him make that promise since he could barely speak English, let alone read it.

That evening through sheer persistence, Tato phonetically sounded out the words that I needed to learn in my reader. He amazed me. The next day, when Sister called on me, I read every word without making a single error. From that day forward, I became an excellent reader.

My parents always expected and encouraged me to do my best work at school. They would also ask me about my homework assignments. One evening, Tato noticed that I was adding instead of subtracting while doing some of my arithmetic problems. So he took a bunch of apples and oranges out of the refrigerator, put them next to me, and in his unorthodox but effective manner, demonstrated how to subtract items.

Religious education was essential to our curriculum. My classmates and I welcomed *Otech*, (Father) a Basilian priest, with the traditional religious greeting, "*Slava Isusu Chrystu*" (Glory to Jesus Christ). He would reply, "*Slava Naviky*" (Glory Forever).

Otech spoke to us about our Byzantine Rite, taught us prayers, and told us Bible stories. I looked forward to his visits because he could tell a Bible story in such a dramatic and descriptive way that I could almost see the characters and their surroundings. Otech would also bring in small religious articles such as holy cards and distribute them for various occasions or as rewards for good work. My classmates and I enjoyed learning our catechism.

First grade was going well for me that year despite two mishaps on my way home from school. The first occurred when I was standing on the corner, waiting for a bus to take me home. I reached into my pocket to take out my twenty-cent fare. Instead of finding two dimes, I found only one. Thinking that I might have misplaced the other dime, I kept searching for it. Then it dawned on me I must have inadvertently used it to buy candy during recess. Tato usually gave me enough money to pay for my bus fare and to purchase a snack such as potato chips or candy. But that day I must have used most of my change on the snacks. When I realized my mistake, I began to whimper.

Luckily, a couple of older boys from my school were also waiting for the bus. The taller boy asked, "Why are you crying?" I replied that I could not find my other dime to pay for the bus fare. He reached into his pocket, pulled out a dime, and gave it to me. I offered to repay him another time, but he told me not to worry about it. I thanked him and learned a big lesson that day: to set aside enough money for my bus fare before buying any lunchtime treats. That day, I told Mama and Tato about what had happened. They were very grateful that the kind boy had helped me out. As Tato handed me some extra coins for the next school day, he reminded me not to spend my fare money on snacks.

The second incident occurred on the bus going home from school. I was busy chatting and not listening for my stop. When

I finally looked out the window, I realized that my stop was coming up, so I dashed to the front of the bus and got off. In my haste, I left my schoolbag on the bus. I went home and told Mama what had happened. She said that I should speak with Tato about getting it back. That evening, I told him what had happened and that I needed to do my homework. He replied that there wasn't much he could do about the homework, but he promised to contact the bus company. The next day, Tato called and spoke in his best English with a knowledgeable employee who said that the bus driver had already turned in a schoolbag. He told my father where to go to pick it up. That evening, I was relieved when I saw my father walk in with my brown schoolbag.

I learned some of my educational lessons outside of school. On a cold and partly cloudy day in 1953, Tato was picking up newspapers left behind by Chicago and North Western Railroad riders. When he glanced at the front page of the *Chicago Daily News*, a black-and-white photograph of a mustached man startled him. He immediately walked out of the train's car to find his American coworker, Frank, who also spoke Polish. When he spotted him, Tato ran over with the newspaper and asked Frank to read the headline. "Stalin in Coma, Dying," replied Frank. Tato stood there silently while Frank continued to read the paper. Frank remarked that President Eisenhower was extending his sympathy to the Russian people.

Tato pointed to Stalin's photo and emphatically stated, in his best English and Polish, that Stalin had systematically starved millions of Ukrainians in their homeland by imposing exorbitant grain quotas from Ukraine. Stalin knew full well the quotas would exhaust the people's food supply and inevitably cause mass starvation. Looking shocked, Frank uttered, "I knew about the tragic Jewish Holocaust but had never heard about the starvation of Ukrainians."

Tato recounted that in 1932 squads of Soviet agents descended upon Ukraine, imposing the quotas, inspecting the peasants' cottages, scouring their cellars and hiding places beneath wooden floors to confiscate wheat, barley, potatoes, and beans. Stalin also authorized that all grains and livestock be considered state property: pilfering of Soviet goods was considered a capital offense, subjecting peasants to death or imprisonment.

Holodomor monument
in Washington, D.C.

Holodomor monument in Kyiv, Ukraine

Tato stressed that in 1932 and 1933 while countless Ukrainians starved to death, the Soviets sold over a million and a half tons of grain abroad. The coworker acknowledged that it was difficult for him to comprehend how Stalin could have engineered such a horrific famine. My father lamented that the artificial starvation (*Holodomor*) had killed over seven million Ukrainian people. (According to some historians, the number of fatalities exceeded ten million victims.)

That evening, when Tato came home, he told Mama about Stalin's impending death. Mama placidly replied, "I envision Stalin standing before God, trying to explain why he had inflicted so much pain and suffering upon so many innocent men, women, and children." Her eyes started to tear when she recounted that the Soviets had annihilated an entire generation of Ukrainians. I couldn't believe that Mama and Tato broached this traumatic topic in front of me. Most of the time, they talked about such matters in private. And then I realized that I was getting older. My parents wanted me to know that Stalin, a ruthless tyrant, had initiated and spearheaded the *Holodomor*.

My parents had survived the famine because they lived in the western region of Ukraine. Their relatives, friends, and fellow villagers were not fully aware of the horrors devastating the eastern part. Still, many of the villagers suspected that something was terribly wrong, but the lack or suppression of communication kept them in the dark. When the truth finally surfaced, the Ukrainians in the western region vowed never to forget the millions of people who had perished during that terrible starvation. I wanted to know more about Stalin and particularly about the victims of the *Holodomor*. However,

Tato said that I needed to be much older to learn about the ghastly genocide.[1]

---

1 The film "MЯ JONES" tells about the Welsh journalist Gareth Jones, who risked his life to seek the truth about the famine that was devastating Ukraine. Released on April 3, 2020, the film was directed by Agnieszka Holland and starred James Norton, Vanessa Kirby, and Peter Sarsgaard.

Chapter

10

One Saturday afternoon, Mama tapped me on the shoulder and said that Tato had some wonderful news. I was so absorbed in my "Little Lulu and Tubby" comic book that I asked her to let me finish reading the page before I dog-eared the next one. As soon as I closed the comic, Tato proudly said, "We will soon be moving into our own *chata* (house)." "What, our own chata!" I exclaimed. I couldn't believe what I was hearing. I enjoyed living in Pani Olya's house, but I was getting older and needed my own room. Mama laughingly concurred as she handed me a bowl of strawberry ice cream to celebrate, and Tato handed me a brand new issue of "Superman." I excitedly thanked them both.

My parents always wanted to purchase a brick home in the neighborhood near St. Nicholas Ukrainian Catholic Church. However, after carefully checking the available properties, they discovered that the spacious one-and two-flat brick buildings were too expensive. My parents also looked for houses near Humboldt Park but didn't find any that they wanted to purchase.

Tato and Mama sought Pan Volodymyr for his advice. A good friend, businessman, and property owner, he recommended that they look for property that would provide a good future investment. He suggested that they look in a different location where larger buildings were more affordable. My parents took Pan Volodymyr's advice to heart. They even invited him to join them in their search since he knew a lot about real estate. After months of searching and inspecting numerous buildings, my parents found a building that appealed to them. After careful consideration, they decided to purchase it.

Mama and Tato weren't in America very long when they put a down payment on an apartment building located farther south and populated by Polish-American families and other Slavic peoples. The solid brick building was well constructed but needed interior repairs. Tato didn't mind the challenge because he was young, eager to learn, and ready to take on the role of landlord. Mama was going to be the landlady, and I would be their secretary. I could read and write in English and fill out rent receipts.

Pan Volodymyr helped Tato load a rented truck with our belongings, including clothing, household items, and some furniture. When they arrived at our new home, they unloaded the truck and carried our possessions to the second floor. Soon after, Pan Volodymyr drove back to our old apartment where Mama, Roman, and I were patiently waiting. When he arrived, we said our good-byes to Pani Olha and Pan Dmytro and thanked them for their kindness during the time that we had lived in their building. From there, we headed toward Pan Volodymyr's home, where his wife, Pani Olena, had prepared a tasty lunch for us. Roman and I stayed with Pani Olena, while Pan Volodymyr drove Mama back to our new home.

Pan Volodymyr returned to drive my brother and me to our new place. When we arrived, I noticed several "wing-tipped" cars parked in front of a three-story brick apartment building on a block of mostly single-family homes. On the left of that building, a door led to a first-floor apartment, and to the right, a door led to the second-and third-floor apartments. I heard Pan Volodymyr calling me, so I quickly followed him and my brother up the front steps to the right door. Pan Volodymyr opened it. We walked up a flight of stairs to the second floor where Mama was waiting to welcome us.

I stepped into a brightly lit spacious kitchen with a brand new table and puffy chairs. A sunshine-filled living room caught my eye. I strolled toward the center of that room and stared at the impressively large windows flanked by white curtains. The walls were covered with wallpaper decorated in dainty pastel flowers. I was surprised to discover another room to the left of that cheerful living area. I stepped inside and recognized the framed print of my Guardian Angel hanging over my brand-new bed. Next to the bed was a small white dresser with a mirror. And close to that dresser was a window. I could look out every morning to check the weather and observe any activity near the small Polish grocery store across the street. A gigantic billboard loomed on the corner of a busy thoroughfare.

That evening, the four of us sat around our modern, steel-chromed kitchen table, eating and talking about how good it felt to be living in our very own home. Tato even started discussing his plans for renovating the apartments when suddenly loud rumblings and screeches startled us. I asked him if a storm was approaching. Mama just kept on eating while Tato explained that the thunderous noises were actually made by trains running past our building. I had never seen or heard of elevated trains. I was familiar only with buses. Tato said that we should not be concerned about the startling noises because after a while we would get used to them. Tato was right. Before long, I would become oblivious to the trains that regularly vibrated behind our building.

On Sunday morning, we donned our finery to attend St. Nicholas Ukrainian Catholic Church. The four of us walked to the corner where we waited for our bus. There was a tavern on that corner, but it was closed on Sunday. When the bus arrived, Tato paid our fares and asked for transfers. Since I would be traveling a new route to school, I sat near a window so that Tato could point out street names and landmarks on Damen Avenue. We got off at Chicago Avenue, crossed the street, and waited for another bus. After a short ride to Oakley Boulevard, we walked a couple of short blocks to the church.

On the way home, my father told me that I could wait for the first bus on Chicago Avenue just as I did when we lived at Pani Olya's. However, I would have to get off the bus at Damen Avenue, cross the street, and wait by the Italian restaurant for the second bus that would travel south to our home. Tato reminded me that I could simply walk from school to Damen Avenue and then board the bus, if I preferred.

On Monday morning, Mama walked me to the corner and waited with me for the bus to arrive. When it did, she gave me a quick kiss and wished me well. I paid my fare and sat near the driver.

When I returned from school, Mama admitted that she had been a bit anxious waiting for my arrival. I told her she had nothing to worry about because taking two buses was a lot more fun than taking one. I also hinted that the aroma coming from the cheese blintzes made the trip well worth it. Mama chuckled as she headed toward the stove. While I was eating, she told me that she, too, had a new route to get to Marshall Field. As soon as Tato arrived from work at five o'clock, she would leave, walk a short distance to the train station, board the elevated train, and take it to State Street.

Traveling by bus to school was never a problem. I enjoyed the responsibility and freedom of being an independent young person. My trips were interesting because I got to see different neighborhoods as I made my way to and from school. For example, one area of the city intrigued me because it had so many houses of worship in close proximity to one another with the word "Baptist" imprinted on most of them. I believed that they belonged to my Black American neighbors, who made God a priority in their lives.

Most of my trips were uneventful, and the best part of riding the bus was my interaction with the bus drivers. Always kind to me, they often greeted me with a friendly "hello" whenever I boarded their buses. The bus drivers were probably protective of me even though I did not realize it at the time. One of them, Mr. Andy, would hand me a candy bar along with a transfer. Moreover, he did not want me to cross the busy Chicago Avenue, so he would insist that I stay on the bus until he drove through the intersection. I would always thank him as I made my way out the door. Then I would walk a few feet where I waited for the second bus that would take me near my school.

Another bus driver that I really liked was Mr. Henry. One morning, when I was paying my fare, I mentioned that my brother and I sometimes liked to play "bus driver," but it would be more fun if we had some transfers. Well, the next day, Mr. Henry handed me a huge pack of them. I thanked him several times and then stuck them in my school bag. When I arrived home, my parents and Roman couldn't believe that I had so many transfers from such a considerate driver. Transfers were popular with many of the kids who loved to play with them.

Some of the drivers would ask me why I was traveling so far to school when so many good schools were in the area. I would tell them that I was Ukrainian and that I went to a Ukrainian Catholic School. They would often ask me, "What's Ukrainian?" and "Is that like Russian?" I would tell them, "Ukrainians are not Russians." I got the feeling that they had never heard of Ukraine or its people. I was just a kid, but I learned early on from my parents and teachers that Ukraine was dominated by the Russians who had taken away its freedom. I also accepted the fact that I would always have to explain my nationality. One day, I complained to Mama, "Americans do not know about us or our country." She replied, "Someday, Ukraine will be free, and then everyone will know about our homeland." I tried to believe her, but there were times when I was convinced that Americans knew only about Russia and its leaders. And they didn't particularly like them because of the Cold War.

Chapter

11

One evening, Tato excitedly informed Roman and me that a fine American family lived below us. They had a daughter, Karolina, only a year older than me and a son about two years older than Roman. Mama was thrilled to learn that American-born Harriet and her husband, Frank, could also speak Polish. Tato said that when they initially learned that an immigrant family had purchased the building, the couple feared that they might have trouble communicating with the landlord. Frank and Harriet were also concerned that Tato might ask them to move out so that his family could move into their apartment. After all, first-floor apartments were the most desirable because they were closest to the street. Tato reassured Frank and Harriet that he did not intend to evict them. My parents also informed my brother and me that an elderly lady lived above us on the third floor. They asked that we never disturb her.

Roman and I finally had an opportunity to meet the boy and girl who lived in our building when we spotted them standing outside their first-floor apartment with their mother, Harriet. A neighborly lady, Harriet had short brownish hair and wore wire-rimmed glasses. She smiled and said, "You must be the landlord's children." I then introduced myself and my brother, Roman. Harriet was a stay-at-home mother while her husband, Frank, was the family's breadwinner. Born in America, they spoke only English to their children. Their daughter, Karolina, was a friendly, eight-year old brunette with a stylish short haircut. She said, "It's really nice to have someone close to my own age in the same building." Her brother, Frankie, was about five years old, wore glasses, and was about a head taller than my brother. Frankie appeared shy when he shook hands with Roman. Harriet exclaimed, "Quite a few boys and girls live in the area. As a matter of fact, a ten-year-old boy named Bobby lives next door. He knows most of the kids in the neighborhood." That day, Roman and I made plans to get together with Frankie and Karolina.

It didn't take long before Karolina and I became friends. We played with our dolls, jumped rope, hop-scotched, talked about school, television, movies and all kinds of girlish hopes and dreams. Frankie would come outdoors with his sturdy red Radio Flyer wagon and play with my brother. He would also talk about baseball and the Cubs. Tato talked to Roman only about soccer so my brother didn't really know much about running bases and hitting home runs. When Frankie mentioned that he and the other boys in the neighborhood loved to "throw the ball around" and play baseball at Gads Hill Center, Roman knew that he had to learn more about the popular American sport.

Chapter 11

It was the weekend. Karolina and Frankie were gone for the day, so Roman and I decided to meet some of the other kids on our block. Tato, who considered himself a part-time barber, insisted that Roman get a haircut before venturing outdoors. He already had his special scissors out and was ready to give his son a trim.

After Tato brushed some stray hairs off my brother's collar, Roman walked up to me. He looked like Tato had placed a bowl on his head before cutting his blondish hair. I was just grateful that Mama cut my naturally curly hair.

Four boys who looked to be older than me were chatting in front of the three-story brick house next door. My brother and I had just made our way down the front stairs of our apartment building when a tall, muscular boy blurted out, "Hey, you must be the new DPs that just moved into our neighborhood."

I didn't know what "DPs" stood for but suspected that it wasn't complimentary. Roman also realized it was a derogatory term because it was delivered in such a mean-spirited way. I replied, "My brother and I do not like being called names," and then asked, "Why are you calling us DPs? You don't even know us."

" 'Cause I heard that you and your family are off the boat and not real Americans like us. You speak a language we don't understand. You should only speak English like the rest of us."

"We speak Ukrainian because we are Ukrainians, but we are also learning to speak English."

I informed Bobby that whether he liked it or not, my father was now the landlord of the building where his friends, Frankie and Karolina, lived.

The toughie was ready to say something when Roman

walked up to him and asked, "Are you Bobby?"

"How do you know my name, Shorty?"

"I'm not Shorty. I'm Roman."

I heard Mama calling us, so I turned to my brother and signaled for him to follow me to the gangway. As soon as I got there, I saw Mama's head sticking out the window. She wanted my brother and me to come upstairs for lunch. As we headed back home, we could hear Bobby shouting, "So long, DPs," while his friends laughed.

That evening, I told my parents that the boy next door and his friends had called us "DPs." I asked Tato what it meant. He said it meant "displaced persons," or refugees. Unfortunately, he said, some people don't like immigrants because they don't understand the foreign language or culture. Tato told me that he had been called a "DP" but didn't let it bother him. He jokingly added that some of his tenants probably resented that a DP was their landlord. "But I don't care what they call me, just as long as they pay their rent on time!" He asked us not to overreact to the term "DP" because in time we would be accepted.

Chapter

12

When my Ukrainian classmates and I had first entered our makeshift classroom in the church hall, we had been like blank slates. Under Sister's strict tutelage, we completed our first year as first graders in America. We could speak, read, and write in English and do arithmetic problems. We also attended Byzantine Rite church services and learned about religious vocations. Sister encouraged the girls to become nuns and the boys to consider the priesthood. To inspire us, she rewarded our achievements with religious cards showing images of Jesus, Mary, Joseph, the angels, and saints. Sister also kept a stash of small religious plastic statues, medals, and rosaries that she sold to us for special occasions. Tato gave me a dollar to buy Mama a small plastic statue of the Blessed Mother. I wrapped it in brightly colored paper and gave it to Mama for Mother's Day, which I had learned was an American holiday. I knew she would be excited to receive her first Mother's Day gift from me.

My new friend, Karolina, told me about a large facility on our block called Gads Hill Center. It housed a library and social center where boys, girls, and young adults could enjoy various activities: reading, music, drama, and carpentry workshops. I was ready to read novels without pictures, so I was thrilled that a library was only a short distance from my home. I headed toward Gads Hill, entered the building, and readily found the library. The imposing bookcases neatly stacked with famous books prompted me to ask a librarian to help me to find some exciting books. She said, "Yes, of course," and escorted me to the children's section. While I browsed through the children's books, she looked for some adventure books for me. Before long, the librarian pulled out some Nancy Drew mystery novels written by Carolyn Keene. She said, "You will enjoy reading about a young female sleuth who solves mysteries." Then she left me to look over the mystery novels.

I walked up to the librarian's desk with a handful of Nancy Drew books. I was eager to begin reading my first novel about a young female detective. "Do you have a library card?" asked the librarian.

"I don't have one, but would like to apply for one."

She smiled and asked, "How old are you?"

"I'm seven years old."

"You're old enough to get your very own library card. Just fill out this form."

After I filled out the small form, she handed me my first library card. I was thrilled. I could officially take out books whenever I wanted, just as long as I returned them on time. The librarian, Miss Sandra, gave me a terrific first impression of the Gads Hill Center's library. She and I would become good book friends.

I walked home with my Nancy Drew books, sat on the front steps of our building, opened up my first mystery novel, and started to read. When Karolina came out to play, I showed her my library books. She was almost as happy as I was when she recognized the titles. Karolina said that I would really enjoy reading my Nancy Drew books, and she was right. I finished reading my first Carolyn Keene book in no time. A couple of days later, Karolina and I agreed that Nancy Drew mystery books were perfect for girls our age, since Nancy was intelligent, shrewd, and creative.

It was time for summer vacation. I had been promoted to second grade and was looking forward to getting together with my neighborhood friends. Bobby and his buddies stopped calling my brother and me DPs and accepted us as their friends. In fact, Bobby became one of our best neighbors. He was always polite, friendly, and even became protective of me. Roman eventually became a close friend of Bobby's despite their age difference.

It was a wonderful time to grow up in America. General Dwight D. Eisenhower was president, and Americans were relieved that the Korean War was over. In Chicago, boys and girls left political issues to the adults and enjoyed their childhood outdoors. Roman and I were fortunate to be living in an area of the city where children knew how to have fun and appreciate the simple things in life. They shared ideas, Coca Cola, bubble and stick gum, Popsicles, chips, various candies, marbles, kites, water balloons, squirt and cap guns, and so many other toys. The children kept themselves busy playing a variety of games and riding their bicycles until late in the evening under street lights. Occasionally, they had trivial squabbles, but they never lasted very long.

On rare occasions when Karolina wasn't around, I would walk over to Gads Hill Center to watch the boys play baseball, because I wanted to learn more about this popular sport. One afternoon, I asked if I could play. The boys looked puzzled and asked why I wanted to be in a "boy's" game. Then, they looked at each other and nodded "okay." After one of the games, Tommy took me aside. He said that I was the only girl the boys had ever allowed to play baseball, since they had a "no girls allowed" rule. Whenever it was my turn to bat, they always shouted out instructions so that the pitcher would "walk me to first base."

That summer I made my way to the local grocery stores to spend the pennies, nickels, dimes, and quarters that my father (who had a penchant for sweets) handed me every evening. He understood my need to purchase ice cream and other treats during the day. Since there was a store directly across the street from my home, I decided to go there first. The owner, a congenial older Polish gentleman, was waiting on a customer who was purchasing milk, bread, and some canned soups. I looked around the small store and quickly realized that the proprietor didn't carry the kind of items I wanted.

I left and made my way toward the other store on my block called *Poskonka*. When I entered, a ringing bell announced my arrival. I noticed a young Polish couple conversing with a couple of customers, so I took a short stroll around the store. The store owners carried an assortment of items that appealed to kids as well as adults.

My eyes lit up when I found a candy counter filled with all kinds of delicious confections. All of a sudden, I had a feeling that *Poskonka* would be the place where I would spend most of my money. The woman proprietor asked if she could help me. I told her that I was trying to decide which candies to purchase. She smiled and asked me to let her know when I had made up my mind.

That day, I joined countless other kids in our neighborhood who made daily trips to *Poskonka*. Like me, they not only found the items that they were looking for but were always treated with courtesy and kindness. *Poskonka* proprietors knew how to make everyone who entered their store feel welcome and appreciated for their business.

I often purchased penny candies such as lollipops, colored dots attached to a long narrow sheet of paper, and powdered candies in paper straws called Pixy Stix. The latter were especially popular because kids liked to pour them into their mouths for an instant burst of sweetness. The other popular treat was bubble gum. It came with a tiny cartoon, joke, and instructions on how to order a cheap toy. Whenever I had a taste for something cold and creamy, I would purchase a Creamsicle, Fudgsicle, or orange Push-Up for about seven cents. When I was thirsty, I would open a small square-looking refrigerator, pull out a glass bottle of Coca-Cola, grape, orange, or some other flavored pop and then use the bottle opener attached on the side of the refrigerator to open it.

When I discovered that pop bottles could be returned for a penny, my friends and I started scouring the neighborhood for empties. The best ones were the quart-sized bottles worth a whole nickel. I asked my parents to save them for me. Collecting bottles was a great way for kids to make some quick spending money.

Poskonka also sold three slightly used comic books in a see-through package. The top portion of the front covers was neatly cut off, and the comic books sold for ten cents. The kid-friendly store also carried giant-sized special edition comic books, which sold for twenty-five cents. Some of my best issues included *Archie and Veronica, Little Lulu,* and *Superman.* The special editions offered not only much more reading material but were packed with jokes, puzzles, and unexpected anecdotes. Whenever my friends and I traded comic books, I would bring out my regular and special edition issues and bargain for issues I had never read before. I especially liked to trade with Bobby, since he had the largest collection of regular and special edition comic books on the entire block. Often, I had to give him at least one of my special superhero editions as he was very stingy about parting with any of his special editions.

Chapter

13

Summer in the city could be a challenge. On June 19, 1953, the mercury soared above 100 degrees, causing misery in the city. Mama had loud fans blowing in our kitchen, but they didn't help much since the heat was so stifling. All I could think about was jumping into a pool of cold water. I asked her if she could please take us to North Avenue beach. Mama appeared sympathetic but replied that there wasn't enough time to go, since she needed to finish her chores and make a light supper for us before going to work.

What she didn't tell me was that she, Tato, and millions of other parents were afraid to take their children to beaches or other public places where they could be exposed to polio, a horrific childhood disease. Polio attacked a child's nervous system, causing paralysis and sometimes death. While school children across the country eagerly looked forward to the summer months, their parents dreaded them.

My brother and I were disappointed, so I suggested that we walk to *Poskonka* to buy some Popsicles. The Popsicles were especially yummy that day, since they had two different flavored bars under one wrapper. When we returned, Karolina, Frankie, and Bobby were sitting on the front steps complaining about the heat. They asked us to sit down and join them. That old adage "misery loves company" made a lot of sense that day.

While we were commiserating with each other, I noticed that John, the owner of the corner tavern, was standing near his imposing Pontiac with a bucket, hose, soap, and car polish. Car owners took great pride in their automobiles and regularly washed, buffed, and polished them. Bobby abruptly yelled out that he wanted to be drenched with the cold water.

John looked up, picked up his hose, and aimed it at the five of us. We screamed with delight when the cold water struck our over-heated bodies. He laughed and then suggested that we run home and change into our bathing suits. Everyone but Bobby disappeared for a brief time and then reappeared in bathing suits. John aimed the hose at the four of us but purposely missed Bobby. That didn't stop Bobby from jumping in front of us, getting soaked and boasting that his wet clothing felt refreshingly cool. That afternoon, we realized that John, a thoughtful and fastidious neighbor, cared not only for his property but for his youngest neighbors.

Not long after John cooled off my brother and me with the water hose, Mama told us that Tato was thinking about purchasing a swimming pool. Then I remembered that most pools were usually located in backyards and we lived in an apartment building. Our chances of getting a pool were as likely as Tato's ordering a telephone for our home. That evening, I told my father that having our own swimming pool would help keep us cool when the weather was too hot for us to play outside. Tato understood how we felt. He said, "During the summer time, when I was a young boy in Ukraine, my friends and I would head to the *richka* (river) to get relief from the sun's rays." It was good that my father shared a memory of his boyhood.

On Saturday morning, Tato brought home an eighteen-inch high, six-foot wide galvanized pool and placed it in the semicircular space between our gangway and the building next door. He said that it would be the best spot for the pool because we could enjoy it without disrupting the tenants walking through the gangway. After Tato had filled the pool with water, he asked me what I thought of it. I replied, "It looks nothing like the swimming pools that are circular, inflatable, and made of vinyl." He suggested that I should try it out before deciding if I liked it or not. I ran upstairs and changed into my bathing suit.

By afternoon, the water in the galvanized pool was warm enough for me to comfortably splash around to my heart's content. Roman commented that we would have more fun if our friends, Karolina and Frankie, joined us. Before I could reply, a dirty rubber ball plopped right into the clear water. I looked up and there was Bobby crying out, "So that's where it went," as he grabbed the wet ball. Before he left, Bobby briefly gawked at our pool and said that he had never, ever seen anything so cool.

As the days turned to weeks, our pool became overcrowded with rambunctious boys who were repeatedly drenching the girls. When one of Tato's tenants strolled by, he or she would inevitably be christened with splashing water. Luckily, none of them ever complained to the landlord.

By the end of summer, our amazing galvanized pool didn't look so amazing anymore. The jumping, shoving, poking, and kicking had damaged its structure. Tato was surprised to learn that the well-built pool was damaged in such a short time. He had hoped that it would last for a couple more years.

After Tato discarded our pool, I asked him where he had purchased it. He said that he had bought it at the local hardware store. Probably because of his limited English skills, he never realized that he had purchased a galvanized trough that farmers used to feed their animals! To my knowledge, we had the only galvanized pool that ever showed up in our neighborhood.

In those days, food vendors often came through the neighborhoods. My family and I enjoyed Chicago-style hot dogs, condiments, and French fries sold by a vendor who owned a pushcart. The aromas from his small cart enticed a steady stream of customers. Mama savored the vendor's hot dogs and French fries so much that she decided to make a similar version of her own. She purchased a package of Oscar Meyer wieners, buns, and condiments, carefully cut-up potatoes, and deep-fried them. Mama's first batch of French fries were so good, they rivaled the street vendor's.

When lunch was ready, Mama would stick her head out of the kitchen window and call my brother and me to come home. Sometimes, I would ask her if we could eat outside, especially if I was in the middle of an important game. She usually acquiesced and said, "Tak." Mama would carry out steaming hot dogs and fries wrapped in a clear foil and then invite one or more of my friends to join me. Before long, everyone was cheerfully munching away. Sharing with others was always important to my mother.

Chapter

14

In August, my parents received a surprise visit from Pan Volodymyr. Before he left, he invited me to stay with his family for a week at their new home. He even offered to drive me there. I excitedly said I would love to go. I asked my parents and they agreed to let me stay for a week.

The following Friday evening, Mama helped me pack my summer clothing and reminded me to be polite and well-behaved. I felt a little sad that I would be leaving my family and friends for an entire week. But it would give me an opportunity to travel to a new city and experience new adventures.

On Saturday morning, I said goodbye to Mama, Tato, and my brother before Pan Volodymyr escorted me to his automobile. We drove through many neighborhoods since there were no expressways in those days.

We finally arrived in a picturesque suburban neighborhood with solid brick homes in Rockford, Illinois. They were surrounded by huge trees and perfectly manicured lawns and trimmed bushes. Pan Volodymyr parked in front of a large brown brick bungalow with a sizable porch. I followed him to the backyard where I saw the most beautiful fruit trees. One was covered with the plumpest red cherries that begged to be picked and eaten. When Pan Volodymyr opened the back door, I was greeted by Pani Olena and her two daughters, Nastya and Ann. As they hugged and kissed me, I felt overjoyed to be a guest in their lovely home. The girls told me that they were working in the kitchen, mixing ingredients and kneading dough. Ann then asked me if I liked lemon meringue pie.

That afternoon, Ann handed me my very first slice of lemon meringue pie. After I took a bite, I knew that it would become my special dessert. Nastya and Ann said that they had learned how to bake pies and cakes in their home economics class at their public high school. When we were done eating, the girls cleaned the kitchen and asked me to join them in the backyard. I walked outside and found a cozy chair, sat down, and basked in the beauty of the backyard's flowers, shrubs, and fruit trees. Pani Olena came out with a pitcher of lemonade and glasses. She placed them on a wooden picnic table and said that she would return with a basket of apples, oranges, pears, and freshly picked cherries.

The girls and I talked about many things including their experiences as young immigrants. Ann and Nastya recalled how they had to overcome the stigma that brands refugees in this country. But once they became proficient in English, they were able to assimilate to American life. Nastya commented that sometimes adults had more difficulty learning English. However, with a positive attitude and persistence, they, too, could learn how to speak English and improve their quality of life.

Ann and Nastya's mood quickly brightened when they started talking about their friends, classes, and teachers at their public high school. Ann remarked that many of the girls with steady boyfriends were taking home economics classes because they hoped to get married after graduation. Nastya emphasized that neither she nor her sister, Ann, were in a rush to get married. They were young ladies who wanted to do fun things like picking out their prettiest blouses, skirts, neck scarves, and going to school dances. The girls also said that students were expected to be polite and well-mannered at every school dance. Their physical education teacher had instructed them to graciously accept a boy's invitation to dance and thank him even if they were interested in someone else.

After the dances, the girls looked forward to going out with their schoolmates to the local burger and ice cream parlor. There they listened to popular tunes such as Perry Como's "Don't Let the Stars Get in Your Eyes," Teresa Brewer's "Till I Waltz Again With You," and Patti Page's "Doggie in the Window." I told the girls that I had heard the Patti Page song and liked it.

The weather was beautiful with sunny skies and light winds. Nastya and I went for a long stroll through her neighborhood where Buicks, Oldsmobiles, Pontiacs, and brown station wagons were parked in many of the driveways. She and I waved to the friendly neighbors who were relaxing or busy mowing their lawns with rotary mowers. Nastya said her father really liked his mower because it was easy to maneuver and kept the grass looking well-trimmed. We continued walking until Nastya stopped in front of a school building. She said that it was the high school that she and Ann were attending. I gazed at the imposing building and told her that she was very lucky to be living so close to her school.

After dinner, Nastya asked me if I wanted to see her collection of makeup and jewelry. She brought out her brightest shades of Revlon lipsticks and a beautiful fancy lipstick case decorated with tiny jewels. She even demonstrated how she applied a "little natural" color to her cheeks by dabbing rouge on them. Nastya also displayed a lovely jewelry box that contained earrings, necklaces, and matching bracelets. I was trying on a few of her sparkling gems when she pulled out a blue-and-yellow handmade bracelet that looked American Indian. It was woven with hundreds of tiny beads and spelled out the name "Nancy." She placed the bracelet around my small wrist and secured the clasp.

That evening, I learned that Nastya's American friends called her Nancy. She suggested that when I get back home, I start calling myself Nancy. I really admired Nastya. She was older, wiser, and more experienced. I proudly gazed at my new bracelet.

The following day, Ann asked me if I would like to accompany her on an interview for a modeling job. I was not quite sure what an interview was, but it sounded interesting so I replied that I would like to go. Ann told me that she needed to look her best, so she carefully brushed her blond shoulder-length hair, put on a pretty dress with a tight knit top, added a petticoat, and completed her outfit with a cinched belt to highlight her slim waist. Ann remembered that her interviewer wanted to see some photographs of her, so she prepared an album to take with her.

That afternoon, the two of us traveled to the business section of town. We walked into a lobby of an office building and looked for the room where her interview would take place. When she located it, Ann asked me to sit down and wait for her. She patted me on my shoulder and promised that she would be back in a short time. While I waited for her, I recalled a conversation she had had with her sister, Nastya, about getting part-time modeling work. A resourceful and attractive blond, Ann was very photogenic with a face that could easily grace the cover of a magazine. She also mentioned that Nastya had some interest in modeling but was not actively pursuing it.

When Ann came out of the office, she appeared eager to tell me that her interview had gone well and that she would have a chance to do some modeling. She took me by the hand and escorted me to a drug store where she treated me to my first luscious ice cream sundae with a cherry on top.

The following day, the girls told me that in the evening they would take me to see a double-feature movie. I told them that I often went to the movie theater near my home. After dinner, the door bell rang. Ann opened the door to two good-looking young men. They politely greeted Pan Volodymyr and his wife, Pani Olena, before approaching Nastya and Ann. The girls introduced me to their dates and mentioned that I was their house guest.

It was getting dark outside when the five of us drove off in a Ford convertible. The driver had confidently driven through the town's brightly lit streets when he unexpectedly headed toward an open field. I began to wonder if he had made a wrong turn until I saw the boldest and brightest lights and a mammoth movie screen. Strangely enough, it was not located inside of a movie theater but under millions of stars. The driver asked his passengers to keep their eyes open for a good place to park.

When Ann spotted a space, the driver carefully parked near a medium-sized stand that held a metal box with many holes in it. He picked up the box and attached it to the rolled-down window. Nastya explained, "It's an adjustable speaker that will let us hear the dialogue coming from the huge screen." Ann told me, "We are at the local outdoor drive-in movie theater." Since I was a city girl, I had never been to a drive-in theater. Just then one of the young men in the back seat asked me if I would like something to eat. I gladly replied, "I would love an orange pop and some popcorn."

After making their purchases, the two young men returned with armfuls of large boxes of popcorn smothered in dripping butter along with bottles of everyone's favorite pop. The girls were chatting away when the first feature, a black-and-white western called *High Noon*, appeared on the screen. It starred the popular Gary Cooper and the beautiful Grace Kelly. The movie was suspenseful, action-filled, and unpredictable.

When it was over, the five of us discussed *High Noon* and how much we liked it. The young men sheepishly admitted that they were taken aback when Grace Kelly saved her husband's life because in most movies the man was a hero "who won the heart of the fair maiden."

The second movie featured a gargantuan monster that invaded a town, wreaking terror and havoc. After about twenty minutes, the five of us agreed that the plot wasn't realistic, so we decided to leave.

When we returned home, the boys thanked their dates for an entertaining evening. Then they bent over, smiled, and told me that they were pleased to have met me. I smiled in return while Nastya and Ann thanked the boys for their generosity and thoughtfulness. Pani Olena was waiting for us when we walked inside the house. We headed toward the couch where we sat down and enthusiastically gave her and Pan Volodymyr a quick overview of the wonderful western we had just seen.

The days quickly went by, and it was almost time for me to return to Chicago. I felt so honored that my hosts tried to make my stay fun and memorable. The night before I left Rockford, I inadvertently walked into Pani and Pan Volodymyr's bedroom. It was dimly lit, but I could still see that it was neatly decorated. When I looked up, I saw an unusually large black-and-white portrait of a very handsome, blond young man hanging above their bed. The portrait captured his youth, innocence, and boyish smile.

Suddenly, a sadness overcame me, and tears welled in my eyes. I remembered that my parents had talked about how he and several other boys were killed in Germany after World War II when a landmine exploded where they were playing. He was so beloved that his parents felt the need to keep his memory alive every single day of their lives. I walked out of the bedroom and never said a word about seeing that portrait. Maybe I should have, but I did not want to reopen an old and painful wound.

That weekend, Pan Volodymyr drove me home. I was sad to be leaving but I would never forget the time I had spent with him and his incredibly warm-hearted family.

Back home, I began to wear my new "Nancy" bracelet and announced to my parents that I wanted to be called by my new American name. I explained that Nastya from Rockford had given me the bracelet and had suggested that I call myself Nancy. Mama and Tato said that I would always be "Nastya" to them, but if I wanted to be called Nancy in the outside world, that would be fine. My friends liked calling me by my new name because foreign names were neither easy to pronounce nor as popular as American ones. Most of my neighbors, including the tenants in our building, started calling me Nancy, except for Harriet and Frank, her husband, who persisted in calling me by my Ukrainian name.

Roman and I continued to enjoy the final hot summer days of August with many of our new neighborhood friends. When Labor Day finally arrived, I knew that it meant that summer vacation was almost over. It was time to buckle down and return to the classroom.

Chapter

15

I was back on the bus corner with my new school bag, notebooks, and pencils ready to begin second grade. Mama was there the first day, reminding me to be aware of my surroundings and stay away from strangers. When the bus arrived, she wished me a safe trip, "*Budh zdorovenka,*" (stay well) and waved goodbye as I walked inside. The bus driver, Mr. Andy, cheerfully welcomed me and said that he had missed me. He even told me that on my next bus ride, he would have a candy bar for me. Mr. Andy kept his word. A fine bus driver, he not only collected his riders' fares, made change, and gave them transfers but also treated them like valued customers.

Whenever Mr. Andy approached my Chicago Avenue bus stop, he would ask me to wait until he drove across the busy intersection so that I wouldn't have to cross it. I would thank him, exit, and wait for my second bus near the corner newspaper stand.

Every day, I would see a short, unshaven, elderly man who wore a tattered dark shirt and old-looking trousers. He was running back and forth between his piles of newspapers handing his customers their paper, collecting money, and making change. Even though he appeared frazzled most of the time, I could tell that selling newspapers was important to him. On occasion when he wasn't busy waiting on his customers, he would glance in my direction as if he wanted to say something. But I didn't feel comfortable around the unkempt stranger, so I turned away.

One morning, he caught me off-guard when he approached and said, "Hello." I didn't want to be impolite so I responded, "Hello," and then continued waiting for my bus. Over the next several days, that brief interaction recurred until I began to realize that maybe this elderly man was nicer than he appeared. And since I had to travel to school five days a week, I thought I might as well make the best of the situation.

Gradually, I began to speak to him. Our brief conversations helped me to realize that he was not someone to be feared. He was simply an elderly gentleman who made his living selling newspapers. A hard worker, he always made sure that his tall stacks of papers were carefully secured on the ground. On exceptionally windy days, he would put bricks on top to keep the newspapers from flying away.

He also had a small wooden shed similar to a lean-to with a slanted roof. It was old, had no front door, and was probably secured to the large pole on the street corner. The wooden slats were cracked and discolored from years of exposure to the sun, wind, rain, and snow. Unfortunately, the shed provided little shelter against inclement weather.

"Pops," as I heard a customer call him, was quite interesting. He moved swiftly like a young buck whenever a driver beeped his horn to get his attention. He hustled to hand-deliver the paper, take the money from the customer, and then make change within seconds. I was amazed that he had a coin changer on his old belt just like the one that Mr. Andy, the bus driver, had. I was impressed that Pops knew his many customers by their first names, including the men and women who just walked over to purchase a newspaper.

Whenever there was a lull in his business, he would chat with me about all kinds of different things. He was happiest during the fall, spring, and summer seasons. However, when the weather changed from warm to blustery, he didn't say very much. Maybe he was so wrapped up in his old black coat, scarf, and cap that I couldn't hear him or see him smile. I felt sorry for him when I saw his old gloves with holes around the finger tips. But then I thought that perhaps he wanted his finger tips exposed so it was easier to collect money and make change.

During the winter months, I really learned to appreciate Pops. He had a large old circular drum that he filled with coals so that by the time I arrived in the morning, it was already giving off some heat. The first time I saw the drum I was hesitant about putting my hands over the coals. Pops recognized my fear and said, "Go ahead, honey. Don't be afraid. The heat will warm you." Then he placed his own hands over the burning coals and rubbed them together. I cautiously followed his example and felt a soothing warmth penetrating my freezing gloves and hands as I waited for my bus.

I grew fond of Pops, who was always good to me. I also admired his work ethic. A conscientious man, he took good care of his customers. Even though he did not make much money selling newspapers, he appeared to enjoy his job. Pops never spoke about his family, so I never knew if he had any children who would care for him when he could no longer work.

Once I arrived at school, I would join my classmates for daily Divine Liturgy, which we were required to attend. I tried to be on time, but often I would come late, especially when the weather was harsh, or I had missed one bus and had to wait for another. On those days, I would run in and join my teacher and classmates as they walked out of the church and headed toward our classroom in the old school building. The best part of that daily ritual was passing by the priests' rectory and fenced-in yard, where a giant St. Bernard was kept. Danube, or Dunaj, looked intimidating but wagged his tail whenever a boy or girl would stop, chat, or try to pet him. At first, I was hesitant to touch an animal that looked bigger than me. When I saw how friendly he was with the other boys and girls, however, I decided to spend some time with him during recess. During that brief encounter, the over-sized St. Bernard gently licked my hand. Dunaj became a kind of mascot for our school long before the students ever heard of that word.

My second grade teacher was a young lay instructor who made her pupils feel at ease in her classroom. She was smart and kind and made learning a pleasant, yet challenging, experience. It was the beginning of the school year, so I decided the time was right to start printing my new Americanized first name on all of my assignments. My teacher must have noticed that I did not use my baptismal name, but she never said anything to me about it. She just called me Nancy.

My classmates and I were also introduced to our Ukrainian language instructor, Pani Maria Ovcharenko. Her professional appearance, rounded eyeglasses, and confident manner suggested that she was dedicated, diligent, and highly educated. (She earned her Ph.D. from Charles University in Prague, Czechoslovakia.) Pani Ovcharenko visited our classroom every day for about an hour to teach us how to read and write in Ukrainian. Although she knew the importance of learning English to become successful American citizens, Pani Ovcharenko appreciated the value of cherishing one's own language and culture. She introduced us to Ukraine's bard, Taras Shevchenko (March 9, 1814 – March 10, 1861). An artist and later a poet, he powerfully described the social and national oppression that the Ukrainian peasantry suffered under serfdom. We studied and memorized some of Taras Shevchenko's poems that encouraged us to learn from other cultures while embracing our own.

Under our teacher's guidance, we learned cursive, became proficient readers, and developed our arithmetic skills. She also reminded us to write the initials JMJ on top of all our written assignments in honor of the Holy Family: Jesus, Mary, and Joseph. We did all that while sitting in sturdy brown wooden desks with a small hole in the corner (inkwell) that we never used.

As second graders, we also prepared for our first Holy Communion. *Otech* (Father) provided each of us with a large booklet of typed prayers to be memorized in both Ukrainian and English. Some of them were rather long, so in the evenings, I would sit down and memorize them with Tato's help. Otech had forewarned us that he would call on any one of us during class to recite one of those prayers, so I wanted to be prepared.

On weekends, I would repeat the process with Mama. One

afternoon, I ran into Harriet, and we started talking about my Holy Communion preparation. She told me that Karolina, who attended a Roman Catholic school, had already made her communion the previous year. But she didn't have to learn as many prayers as I did, let alone in two languages. In addition to prayers, we had to memorize the Ten Commandments. Otech told us that they were valuable guidelines for living better and happier lives in a moral society.

Chapter

16

One Saturday morning, my parents announced that a special purchase would arrive during the week via a Marshall Field truck: a television set! My brother, Roman, and I were so excited that we would finally have a TV just like the rest of the kids on our block. Within days, a large brown, twenty-one inch wooden Zenith Console Television graced our living room. When Mama walked in, she said that it not only looked like a piece of fine furniture but still had that "brand new" smell. She pointed to the antenna, or rabbit ears, that the delivery men had placed on top of the console. That afternoon, I completed my homework assignment in record time because I could hardly wait to watch a program on our very own television set.

Television offered many fine comedy shows. *The Adventures of Ozzie and Harriet* featured real-life family members: Ozzie and Harriet Nelson and their sons, David and Ricky.

Together, they faced life's challenges and weekly problems with affection and a sense of humor. I readily joined Tato to watch the *Red Skelton Show,* Milton Berle starring at the *Texas Star Theater,* William Bendix in *Life of Riley,* and *The Amos 'n' Andy Show.* Amos was played by Alvin Childress, Andy by Spencer Williams Jr., and Kingfish Stevens by Tim Moore. After my father discovered *You Are There* with newscaster Walter Cronkite, he became a faithful viewer. Before long, I, too, became engrossed in Mr. Cronkite's broadcasts. They were not only informative but helped us learn about American history, politics, and world views.

One of my favorite westerns was *The Lone Ranger.* Clayton Moore played the masked rider who dressed in white and rode a horse called Silver. His faithful Indian companion named Tonto was played by Jay Silverheels. The brave duo were from different backgrounds, but when they worked as a team, they defeated outlaws and brought law to the early West.

The Adventures of Superman was one show I never wanted to miss! It starred George Reeves, who disguised himself as Clark Kent, a mild-mannered reporter. He would dash into a phone booth, take off his glasses, remove his fedora and suit, and transform into the man of steel. Superman would fly above the city, fight evildoers, save lives, and preserve American values.

Mama had her own desires for a more upscale life. One evening while we were eating supper, Mama announced that she had found a set of lovely china that she really wanted. Tato reminded her that we already had enough plates and cups and then asked why she needed more. Mama replied that the plates and cups that we had were for everyday use. We needed real china for special occasions. Tato asked where

Mama was planning on putting the china. She cheerfully replied that she coincidentally had found a slim, white china cabinet that would look great in the corner of our kitchen.

Boxes with gold-trimmed plates, cups, and saucers decorated with the daintiest lilacs and leaves arrived in a green Marshall Field truck. The following week, a china cabinet was delivered to our home. Several of our neighbors had watched the uniformed delivery men make their way toward our apartment building. The curious ladies probably wondered which lucky neighbor had not one but two deliveries from the well-known Marshall Field and Company.

Meanwhile, at St. Nicholas School, my classmates and I were steadily making progress in our second grade studies. In October, we learned about Christopher Columbus and his voyage across the Atlantic Ocean to America. Our teacher told us that Columbus initially planned to sail to the East Indies where he could obtain valuable goods such as silks, spices, and gold. He received permission from Queen Isabella to sail to the Indies with some ninety sailors on three ships: *Niña, Pinta,* and *Santa Maria.* On October 12, 1492, Columbus landed in America and called its Native inhabitants Indians. In honor of his discovery, school children received the day off. Many memorized the rhyme, "In 1492, Columbus sailed the ocean blue."

By November, my classmates and I were discussing pilgrims and drawing turkeys. On the fourth Thursday of that month, we would be off from school celebrating Thanksgiving with our families. Mama finally bought a big turkey and figured out how to stuff it. One of the ingredients she used was onions. Every time she cut up the fresh bulbs, their juices permeated the air and made my eyes water. It wasn't until

Mama sautéed them that my watery eyes began to clear up. After she stuffed the bird with her own special dressing, she used an actual needle and thread to sew the contents inside the turkey. Mama's first turkey dinner was so delicious that Tato couldn't stop talking about how much he enjoyed this America tradition.

When classes were over, I would walk down Chicago Avenue to catch the bus at Damen. When the temperatures began to drop, and sunny days turned cloudy and wet, I would take a bus to that busy intersection. After my short trip, I would take refuge from the bad weather inside an Italian restaurant's foyer. A kind young woman with blond hair, who always had a smile for her customers, worked there. She never complained about my presence, even when I showed up with a dripping umbrella or snow-covered galoshes. She reminded me of Mary Hartline, the performer who starred in the *Super Circus Show* on Sundays.

In late December, I was still riding buses to attend classes at my school while the rest of the boys and girls in my neighborhood were enjoying their Christmas vacation. One of the bus drivers asked me, "How come you're not at home vacationing with the rest of the kids?"

"I'm Ukrainian, and I attend a Ukrainian Catholic school. We celebrate Christmas on January seventh according to the Julian calendar, while my neighborhood friends celebrate Christmas on December twenty-fifth, according to the Gregorian calendar."

The bus driver didn't say much after that explanation, but the confused look on his face confirmed my suspicion. He had absolutely no idea what I was talking about, though he politely nodded as if he did.

Pops, the newsstand owner, said that he would miss me during my time off from school to celebrate Ukrainian Christmas. He also noted that I was much better off taking my vacation in January since it was a much colder month than December.

In January of 1954, I was officially on my Christmas vacation from school to celebrate Jesus' birthday with my family. Our apartment looked festive after Mama attached velvety red ribbons to the fancy white curtains in the living room and Tato set up a tall, fresh evergreen tree that Roman and I had helped pick out at the local Christmas tree lot. What made our tree look extra special that year were the real electric light bulbs that Mama had purchased and Tato had carefully woven through the tree's aromatic boughs. That full Christmas tree sparkled from top to bottom, starting with a gleaming star and exquisitely decorated ornaments and finishing with long silvery shimmering icicles. Mama reminded my brother and me that even though the Christmas tree symbolized the Christmas season, the true meaning of that religious holiday was at the foot of the tree: a crèche with the baby Jesus, Mother Mary, and Joseph, a few stable animals, visiting shepherds, and the three kings.

During my break, I usually slept in late. One morning, Mama walked into my bedroom and said that she had a surprise for me. She was holding a thick woven cloth called a tapestry. She told me that she had purchased it from a street vendor and had been saving it for me. Mama emphasized that tapestries were fashionable and thought that I would like to have one in my room. I looked up and saw a pattern with a bright blue sky, sun, and a white fluffy kitten basking in the sunshine in a field of grass. I told her that I liked it but would have preferred a real live *kotyk* (kitten). Mama didn't respond to my comment because she did not like cats. She said that Tato would hang the tapestry on my bedroom wall after the holiday.

I jumped out of bed and felt a chill. My window was entirely covered with beautiful, intricate patterns of crystal snowflakes. I tried scratching off nature's one-of-a-kind frozen wonders until I realized they had formed outside. That morning, *Did Moroz* (old man winter) left his artistic imprint on my bedroom window pane.

I found Mama in the kitchen ready to turn on the radio and listen to her favorite weekly program sponsored by the priests of St. Nicholas Ukrainian Catholic Church. It featured sermons, prayers, hymns, and native music. Those programs were especially meaningful for shut-ins who could not attend Mass. Since it was the Christmas season, Mama was looking forward to hearing the traditional Ukrainian *kolyady*, or Christmas carols, along with holiday greetings.

During the year, those radio programs also gave parishioners an opportunity to send greetings or personal messages to family members on their birthdays, weddings, or anniversaries. Sometimes the priests would notify their listeners about a parishioner's passing. The Church members showed their appreciation for the weekly broadcasts by donating to help defray their cost.

On January sixth, we celebrated Christmas Eve with our traditional *Sviata Vechera*, or Holy Supper. Earlier in the day, Mama put some hay underneath her embroidered tablecloth to signify that Jesus was born in a manger. We shared twelve meatless foods representing Christ's twelve apostles. Mama would also put an extra place setting on the table for departed family members. Roman and I changed into our traditional Ukrainian shirt and blouse and waited for Pan Ivan and Pan Jaroslaw, our dear bachelor friends, to join us. When they arrived, they greeted us with the words *"Chrystos Rozdayetsia,"* or "Christ is born."

The six of us stood by the table as Tato led everyone in prayer and invited the departed members of our families to join us. When we sat down, Mama passed around the *kutia*, a mixture of bulgur wheat kernels and poppy seeds, walnuts, and honey, which symbolized prosperity for the family in the coming year. She served a beet soup that contained little mushrooms wrapped and folded into small dough squares that resembled "little ears," called *vushka*. On the table were *holubtsi*, or stuffed cabbage rolls with rice. A Christmas bread called a *kolach* was in the center of our table. The adults ate sardines and herring. Roman and I passed on the fish and ate Mama's homemade potato pyrohy sautéed in onions. For dessert, our guests enjoyed her deep-fried *pampushky* containing various fruit fillings like apples and jelly and a poppy-seed bread called *makownyk*.

We were now the only family on the block to still have a large snow-covered evergreen wreath hanging on our front door, along with bright holiday lights streaming through our living room windows. At first, some of our neighbors made joking comments about our Christmas decorations, but after a while the word got out that the immigrant landlord and his family were celebrating their Christmas in January.

Chapter

17

By early February, my teacher was discussing America's sixteenth president, Abraham Lincoln. She said that many historians consider him America's greatest president. He freed the slaves during the Civil War with his 1863 Emancipation Proclamation and saved the Union. Our teacher also told us that people who knew Mr. Lincoln called him "Honest Abe." She said that when he was a young man, he walked many miles back to his local country store to return extra change mistakenly given him. My classmates and I not only learned important facts about Mr. Lincoln but looked forward to taking Lincoln's birthday off from school to honor his memory.

Two days later, on February fourteenth, Tato walked into our kitchen carrying a large, red heart-shaped box and handed it to Mama, blurting out a "Happee Valenteeno" greeting in broken English. I tactfully corrected him by saying, "Tato, it's Happy Valentine's Day." Mama chuckled as she opened the box and found an array of chocolate-covered candies. He leaned over and kissed her, as she gleefully asked him what made him finally decide to observe the charming American holiday. Tato admitted that some of his American co-workers had invited him to come along on a shopping spree to buy Valentine candy for their wives. That day, Tato bought a smaller box of chocolates for Roman and me. Tato promised that every year he would continue to bring chocolates home for "Valenteeno" Day.

On February twenty-second, we had another day off from school to honor the "Father of our Country," George Washington. Our teacher explained that during the Revolutionary War, George Washington led his ragged colonial army to victory against the British troops. The colonists recognized his wisdom, leadership skills, strength, and courage, electing him as their first president. George Washington was also known for telling the truth. According to a legend, his father once asked him when he was a child, "Who cut down my cherry tree?" George replied, "I cannot tell a lie. I did."

The following week, I heard Tato notifying Mama that he needed to begin work on the dingy, unfinished front basement to convert it into a livable unit. Mama said that there was too much work for one man. Tato replied that he had never been a landlord before, yet he was successfully handling the plumbing, carpentry, and other repairs in his building. He would, however, hire an electrician to do the electrical work.

Tato invited me to take a peek at the basement before he started renovating it. He and I walked down the back stairwell to the lowest level of the building. He inserted an antique key into the lock of the timeworn front door and joggled it until the door opened.

The chilly basement looked more like an underground vault than a future apartment. Dust particles floated through the air as Tato inspected the sizable room for signs of dampness or water leakage. When he was done surveying the area, we left the room, and he locked the heavy door. We headed back upstairs to our second-floor apartment where Tato reassured Mama that the basement would be refurbished and ready for tenants within a few months.

Tato toiled from early morning until dusk on Saturdays, taking few breaks and eating only when Mama came down with some freshly prepared food. One Saturday evening, he tried to convince her that the repairs would be completed sooner if he could just work a few Sunday afternoons. Mama couldn't believe that Tato would even consider working on the Sabbath Day. She said that he should not only "Keep Holy the Lord's Day" by attending church services, but by refraining from manual labor. Respecting the Sabbath Day was important to Americans for generations. Employers acknowledged their employees' need to spend time with their families. Grocers, retailers, car dealers, and tavern owners regularly displayed "Closed Sunday" signs on windows and doors.

Men, women, and children donned their best Sunday apparel and traveled to a church or house of prayer. Mama, like other properly dressed ladies, wore a hat and small white gloves while gentlemen like my father sported a suit, dress shirt, and tie. During the services, the congregation learned about their faith and the importance of working together as a community. Worshipers organized potluck dinners, dances, and picnics. They also sponsored local craft shows and bake sales to raise money for worthwhile causes.

St. Nicholas Ukrainian Catholic Church also held parish events, including a church picnic. Parishioners were encouraged to attend and purchase raffle books for the annual fund raiser. The first prize was a brand-new automobile donated by a generous local car dealer. Tato always purchased two raffle books, hoping that he would be the first-prize winner. One year, he and some of his fellow parishioners were disheartened to learn that a non-parishioner had purchased a single ticket and won the prized car. Over time, Tato would laughingly remark that if he couldn't win the car, he would settle for one of the other prizes. Needless to say, he never won anything. That never stopped him from being a good parishioner and purchasing raffle books each year.

On Sundays, when religious services were over, American families including grandparents gathered around the dinner table to show their love and appreciation for one another. The younger generation admired and respected their elders. They often communicated with them, sought out their advice, and drew upon their experiences. My brother and I never had a chance to meet our grandparents, so we envied the boys and girls who were fortunate enough to have a grandmother, grandfather, or both in their lives.

Occasionally, I accompanied my mother to deliver bags of fresh and canned food to the nuns' residence near the Ukrainian Catholic Church. Besides teaching children, the nuns helped with liturgical preparations, various parish events, and kept the church sanctuary in pristine condition. The immigrant parishioners recognized the Sisters' selflessness by regularly bringing them food and household goods. The parishioners took to heart Jesus' words: "Love thy neighbor as thyself."

During the early 1950s, fear of Communism gripped the country. On April 22, 1954, Tato and I, along with millions of Americans, watched a televised presentation of a subcommittee hearing to investigate Wisconsin Republican Senator Joseph R. McCarthy's claim that many communists had infiltrated the federal government. South Dakota Republican Senator Karl Mundt chaired the subcommittee probing the conflict between Senator McCarthy and Joseph Welch, the special counsel for the United States Army.

Tato and I listened intently to accusations of Communist influence and the emotionally charged denials. Tato wanted to form his own opinion of Senator McCarthy, Joseph Welch, and other participants, so he asked me to define certain vocabulary words and phrases used during the inquiry. After an extraordinary thirty-six days of riveting testimony, Tato was confident that the Senate would finally reach a decision. Unfortunately, it did not. Instead, my father and millions of other viewers would have to wait to see what action, if any, the Senate would take. In the end, the Senate censured Senator McCarthy for violating the ethics of the Senate.

Chapter
18

Not long after the hearings, I saw my father sitting in the kitchen staring at a blank sheet of paper. I asked what he was doing. Tato replied that he was trying to gather his thoughts to compose a letter to one of his best friends whom he had never expected to see again. He had known Pan Petro ever since they were mischievous boys in the same village in Ukraine. Their friendship endured even after the wretched days of World War II drove them apart.

Tato had recently learned that Pan Petro had immigrated to France. He was living and working on a small farm with his wife and children. A conscientious worker, Pan Petro realized that farming would not provide the kind of livelihood he had envisioned for his family. He wanted to leave Europe and immigrate to America where he could explore other fields of employment to provide a better life.

The following day, I spoke with Mama about my conversation with Tato. She said that he was grateful and relieved to hear that his old friend, Pan Petro, was still alive. Tato also emphasized that Pan Petro would need assistance to come to America. Mama wholeheartedly agreed. She remarked that he should have the opportunity to realize his dream.

Tato sought legal advice from people in the Ukrainian community on how best to initiate a sponsorship. When he secured the information, Tato filled out the necessary paperwork. His next step was to secure housing for the incoming family. Ordinarily, that wouldn't have been a problem; however, that year every apartment in Tato's building was occupied. Eventually, a family on the first floor in the rear of the building gave Tato notice that they were moving. Once they vacated the premises, Tato started to clean, repair, and repaint the apartment. He also furnished it with beds, a table, and chairs. Mama purchased household items and even put up attractive curtains on the windows. Lastly, Tato obtained a full-time job for Pan Petro. Once all the legal requirements were satisfied, Tato wrote his old friend and asked him to purchase one-way tickets for himself and his family to America.

My family and I excitedly awaited the arrival of Pan Petro, his wife, and children. When we heard a knock on the door, Tato rushed over to open it. A boundless sense of joy filled our home when we saw a smiling man holding a little boy, while his wife and two other children stood behind him in the doorway. Tato and Pan Petro embraced like two lost brothers who had never expected to see each other again. That afternoon, Tato proudly presented his old friend to my brother and me as *Vujko*, or uncle. Vujko in turn introduced his Ukrainian wife Maria, daughter Anna about six-years-old, and two sons: Ivan, three and Michasko, about a year old.

Our guests were welcomed with heartwarming words and Mama's delicious cooking. The adults reminisced about the past and discussed the possibilities for a brighter future. I was the oldest, so it was my responsibility to keep the youngest children occupied with games and toys. I noticed that several of our guests spoke with a French accent and all five interspersed French words into their conversations. Anna said that she spoke fluent French. I told her to develop her ability to speak French and not forget it even when learning to speak English. That evening, our humble home became the center of new and rekindled friendships.

By evening, Pan Petro and his family were tired, so Mama suggested that Tato take them downstairs. He obliged by picking up their suitcases and escorting them to their first-floor rear apartment. Tato opened the door, turned on the lights, and welcomed Pan Petro and his family to their first American home. While the adults were examining their new surroundings, Tato pointed to the back door and said that it led to a relaxing back porch. He jokingly mentioned that the view was not the best because it faced a garage and "L" tracks. He said, *Dobranich* (good-night) and left so that the family of five could unpack and get a good night's sleep.

Pan Petro and his family slowly became acclimated to their new surroundings. Mama shared her home cooking, household appliances, and information about American and Ukrainian community events. Tato encouraged his new neighbors to learn English and familiarize themselves with American traditions. He also provided directions to the local stores, Ukrainian Catholic Church, and school. Before long,

Pan Petro and his family were traveling by public transportation and successfully navigating the city.

Back in school, my classmates and I were getting closer to a special day in our lives. The priests and sisters had been diligently preparing us for our First Holy Communion to take place during the beautiful month of May. Boys and girls were encouraged to go shopping with their parents for dark suits and traditional white dresses. In addition, the Sisters suggested that all the girls purchase their veils or headpieces from the school so that everyone would look coordinated on Communion Day. Every second grader also received a rosary and a prayer book.

Gentle winds stirred the huge leafy green trees, and the scent of newly blossomed flowers wafted through the air when we gathered at the back of the church for our first confessions. Many of us were somewhat nervous as we made our way into the confessionals. We entered one at a time, knelt down, and proceeded to divulge our most secret venial sins to the patient priest. After receiving absolution, we hurriedly walked out of the dark confessional with a sigh of relief into the brightly lit church. After reciting a prayer or two as a penance, we were all ready for our First Holy Communion on Sunday.

I woke up early Sunday morning, having fasted for twelve hours, washed up, and put on my new petticoat, white socks, and ankle shoes. Mama helped me with my beautiful white, short-sleeved ruffled dress and white satin ribbon belt with an attached white flower.

When I walked out of my room, Tato presented me with a gleaming gold crucifix and matching gold link-chain. Mama commented that he had a difficult time finding a cross with Jesus' image on it. He finally found the crucifix at a small

134

Greek jewelry store. I kissed and thanked my parents for their special gift.

Tato surprised me with another small box. I opened it and found a gold-plated wristwatch that I had wanted and hinted about for quite some time. While I put on my new wristwatch, Mama placed the lovely white headpiece and long veil over my long, thick, wavy hair that she had curled the night before.

Just before leaving the apartment, I put on my small white nylon gloves to complete my ensemble. The four of us left the house early to catch the bus so that I would be on time to walk in the procession with my classmates into the church for the Liturgy. There were four classes of second graders – some two hundred communicants. The girls looked angelic in radiant white dresses, headpieces and veils; the boys looked like perfect little gentlemen in dress shirts, ties, and dark suits.

From the moment the second graders entered the magnificent church with its stunning stained-glass windows and icons, they knew they were in God's house to take part in a solemn religious experience. Their parents and relatives beamed as the First Communicants walked reverently toward the front of the church to sit in designated pews decorated with white bows and flowers.

During one of the most sacred moments of the Liturgy, the communicants made their way toward the priests, each of whom held a shiny golden chalice. With a tiny spoon, the priests dispensed the body and blood of Jesus Christ under the form of bread and wine. At the end of the Liturgy, the sisters directed the First Communicants to assemble on the front steps and sidewalk of St. Nicholas Church for a group photograph. When everyone was ready, the sisters and priests posed with the smiling boys and girls.

After a long church service and the group photograph, my parents still insisted that we take a bus to a professional photography studio on Chicago Avenue. They were strong believers in the value of photographs to commemorate rites of passage. A photographer snapped various poses of me holding my prayer book and rosary. My brother joined me for one of those photographs.

Finally, we made our way home to prepare for my First Holy Communion Day celebration. When our guests arrived, they were welcomed and feted like family members. Some of the well-wishers included my godfather, Pan Ilko, his wife, Olena, and younger son, Roman, a fellow communicant; Pani Olya and her husband; and our newest neighbors, Pan Petro and his family. It was a glorious day, the culmination of yearlong preparations.

Chapter

19

On April 12, 1955, the *Chicago Daily News* proclaimed in large, bold print: VICTORY AGAINST POLIO! SALK'S VACCINE WORKS. The announcement brought tears and sighs of relief to millions of parents who dreaded the childhood disease that had killed thousands of children and crippled many others including adults. Dr. Jonas Salk, the son of Russian-Jewish immigrants, had successfully developed a vaccine against Infantile Paralysis. President Dwight David Eisenhower awarded Dr. Salk the Congressional Medal of Honor for this achievement.

Also, during that month, Tato mentioned that his co-workers were preparing to vote for a new Mayor of Chicago. After numerous discussions about the different candidates' qualifications and positions on various issues, they all agreed that Chicago needed a strong leader to work for the people. On election day, the citizens cast their votes, electing an Irishman named Richard J. Daley as Mayor of Chicago.

I could hardly wait for summer vacation to begin so that I could take a hiatus from riding buses to and from school five days a week. I could sleep in late and not have to rush through my mother's creamy kasha made with Farina, oats, and fresh whole milk. Mama had stopped purchasing milk at the grocery store when she discovered that dairy companies such as Borden and Bowman made home deliveries. She even added bottled orange juice to her dairy order. Mama would wash out the empty glass bottles and leave them downstairs for the delivery man to pick up and replace with new bottles of milk and juice.

My neighborhood friends and I planned to spend our summer vacation engaged in challenging outdoor physical activities. Practically every day, my brother and I would hear one or more of our friends shouting from our gangway for us to "come out and play." We would stick our heads out of the kitchen window and shout back that we would be right out.

Both boys and girls would participate in various games such as dodge ball, kick-the-can, red-light/green-light, regular or freeze tag, and everyone's favorite, hide-and-go-seek. The latter game required its players to use their imaginations to find the most daring and unusual places to hide. One such place was a "forbidden" garden that had perfectly manicured greenery and a mammoth assortment of shrubbery. For an adventurous kid willing to take a chance, it was the ideal hiding place.

The garden belonged to a robust, good-natured middle-aged Polish woman, Babusia, who took great pride in her meticulously sculptured garden. She worked tirelessly throughout the spring and summer months planting, watering, and shaping her garden, creating the most eye-appealing display of flowers: azaleas, daisies, dahlias, day lilies, gladiolas, hydrangea, rhododendrons, roses, and many others. Whenever kids congregated near her garden fence, Babusia shouted an amicable warning not to scale her wire fence.

Once, when my friends and I were about to start playing hide-and-go-seek, Bobby showed up. He excitedly told us that his grandma, Babusia, and her husband had left and wouldn't return until evening. When I heard the good news, I decided finally to make my way inside the forbidden garden. As soon as the "hiders" scattered, I ran toward the garden and carefully lowered myself over the jagged fence. While moving gingerly around the sprawling bushes and shrubs, I felt sharp branches grazing my bare arms and legs. I was about to check for scratches when I was startled by strange rustling sounds. Fearing that someone else was in the garden, I quickly stooped down between two spiky bushes and waited until the coast was clear. Lo and behold, instead of a person, two striped chipmunks with bushy tails were rapidly chasing each other in a circle. I felt as if I were in a Chip-and-Dale cartoon. Those playful chipmunks kept circling until one raced up a nearby tree and the other followed close behind.

As I was making my way back to the fence, I noticed about a half-dozen Monarch butterflies fluttering around a striking array of coneflowers, salvia, and the beautiful flowers that had majestically scaled a white trellis. I was tempted to inhale the scarlet roses' fragrant aroma until I accidentally touched their prickly stems. After removing a tiny thorn from my finger, I knew it was time to leave the "Garden of Babusia" with all of its beauty and unexpected hazards. As I began to climb over the fence, I spotted Nick and another boy climbing into the garden. I tried to warn them to stay out, but they wouldn't listen.

A sense of relief came over me when I was back on the sidewalk with my fellow hide-and-go- seekers. When they asked me about my hiding place, I proudly responded that I had hid inside Babusia's unbelievable garden!

Suddenly, Bobby started shouting that Babusia and her husband, Carp, were pulling up in their car. The driver parked and then helped his wife out of the car. Instead of heading home, Babusia pointed to the gate and blurted out that she had just seen a boy hightailing it out of her garden. She walked over to the fence and found another boy squatting in the garden. Babusia shouted a warning before demanding that her husband "chase that kid out of there!" By the time Carp had made his way to the gate, Nick had made his way out of the garden. Carp wanted to keep his gardener happy, so he told all of us kids to "stay away from Babusia's garden!"

When Carp wasn't lecturing us, he was a friendly, down-to-earth man who liked and respected his neighbors. A humble fisherman, he relished talking about his frequent expeditions while the other men preferred to discuss their jobs, politics, and neighborhood happenings.

After supper mothers, fathers, grandparents, and young people would sit on their porches or front steps to enjoy the occasional breezes that would waft temporary relief from the summer's heat. The adults would discuss the day's events while the children played a variety of games until it was time to go home and get ready for bed.

One evening after the other children and their parents went home, Karolina and I got permission from our fathers to stay out a little longer to experience the serenity of the night. I was sitting pensively on our front steps when I glanced up at the vast sky illuminated with thousands of brilliant sparkling stars. Frank, standing nearby, was also gazing at the heavens. After pointing out the Big Dipper and other constellations to us, he recognized a shooting star. "Make a wish!" he shouted as it flashed through the sky. I stared in awe and almost forgot to make a wish since I had never heard of, let alone seen, a shooting star. And then, in the blink of an eye, it disappeared! That summer night, a city girl had the good fortune to observe an extraordinary display of stars from the front steps of her Chicago home instead of having to travel to the countryside.

With no air conditioning, we weren't prepared for the steamy temperatures that descended on Chicago in 1955. Children were especially vulnerable that summer because they loved spending time outdoors. I was on my way home carrying an issue of <u>Archie and Veronica</u> and sipping Coca-Cola from a sweaty glass bottle when I saw several older boys sauntering toward the fire hydrant. One of the boys turned around, reached into his pocket, and pulled out some kind of tool. He twisted and rotated the fire plug's cap until water started gushing out onto the street! His buddies howled with approval before they kicked off their shoes and lunged toward the streaming hydrant. The sight of that cold rushing water made me wish that I was across the street getting some cool relief from the miserable heat.

Word of the spraying hydrant rapidly spread throughout the neighborhood and became a rallying cry for every heat-oppressed kid on the block. Boys and girls came running from every direction to feel the ice-cold water douse their overheated bodies. I was tempted to sprint across the street when I realized that I was still holding my unread comic book and half-empty coke bottle. I ran toward our apartment building, opened the front door, and placed them inside the hallway.

When I came back out, Karolina and her mother were coming out of their apartment. Harriet wiped her forehead with a white handkerchief and complained that her apartment was so stifling they had to come outside just to get some air, even if it was hot! I told her and Karolina about the opened fire hydrant and that I was going back there to get cooled off. Karolina immediately asked her mother if she could come along with me.

Surprised by the news, Harriet wanted to see for herself, so she walked down the stairs and looked over to where the kids were darting in and out of the hydrant. Harriet smiled and told her daughter she had better hurry and change into her bathing suit before a policeman showed up and shut off the hydrant. An understanding mother, Harriet realized that on a sweltering day, boys and girls must try to stay cool, even if under a fire hydrant!

The miniature waterfall was already overcrowded with sopping wet kids when we arrived. As Karolina and I enthusiastically approached the hydrant, a boy with a mischievous grin cupped his hands around the rim of the plug and aimed the freezing water right at us. Splat! We ran from the hydrant while Bobby and his friends roared with laughter and then continued annoying the rest of the girls with their water antics.

Shivering, Karolina and I dashed toward the sidewalk where we warmed up under the sun's rays. After wringing out our dripping hair and squeaky shoes, Karolina and I made our way back to the fire hydrant where we had a great time.

That spurting plug kept flowing throughout the day, keeping the neighborhood kids cool and content. It also left wet tire tracks whenever automobiles drove through the puddles. By evening, someone had shut off the hydrant, forcing all the young frolickers to head home.

The summer finally ended, and in September, my classmates and I entered the new school building with its modern classrooms, large blackboards, and windows that could easily open to let in fresh air. The best part was having a third-grade teacher who was kind, thoughtful, and understanding. A patient educator, she would make coming to school a daily joy and not merely a necessity. Over the years, I would remember her fondly as my favorite teacher at St. Nicholas School.

My classmates and I started our school day by reciting prayers and the Pledge of Allegiance. That September, the Pledge of Allegiance included the words "under God" because President Eisenhower had approved the phrase "one nation, under God." On Flag Day in 1954, President Eisenhower had expressed his reason for making the change. "In this way we are reaffirming the transcendence of religious faith in America's heritage and future; in this way we shall constantly strengthen those spiritual weapons which forever will be our country's most powerful resource in peace and war."

Our up-to-date school building had a kitchen facility and a spacious cafeteria that served all the ravenous boys and girls during lunchtime. The cafeteria was not only a place to eat but also provided my friends and me an opportunity to chat, tell jokes, and laugh without getting into trouble. The mothers and fathers who volunteered their time and cooking skills superbly prepared the food. Parents paid a nominal weekly fee to the school so that their child or children would eat savory home-cooked meals: traditional Ukrainian fare such as *borscht,* or beet soup, and popular American meals with meat, potatoes, and vegetables. The meals were so scrumptious that my friends and I would often go back for seconds and even thirds. That was especially true on Fridays, when *varenyky* (boiled dumplings stuffed with potato, cheese, or other fillings) were served, since Catholics were not permitted to eat meat on that day. It was not uncommon to see long lines of pupils eagerly waiting to refill their plates with the popular dish.

The new school building also housed an auditorium with a splendid stage. Boys and girls from different grades would perform for their families, priests, educators, and guests. Sister was instrumental in preparing the pupils for their public appearances. A young and enthusiastic music teacher, Sister instructed the boys and girls on how to read music, carry a tune, and harmonize in a school, church, or public setting. She made singing fun and rewarding by her encouragement and her excellent selection of American and Ukrainian songs. A caring nun, Sister never raised her voice when her pupils were distracted or singing off-key during their rehearsals. She was a great role model for the boys and girls who aspired to be singers or musicians.

St. Nicholas School was more than just an educational institution. It was a testament to the hopes and dreams of the immigrants who valued education and appreciated the teachers committed to educating a new generation of Ukrainian American citizens.

Chapter

20

Tato finally invited me to come downstairs to see the unfinished basement he had worked on for months. We went out the back door and down the middle staircase to the ground floor. When we arrived, Tato asked me to shut my eyes. When he said to open them, I found myself staring at a newly installed door. Right away, I told him that I was so glad that he had replaced the creaky and spooky-looking one. Tato surprised me by saying I was looking at the old door after he had repaired, sanded, repainted, and replaced its lock and door knob.

He unlocked the door, stepped inside, and flipped on a switch. In the bright light, I saw a cheerful kitchen with a sink, refrigerator, and stove. Tato pointed out the pantry and then asked me to look down. I found myself standing on a leveled floor covered with attractive linoleum. Moving around the small but immaculate apartment, I discovered a bedroom and a bathroom with a bathtub. My last stop was the living room that had previously looked like a dark cave. It was now a cozy unfurnished room with a neutrally designed wallpaper. But what really caught my attention was the bright light that entered through the once darkened window.

I complimented my father for having created an apartment in a previously uninhabitable basement. He humbly responded he had received valuable remodeling advice from his knowledgeable friends. He had also hired a professional electrician, plumber, and heating expert.

Tato said, "No man is ever born with a hammer in his hands."

"What do you mean?" I asked.

"No man is born knowing how to do a job. Education, experience, and hard work are necessary."

Tato emphasized that age should never be a factor when it comes to learning something new. He never wanted to stop learning so that he could improve his skills at home and at work. As the two of us headed back upstairs, Tato asked me to make him a "For Rent" sign so that he could find a good tenant to occupy the new apartment.

We were also enjoying our new television set. Every Sunday night, my brother and I watched a show called *Disneyland*, narrated by Walt Disney himself. He welcomed his audience and then introduced one of four Disney realms of wonder: Adventureland, Fantasyland, Frontierland, and Tomorrowland. I especially liked Fantasyland and Frontierland. The former featured wonderful Disney movies and cartoons. I liked Frontierland because I admired American heroes such as Davy Crockett, played by Fess Parker. Mr. Crockett's easygoing sidekick George Russel, played by Buddy Ebsen, added comic relief. Whenever my brother watched Davy Crockett, he wore his coonskin hat. Tato would often join us. He especially liked the episodes when Crockett clashed with his archrival Mike Fink, who dubbed himself "the King of the River."

Families had a myriad of excellent television comedy shows from which to choose. *The Honeymooners* was one of the funniest comedy shows on television. It starred Jackie Gleason as Ralph Kramden, a New York bus driver, and Art Carney as Ed Norton, his upstairs neighbor, friend, and sewer worker. Faithful Raccoon members and bowling buddies, Ralph and Norton often got themselves in trouble especially when they concocted preposterous get-rich schemes. Fortunately, their wives, Audrey Meadows as Alice Kramden and Joyce Randolph as Trixie Norton, were always there to love and forgive their husbands. Another comedy show was *The Phil Silvers Show*. Funnyman Phil Silvers played M.Sgt. Ernest Bilko, a conniver in charge of the Army Motor Pool's zaniest soldiers.

A daring new adult western called *Gunsmoke* immediately attracted grown-up viewers like my father. James Arness starred as Marshal Matt Dillon and Dennis Weaver as Deputy Marshal, Chester Goode. Supporting actors included Milburn Stone as Doc Adams and Amanda Blake as Kitty Russell, owner of the Long Branch Saloon. *Gunsmoke* would eventually become one of the most celebrated and longest-running westerns of all time.

An unconventional drama called *The Millionaire* featured Marvin Miller as Michael Anthony, an employee of a rich benefactor whose weekly assignment was to give away a million dollars to a stranger. Curious audiences would tune in to see how an ordinary person's life would change overnight when he or she unexpectedly became a millionaire.

There was another modern convenience that I really wanted to have. One evening after supper, Roman asked Tato if he could go outside to invite Frankie to play with him. Before my father could reply, I asked him when were we going to get a telephone so that Roman and I wouldn't have to go outdoors every time we wanted to call one of our friends. I also mentioned that a Ukrainian classmate of mine had recently asked me for my telephone number, and I was embarrassed to tell her that we did not have a phone.

Tato retorted that most of his Ukrainian friends and acquaintances didn't have telephones. If he or Mama ever needed to make an emergency call, he would simply ask one of his tenants if he could use their phone. Tato also reminded me that several public phone booths were in the area. When I realized I couldn't change his mind, I changed the subject.

"Tato, I finished my homework and I'm ready to watch some television."

"You can watch TV after you go upstairs to Mrs. Panic's third-floor apartment. Earlier this afternoon, she wasn't feeling well, so Mama brought her some homemade *rosil* (chicken soup). Mrs. Panic asked Mama if a family member could come upstairs in the evening to pick up her rent money." I had never visited her third-floor apartment so I was curious to see it.

And then I remembered: Mrs. Panic was the only adult in the neighborhood I didn't get along with. I didn't see her very often, but during the summer months, she would stand outside our apartment building and talk with some of our neighbors. One evening when I said "good night" to my friends, I noticed that she was still standing outside.

Without any warning, she approached and started

reprimanding me for disturbing her during the day. While Mrs. Panic was scolding me, Tato showed up. He said hello to her, and she politely responded. But then, she began to complain about me. She said that whenever she had her kitchen or living room windows open, she would hear ear-piercing voices. Mrs. Panic said she could always pick out my loud voice. She said I should lower my voice. That night, Tato asked me to respect her wishes and lower my voice.

I was about to start my journey to the third floor when Tato asked me to wait a few moments. He briefly left the room and returned with Mrs. Panic's rent receipt.

"Nastya, proshu (please) give this rent receipt to Mrs. Panic." I grudgingly walked up the stairs and knocked on her door.

Mrs. Panic asked, "Who's there?"

"It's me, Mrs. Panic," I replied. There was a pause and then the door slowly opened. I gazed up at my neighbor who was sternly gazing down at me. Mrs. Panic, rather tall but fragile looking, wore wire-rimmed glasses and no makeup. Most of the time her gray hair was in a bun, but that evening it fell down to her shoulders. She wore a long, off-white cotton nightgown and worn-out slippers.

Mrs. Panic said, "Come inside."

"How are you feeling, Mrs. Panic?"

"I feel fine, and please thank your mother for the delicious chicken soup."

"Okay, I will, Mrs. Panic."

I walked into her apartment, and it was like being transported back in time. I saw worn furniture, adorned fixtures, and a faded oriental rug in her living room as well as a davenport with a dark and unusually carved hardwood frame and greenish upholstery with a floral pattern and French legs. Directly across from the davenport stood a wing chair with a slightly different upholstered pattern but similar French legs. A lovely circular hand-crocheted cover – faded but beautiful – decorated the middle of the wing chair. On a nearby table stood a wrought-iron lamp with a beige-fringed shade that I had seen only in old movies.

In the far corner of the room, an array of striking knickknacks rested on an end table. Several of them appeared to be figurines of ladies dressed in clothing from a different era. I was tempted to pick one up but knew better than to touch something that didn't belong to me. Mrs. Panic must have read my mind because she asked me to sit down while she went into another room. I sat on the vintage davenport and noticed a Phillips radio encased in a dark wooden cabinet but no television set. Mrs. Panic seemed to be living in the 1930s or 1940s and not the 1950s.

She reappeared with a sealed envelope, sat down, and handed it to me.

"Thank you, Mrs. Panic. Here's your rent receipt."

I made up my mind to listen politely and respond to her queries about my school work and outside activities. In the middle of our friendly conversation, Mrs. Panic started talking candidly about herself.

She told me, "I don't get out of my apartment very often during the cold and wintery months, except to buy groceries or to visit a doctor. However, during the warm spring and summer months, I look forward to going outdoors and visiting with my wonderful neighbors."

Mrs. Panic only smiled when she revealed, "I once had a kind and loving husband."

I was startled to learn that she had been married because Mama and Tato told me that she lived alone.

Mrs. Panic proudly told me, "My husband was a brave Chicago firefighter a long time ago."

I could tell from the way she spoke that she still loved and missed him deeply despite all the years that had passed since they were together. At that moment I felt so sorry for her. She must have sensed my sadness because she happily informed me, "I still have my brave husband's firefighter's hat and other treasured mementos."

Mrs. Panic had suffered a deep loss and was living as if time stood still. Even though she had lived in the same apartment for many years, surrounded by her memories and possessions, I couldn't ever recall seeing anyone visiting her. That evening, I realized that she really was a good person, a lonely lady who needed kindness, understanding, and loving people in her life. She and I would become better neighbors, even though I didn't really change into a much quieter person. After all, I was still a kid who just happened to have a rather resounding voice. Mrs. Panic must have finally understood that fact because she never again complained about me to my parents. And I continued making efforts to be more considerate of her need for peace and quiet.

Chapter

21

Toward the end of summer, most parents were ready to send their children back to school. Like Mrs. Panic they, too, were looking forward to some peace and quiet during the day. They were also hoping for cooler temperatures that usually arrived with the autumn weather.

I was back in school wondering who our new fourth-grade teacher would be. And then my classmates and I met her. A no-nonsense teacher, Sister had a set of classroom rules that she expected everyone to follow. She demanded that we keep our eyes fixed on our own work at all times and refrain from whispering or talking with any of our classmates. An uncompromising disciplinarian, she made me fear that the coming year would lack the pleasant and relaxed tone set by my third-grade teacher.

My intuition was right. After only a short time, I began "creeping like snail / unwillingly to school"[2] and experiencing a sinking feeling at the pit of my stomach as I approached Sister's classroom. With her rigid teaching style, she prepared us for challenging work ahead.

As the weeks went by, I hoped that Sister would eventually relax her rigid style once she had gotten to know her smart and hardworking pupils. Of course, that never happened. Luckily, some brave boys occasionally injected some levity into our classroom by challenging Sister's strict rules. Whenever one of the boys got caught for talking or not paying attention, Sister would purposely question him about what we were discussing. An absurd answer usually followed, triggering uproarious laughter from everyone except our fuming teacher!

At the end of the school day, I usually walked to the corner of Damen Avenue where I waited for a bus. One day, I saw an Oscar Mayer Wienermobile zooming toward me. I recognized it from the television commercials but never dreamed I would actually see it in person. As the Wienermobile drew closer, a small man dressed in white wearing a chef's hat popped out the top. He waved to me like an old friend and threw a large batch of Oscar Mayer wiener whistles in my direction. I excitedly waved back, retrieved the whistles, and then stashed them in my coat pocket. I could hardly wait to tell my friends about my encounter with the Wienermobile. Mama would also be happy because she often purchased "Oskey Mayer" products for us.

---

2   William Shakespeare, *As You Like It*, ed. Peter Hollindale (London: Macmillan Education, 1974) II, vii, 146-147.

That first sighting of Oscar Mayer and his Wienermobile would not be my last. Luckily, I would see him a second time and get some more wiener whistles. I felt fortunate to have a traveling route that occasionally brought me some unexpected surprises.

In late September, news broke that President Dwight D. Eisenhower had suffered a heart attack. When Tato arrived home from work, he asked me if I had heard anything more about the President's condition. Apparently, some unsettling rumors had circulated earlier that day. My parents really liked "Ike." Fortunately, President Eisenhower recovered rapidly and returned to his job as the nation's Commander-in-Chief. In the meantime, a lesser known leader named Dr. Martin Luther King, Jr., was also making news. A black minister, he preached nonviolence and equality for all. At that time, most Americans had no idea that Dr. King would wield enormous influence as a civil rights leader in the coming years.

Back in my fourth grade classroom, while Sister wasn't watching, my classmates were whispering about a new Walt Disney television show called the *Mickey Mouse Club*. Led by Musical Mouseketeer, Jimmie Dodd, a group of talented boys and girls including the popular Annette Funicello regaled their young audiences with singing and dancing. Wearing Mickey Mouse ears, they called themselves the Mouseketeers. Like millions of other children, I looked forward to watching the *Mickey Mouse Club* whenever I came home from school.

One chilly weekday, Mama surprised my brother and me with the announcement that we would be going downtown on Sunday to Marshall Field for its annual Children's Christmas Party. The store would be closed to the general public so that Marshall Field employees could bring their children to see

Santa and Mrs. Claus at their Cozy Cloud Cottage. I could hardly wait to visit the store with escalators and the Great Tree in the Walnut Room. That colossal Christmas tree was always exquisitely decorated with one-of-a-kind ornaments that delighted guests of all ages.

I changed into my velvety red dress and attached a matching hair bow to my long hair for the special visit. Mama, Roman, and I walked to the train station and boarded the elevated train. Once it picked up speed, I peered out the window to watch it whiz past the backs of houses and yards, including our building's back porches. I was intrigued by the different neighborhoods, empty lots, trucks, old cars, and smattering of people. When the train began to ascend the tracks, I was exhilarated and scared at the same time. As it reached the highest level, I looked down but couldn't see the tracks— just a sheer drop! I was glad when we finally arrived at our downtown destination and headed toward the store with the famous green clock on State Street.

The elaborately decorated store evoked the kind of holiday spirit that inspired me to tell Mama how lucky I felt to be inside such a beautiful store. She told me that the staff and employees helped build Marshall Field's outstanding reputation because they treated their guests with courtesy and respect.

A uniformed female elevator operator smiled and greeted us, then took us to the seventh floor and pointed out the Cozy Cloud Cottage. Mama asked that we take off our coats before meeting the American *Mykolaj*. I was about to remind her that he was called Santa Claus, when I recognized Uncle Mistletoe. He was wearing his trademark black hat with a sprig of mistletoe sticking out of it, a bright reddish jacket with a long white scarf, and wings that protruded from his back. Uncle Mistletoe was making his way among the boys and girls meandering or running toward him. I was tempted to run toward him as well, but changed my mind because I didn't want to lose my place in the long line.

As we approached the Cozy Cloud Cottage, I saw Santa gently stroking his thick, white flowing beard and twirling his mustache while patiently listening to a boy reading from his list of toys. Mama laughed when Santa motioned for Roman to come over and then lifted him onto his lap. My brother appeared a bit awestruck by the jolly man but still managed to ask Santa Claus for a Tonka Truck and a brand new double holster with cap guns. When Roman got off Santa's lap, I took his place. I asked Santa to bring me a pink diary with a key, a bigger pair of roller skates, a Mr. Potato Head, and a plaid skirt with a matching cardigan sweater. After I spoke with Santa Claus about my wish list, his wife complimented me on my velvety red dress. I thanked her and Santa Claus as I exited the Cozy Cloud Cottage.

Mama told us to follow her to the white tables covered with many tasty cookies. Baked for Marshall Field's youngest guests, they contained the finest ingredients such as pure butter, sugar, vanilla, cinnamon, and other spices. We descended on the holiday treats like bees on honey and then headed toward the crystal punch bowls to wash them down. Mama also tasted the Christmas cookies and suggested that we bring some home to share with Tato, who would love to sample the Marshall Field pastries that she had often bragged about. That afternoon, Roman and I munched our way through a number of holiday cookies and downed them with delicious creamy red punch.

It was getting late, so Mama suggested that we get ready to go back home. When we stepped outside, a large group of children and adults were winding around the Marshall Field windows. I asked Mama if we could stop and look at all of the animated characters, but she insisted that we had to go home. She promised we would return to view the famous Marshall Field displays another day.

Later that evening, I handed Tato the Christmas cookies that we had wrapped in napkins and placed in Mama's purse for safe keeping. He asked about the Christmas party as he took a bite out of one of the cookies. Mama said that she was pleased with the way the Marshall Field staff welcomed all of their guests. I told her that Roman and I were probably the only kids on our block invited to the Marshall Field Christmas party.

Chapter

22

In the 1950s, movie theaters were a major attraction. Throughout the year, theater owners lured audiences with brightly lit marquees where hundreds of lights flashed nonstop. Oversized colored posters displayed actors in exciting scenes from their latest movies. Many patrons sat in baroque-style theaters where sparkling crystal chandeliers dangled from elaborately decorated high ceilings. Some of the earliest theaters even featured a stage, an ornately carved mezzanine, and a balcony.

During the summer months, my family would stroll to the air-conditioned Illington Movie Theater on Cermak Road. Tato would purchase four seventy-cent tickets and then head toward the concession stand where he ordered several boxes of buttered popcorn for us and a big box of Junior Mints, Milk Duds, or Good and Plenty candy for me. I was ready to watch two features, a newsreel, and a cartoon.

Adult moviegoers flocked to the theaters to watch Marilyn
Monroe, the reigning Hollywood queen, and Tom Ewell in
a witty comedy called *The Seven-Year Itch*. Marilyn Monroe
attracted scores of male fans, including my father who always
called her "Merri Mon Row." The youngest moviegoers
preferred a Walt Disney animated feature called *Lady and the
Tramp*. It starred a pampered female cocker spaniel named
Lady and a street-smart alley dog named Tramp. Their warm-
hearted romance brought giggles and sighs from both adults
and children, especially when Lady and the Tramp slurped
spaghetti and shared huge meatballs to the tender strains of
an Italian love song, "Bella Notte."

True movie fans were always looking for juicy gossip
about their favorite movie stars. They would trade stories with
their friends and neighbors and then pick up a twenty-five
cent tattler magazine called *Silver Screen* with a headline that
read "Debbie and Eddie: Is Their Love Threatened?" Other
periodicals such as *Screen Stars*, *Hollywood Stars*, and *Photoplay*
also highlighted movie stars and singers. I learned a lot about
movie stars and their latest romances or breakups by listening
to my neighbors or watching the news. I knew whose actions
were scandalous and whose career could be affected.

My sojourns to Cermak Road were always fun because
I was either going to the Illington to see a double feature or
shopping at one of the stores on that busy street. One tiny
shop displayed a pair of pink ballet slippers in its window.
I wondered what it would feel like to try on those beautiful
dancing shoes. After several brief stops at the shop, I decided
to show Mama my great find and ask her if I could take
ballet lessons. I would really love to pirouette to Tchaikovsky's
music just like a real ballerina. Mama listened attentively and

appeared sympathetic but said that it was not a good time for me to take lessons. With so many daytime responsibilities, she couldn't commit to the hours I would need. And then, of course, there was the cost. Tato depended on her to squeeze every penny out of our tight household budget. I was disappointed but still confident that I would find another artistic activity to pursue.

We walked away from the dance studio and headed toward the F.W. Woolworth Five-and-Ten Cents Store. Like most people, Mama appreciated the dime store's bargain prices. She could purchase household items, odds and ends, notions, and sewing paraphernalia to darn socks, replace buttons, or work on her embroidery. Mama also often purchased and sent seasonal fabrics, babushkas, needles, regular and embroidery thread, yarn, etc. to her family in Ukraine. They would use the materials to sew clothing or sell or barter them to obtain other necessities. However, before Mama sent her package, she would write a letter to her family listing the items that they would receive. This was necessary because, unfortunately, every so often, certain things would be missing from the package. While Mama was waiting to pay for her purchases, I reminded her that I needed a new jump rope because my old one was pretty frayed. I also wanted a walkie-talkie so that I could secretly communicate outdoors with my friends. The sales woman told us that there were jump ropes in the toy aisle but didn't think they had any walkie-talkies. I was disappointed but at least I got a new jump rope that day.

A few days after our Woolworth visit, Tato reminded Mama that an installer from the telephone company would pay us a visit. "Am I hearing things?" I asked Tato. He laughingly replied that we were finally going to have a telephone like so many of our American and Ukrainian friends. We were living in modern times where communicating by telephone was essential.

An Illinois Bell Telephone Company representative arrived at our second-floor apartment. He installed a shiny, bulky black telephone with rotary dialing in our kitchen and placed it on a small square end table. When he concluded the installation, he tested the phone. When it rang for the first time, I felt elated. I was so excited that I wanted to call everyone I knew to tell them the momentous news. Tato appreciated my enthusiasm but asked that I make calls only when necessary. Calling my friends simply to "yakyty-yak" would only increase his monthly bill to over four dollars a month. I told Tato that I would try not to make too many phone calls, though I knew that would be nearly impossible for a chatty kid like me. The telephone would become the second most used item in our home after our 21-inch television set.

One morning, Mama cheerfully told me that Tato had found his first tenants to occupy the renovated basement apartment: a single mother with an adolescent son. After breakfast as I made my way outside, I spotted a boy leaning against the black railing above the basement apartment.

I walked up to him and said, "Hi."

"Who are you and where did you come from?" he asked.

"I'm the landlord's daughter, and I live upstairs."

"I'm Patrick and that basement apartment is my new home."

Taller and older, with unkempt brownish hair, Patrick continued leaning against the railing. I was about to leave when I saw him frantically searching through his pockets and turning them inside out.

All of a sudden he looked up and asked, "Do you have a cigarette?"

Stunned, I asked, "What?"

"Do you have a cigarette?"

"No!" I emphatically replied.

What would I be doing with cigarettes? I was just a kid who never thought about cigarettes let alone carried them around with me. Agitated by my response, Patrick strolled over to the curb, scrutinized the open parking spaces, found a discarded butt, and stuck it in his mouth!

Like most kids, I observed adults and teenagers smugly displaying "cigs" between their lips while others flaunted their puffing skills by blowing smoke rings out of their mouths and noses. Always in demand, cigarettes were inexpensive and easy to purchase from stores and vending machines. Billboard and television advertisements offered tobacco lovers many brand names to choose from: Marlboro, Lucky Strikes, Camels, Chesterfields, Pall Mall, among others. During the Christmas season, television advertisements promoted cigarettes packaged in specially decorated holiday cartons as ideal gifts for family and friends for only about two dollars a carton.

After our first meeting, I assumed that Patrick had forgotten about cigarettes and was ready to meet the other boys who were friendly and accepting of newcomers. Sadly, Patrick never showed any interest in approaching or befriending them. Whenever the boys headed toward Gads Hill to play baseball, Patrick remained near his apartment. I was probably one of the few people he ever spoke to. After a while, his cravings for cigarettes were so strong that he keenly observed and noted where his neighbors tossed their used smokes. Patrick also scoured the corner tavern's curbs and sidewalk where patrons regularly tossed their cigarette butts before entering or leaving the bar. He didn't care what anyone thought of him.

Unfortunately, Patrick was not happy unless he had a cigarette dangling from his lips. Patrick's mother worked all day, and his father was never around. Most of the kids on our block had a mother and a father living with them. I didn't have the heart to tattle on him to my parents. He lived in our basement apartment with his mother quietly for about a year before they moved out. Whenever I thought of Patrick, I hoped his mother would encourage him to make friends and enjoy being a kid without thinking about or searching for cigarettes.

Chapter

23

Karolina and I enjoyed playing hop-scotch. We had just purchased some new white chalk to neatly draw the usual pattern of rectangular shapes on the sidewalk and then hop from space to space. Luckily, our neighbors never complained about our artwork, which regularly appeared in front of the building. Neither did Mama. A fastidious lady, Mama always kept her property neat and tidy, yet she never asked us to stop making chalk marks that sometimes lasted weeks before the rain washed them away.

That summer, a new girl showed up in our neighborhood. A confident cyclist, she pedaled her bicycle with such energy and speed that pedestrians had to move out of her way whenever she showed up.

The newcomer shouted a friendly greeting. "Hi, I'm Debbie. Can I join you?"

Karolina and I stopped our hop-scotch game as the girl with strong shoulders and brownish short hair and bangs rode her bicycle toward us. When she spoke, I detected a kind of steadfast confidence that proclaimed, "I can take care of myself!" Debbie parked her bicycle and told us that she didn't live in the area but was staying with her grandmother during the summer months. She pointed across the street and said that her grandmother's modest brick home was located down the block. Debbie mentioned she wanted to make friends with the neighborhood kids. That's when Karolina and I asked her to join us in our game of hop-scotch. We reminded her that it might look like an easy game, but it wasn't. Players had to move quickly from rectangle to rectangle without stopping, stepping outside the lines, changing feet, or repeating a word.

In the middle of our game, Debbie unexpectedly said that she had to leave but would soon return. Karolina and I wondered about her hasty departure but didn't say anything. We just continued to play. We were both competitive and knew that there could be only one winner per game. We also knew that if either one of us lost, it wasn't a big deal because there would always be a next time.

Karolina's mother, Harriet, came out of her apartment and asked her to come home and get ready for supper. Her father, Frank, would soon be coming home from his nearby work place. My father worked in a different part of the city and had to take two buses to get home. Karolina reminded me that we would get together after supper.

"I'll be outside waiting and don't forget to bring your jump rope," I replied.

I sat down on one of the steps trying to decide if I should go back home or wait outside for Tato. I had just decided to go home when I heard a loud familiar voice ask, "Where are you going?" I turned around and saw Debbie crossing the street with her beautiful Schwinn bicycle in tow. She parked it in front of our apartment building, and I asked her why she had left our game so abruptly. Debbie admitted she had to check in periodically with her strict grandmother, an elderly woman who was adamant about knowing where and with whom her granddaughter was at all times. This was especially true when Debbie was spending time with boys and girls that her grandmother didn't know.

That revelation must have been a little difficult for her, since she looked so independent from the outside. Debbie also wanted to know about the boys in our neighborhood. She acknowledged that she had been eyeing them while pedaling her bicycle. I commented that many of the boys were our friends. They would team up with the girls for the usual outdoor games such as hide-and-go-seek and then invent new ones whenever they were in the mood for something more daring and adventurous.

I mentioned the boys by name, including Lloyd, one of my favorites. A cute and soft-spoken boy, Lloyd had invited me over to his apartment to watch *Flash Gordon* with him. We both enjoyed watching the science fiction serials that starred Buster Crabbe as the space hero who battled Ming the Merciless and other villains. Lloyd lived across our alley in the huge apartment building with all the back porches. Like many of the other kids, he entered and exited his apartment through the back porch instead of using the front-door entrance.

Debbie said that she liked *Flash Gordon* and watched it whenever she was at home. Then she mentioned a good-looking boy whom she had recently met while riding her bicycle. I could tell she liked him by the way she smiled when she spoke about him. I asked her if we could continue our conversation another day because Mama was expecting me for supper.

Debbie said, "Okay," walked over to her bicycle, kicked the kickstand up, and straddled the seat.

I told her, "You're really lucky to be riding a Schwinn bicycle."

She boasted, "Riding is so much fun. I can move as fast or as slow as I want to, and still get to my destination quicker than if I had walked! I feel a sense of freedom that only a fellow biker can understand. Would you like to go riding with me sometime?"

"I don't know how to ride a two-wheeler." Debbie was amazed that I couldn't ride a bicycle.

"Could Karolina?"

"I don't know. I never saw her riding one."

I tried to explain to Debbie that not every boy and girl in our neighborhood had a fancy bicycle like the one she rode. And kids who did own their own bikes still did a lot of walking and running.

Debbie laughed. "I prefer riding my bike anytime over walking or running."

Just before she crossed the street, she waved and said, "See you later, alligator."

I waved back, "After while, crocodile."

I had been dreaming of having my very own shiny red Schwinn bicycle for quite some time. Several times, I had asked my parents for a two-wheeler and told them how much fun I would have riding it around the block with the other kids. I even asked them to purchase a bicycle for Roman. They understood how I felt, but always said that it wasn't the right time. That day, I decided to approach Tato one more time. He patiently listened to my reasons for needing a bicycle and then replied that he would talk to Mama about possibly purchasing one for me. "What about Roman?" I asked.

Tato replied that he could not afford to purchase two Schwinn bicycles, but he would consider getting a two-wheeler for me if I agreed to two conditions. First, I would have to learn how to ride a two-wheeler, and secondly, I would have to share my new bicycle with my brother.

"How can I learn how to ride a bicycle if I don't have one?" I asked Tato.

"If you really want that two-wheeler, you will figure out a way."

Coincidentally, that evening, while changing channels on the television set, I came across the Doris Day song "Whatever Will Be, Will Be." I stopped and listened to the lyrics, realizing that they were thought-provoking. Millions of music fans must have felt the same way because that song soared to number five on the 1956 music chart.

The next day Debbie came over with her Schwinn and said she had to go to the gas station to put air in her bicycle tires. The gas station was nearby, so I walked beside her while she slowly rode her bike. As we made our way inside the gas station, we saw customers filling up their tanks with gasoline costing about twenty-five-cents-a-gallon. Debbie and I went to the back where the air pump was kept. Debbie parked her bicycle, loosened the tire screws, picked up the hose, and filled the bicycle tires with air. I was carefully watching every step because I had a feeling that I would soon be doing the same thing.

When we returned, Debbie and I started playing a game of Jacks while we waited for Karolina to join us. Jacks was a game that required speed and good coordination. You had to toss a small ball in the air and try to pick up as many jacks as possible before the ball hit the ground. I had played Jacks many times, so I was really quick.

After I won a couple of games, Debbie suggested that we play *Monopoly* instead, because she loved collecting money, houses, and hotels. I told her that my *Monopoly* game was one of my prized possessions.

I ran back upstairs and returned not only with the *Monopoly* game but a couple of orange Push-ups for us. While we were licking our Push-ups on that eighty-plus degree day, Debbie helped me sort out the paper money, small houses, hotels, deed cards, and chance cards.

I was ready to distribute the game tokens when Bobby and a buddy of his showed up. Bobby asked if I had seen Ben, John, and the other boys.

"No, I haven't," I replied.

"Oh, by the way, Bobby, have you met Debbie?" He turned to Debbie and said, "Nope, but I've often seen you on your bike speeding up and down our street." Debbie took Bobby's comment as a compliment and asked, "Do you boys wanna join us?"

"Can't," replied Bobby, "but we could watch you girls play before our friends arrive."

Whenever Debbie or I made a certain move that the boys didn't agree with, they would comment or joke about it. They laughed whenever Debbie or I landed in jail or lost our money and property.

Eventually, Nick, Gerry, and some of the other boys

showed up and asked Bobby to go with them to Gads Hill to play softball. Bobby said, "See ya," to us as he left with his buddies. Debbie and I continued playing our game until an unexpected gust of wind scattered my cards and paper money all over the stairs. Debbie and I went scrambling up and down those steps to locate all of the missing game pieces. She helped me put them away before she got back on her bicycle. I asked her if I could try riding her bicycle. She replied, "Of course, you can."

Debbie got off her bike and handed it over to me. I took hold of her Schwinn bicycle and sat down on the seat. Debbie offered me some advice on how to properly steer and control a two-wheeler. It was at that moment that I decided to make a deal with her.

I said, "If you will let me use your bicycle for an entire day, I'll pay you twenty-five cents."

Debbie's eyes lit up. She had already spent most of her money and, like the rest of the kids, was making daily trips to *Poskonka* for her favorite treats.

Debbie asked, "Do you have the quarter with you?"

"No, but I'll have it for you tomorrow."

"Okay, but I have to be with you during the lesson. And I'll need to ride it a few times around the block."

After I agreed, she said that she would offer me tips on how to ride her bicycle. The two of us shook hands to complete our deal.

That evening, I excitedly told Tato about my plan and asked him for twenty-five cents. He pulled out a small pile of change and handed me a quarter, three nickels, a dime, and eight pennies. I not only had a quarter for Debbie but extra change to buy bubble gum, ice cream, and a grape pop. I hugged and thanked him. Roman must have overheard our conversation because he quickly came over and stuck his hand out. Tato reached into his pocket and gave his son the leftover change and wished me luck. I thanked him and told him that I wanted only a shiny red sixteen-inch Schwinn bicycle. He suggested that I first learn how to ride it before putting in my order.

The next morning I got up early and made my own *snidanok* (breakfast) with Cheerios and milk. As I put on my pink and yellowish top with matching pedal pushers, Mama reminded me to "keep them clean." I slipped on my black-and-white saddle shoes over my white socks and headed outdoors with my quarter clutched tightly in my palm.

I waited in front of our apartment building for Debbie. About fifteen minutes later, she showed up and asked if I had the quarter. As I reached into my pocket, I reminded her that I would be riding her bicycle for the entire day. She agreed, so I handed her the quarter. Debbie thanked me and swiftly tucked it away in her shirt pocket. I asked Debbie if there was a difference between a girl's and a boy's bicycle. She replied that a girl's bike had no center bar below the handlebars while a boy's bike did.

I was ready for my first lesson. After watching a few of her demonstrations, I sat down on the bicycle seat, placed my feet on the ground, and took hold of the handlebars. "So far so good," I told myself. Then I quickly took my feet off the ground and tried to pedal. The bicycle toppled to one side. So I put my feet down again, straightened out the bike, and tried to pedal once more, but the bike tipped over again. This wasn't going to be so easy. After several more unsuccessful attempts, Debbie took over and got back on to show me how to get started.

As we talked, Debbie confided that while riding her bicycle, she had met a good-looking teenage boy whom she wanted to get to know. The first time she had noticed him, she was riding her bicycle, and he was walking with a friend. The second time she saw him, she said, "Hello." He said, "Hi," and that was the extent of the conversation. Debbie wanted to see him again.

I could tell she had developed a crush on that unknown boy. I told her not to worry because she would probably see him again. I also suggested that the two of us talk about this on our way to the ice cream shop near the train station. It was a favorite stop whenever I had a taste for a creamy hand-scooped ice cream cone. Debbie liked the idea. I got back on the bike trying to pedal, while Debbie continued instructing me on how to steer it properly. Unfortunately, the two wheeler kept wobbling all the way to the ice cream shop and all the way back again. Debbie kept encouraging me and never complained that she had to hold onto the back end of her bicycle.

We slowly made our way toward Gads Hill Center with Debbie still holding on. After a few minutes, I noticed that I wasn't weaving back and forth and had even picked up some speed. I was happy that Debbie was doing such a good job holding the Schwinn steady. I shouted a "thanks" for her help. When Debbie didn't respond, I turned around and saw that she was a few feet away, chatting with a boy! I shouted to get her attention. When she heard me, Debbie looked up and shouted back that I had been riding her bicycle the whole time without her assistance. Debbie was right.

That afternoon in front of Gads Hill Center, I learned how to ride a two-wheeler. We were elated! The rest of the day, the two of us took turns riding her Schwinn up and down the block.

Within a few weeks, I had my brand-new, shiny red Schwinn bicycle with an attached horn. The only problem – it wasn't a girl's bike. Roman had complained to Mama and Tato that he didn't want to ride a girl's bike. They understood his reasoning, so Mama purchased a boy's bike.

It wasn't long before I had skinned knees from riding too fast. Before the right knee healed, I skinned the left one. As a result, I had to ride back home so that Mama could apply iodine to my latest wound. A popular antiseptic, iodine was used to treat all kinds of cuts and scrapes, but it burned like heck. As Mama applied the stinging red liquid to my scraped knees, she lectured me about my riding habits. In the meantime, the iodine made my scraped knees look worse because of the blazing red color.

It wasn't uncommon for bicycle riders to fall on hard cement surfaces after racing or attempting new bicycle tricks. The boys were the worst offenders. They would show off their riding skills by lifting their legs and placing them on top of their handlebars. Some boys allowed a friend to ride on top of the handlebars or on the back of the bicycle, increasing the likelihood that it would topple over.

When my brother learned how to ride my sixteen-inch bicycle, I knew that meant he and I would have to devise a plan for sharing. We agreed to take turns riding the Schwinn every other day. However, if one of us decided to do something else, then the other person could take it. If the two of us needed to ride the Schwinn on the same day, we would toss a coin to see which one of us would get the two-wheeler. Except for a few bumps in the road, our plan worked out fairly well.

Chapter

24

When not riding my bicycle, I liked to play games such as dress-up. Karolina and I would borrow our mothers' long pretty frocks and jewelry that made us feel glamorous and grown-up. Mama let me use her pop beads that she wore with a pretty blouse or casual dress. Popular with the ladies, they came in different colors and enabled the wearer to make a two-three-or four-strand necklace by inserting one pop bead into another. If the wearer changed her mind and wanted a single strand, she would simply pop out the additional beads.

Karolina and I also borrowed our mothers' high heels to look and feel taller. Walking up and down the stairs was especially challenging because our feet were too small for adult shoes. The high heels started to look rumpled and misshapen after we had traipsed around in them all day. Thankfully, our understanding mothers never complained.

For the finishing touches, we borrowed our mothers' makeup, vibrant red lipstick and rouge for dazzling lips and rosy cheeks. One day, the top portion of the lipstick broke off while I was applying it to my lips. Mama told me not to worry because she kept extra tubes on her dresser, but I wanted to replace the one I had broken.

The following day, Mama was on her way to purchase a rolling pin and other kitchen utensils when I asked her if I could come along. The two of us strolled to Woolworth's where she readily found what she was looking for. In the meantime, a friendly sales lady helped me pick out a bright red tube of Revlon lipstick like the one I had ruined. Mama suggested that I keep it for future "dress-up" games. I also discovered an attractive bottle of perfume called "Evening in Paris." The sales lady let me take a few whiffs. I was instantly drawn to its lovely fragrance. Mama took a whiff and liked it. She smiled and asked me if I had enough money to pay for it. I proudly replied that I did. That day, I spent a dollar on my first bottle of "Evening in Paris" perfume.

I was getting older and paying more attention to movies, actors, singers, and popular fashions. The billboard near my home beamed larger than life images of Deborah Kerr and Yul Brynner dressed in majestic costumes and dancing from a scene in *The King and I*. Before long, that gigantic poster attracted local residents and motorists. The musical's delightful tunes also spread via radio and television to captivate audiences everywhere. Karolina and I liked the music so much that we memorized the words to "Shall We Dance?" and "Getting to Know You." Neighbors who could barely carry a tune could be heard humming or singing lyrics from the entertaining movie.

I noticed that many teenagers and women styled their own hair. Saturday evenings were date nights for teen girls and ladies who wanted to look their loveliest without going to a beauty shop. After washing their hair, they would make tightly wound curls, secure them with bobby pins, and then cover their heads with colorful scarves tied behind their necks. By evening, they removed the scarves, pulled out the bobby pins, and combed out a wavy and bouncy head of hair. The teens and ladies were ready for a night out with their family, friends, or dates.

During the mid 1950s, rock 'n' roll revolutionized music. While many Americans listened to spectacular musicals and tunes like Perry Como's "Hot Diggity," teenagers were listening to a young, dark-haired singer from Tupelo, Mississippi. Elvis Presley entertained his listeners with racy lyrics while swiveling his hips provocatively, turning staid females into shrieking adolescents. Despite some adults' assertion that Elvis Presley's music and movements were offensive, his popularity continued to soar.

After a while, I felt that the criticism leveled against him was exaggerated and that he was really a good singer. I even decided to buy one of his records. I took a dollar bill and some change from my cigar box and purchased a large 78-rpm record called "Hound Dog Man" and carefully carried it home. When Mama asked me what I was holding, I reluctantly replied that I had an Elvis Presley record. She looked surprised but didn't say anything. A few days later, I accidentally dropped my Elvis record, and it shattered into many pieces. That slip-up convinced me to refrain from buying another rock 'n' roll record until I was a teenager. Fortunately, by that time records were smaller and unbreakable.

"Poodle skirts" were paired with rock 'n' roll. Girls of all ages wore them including teenagers who danced to the beat of the fifties' music. Wanting to keep up with the latest craze, I asked Mama to buy me a poodle skirt. At first, she didn't think that I needed one, but she changed her mind when she noticed they were in style. She bought me a wide black skirt with reddish musical designs on it. It looked good with my crispy starched white blouse. A red bandanna around my neck completed my "cool" look.

I was not only "cool," but enterprising. I had just finished stuffing approximately fifty bubble-gum wrappers, along with some additional coins, into a long stamped envelope requesting a pair of walkie-talkies advertised in one of the bubble-gum wrappers when a familiar voice called out to me. I looked up and my next-door neighbor, Carp, gestured for me to come over. I put away the envelope and went to see what he wanted.

Carp was sitting on his front porch like an oversized bird perching on his nest. He seemed genuinely glad to see me.

"Can you do me a favor?" he asked.

"Of course," I replied.

Carp explained that he wanted me to go to *Poskonka* and pick up a Polish newspaper for him. I told him that I would be happy to go. Carp dug into his pocket, pulled out some money, and asked me to bring him the *Dziennik związkowy* (Polish Daily Zgoda). When I repeated the name correctly, Carp looked surprised and even complimented me on my pronunciation. I didn't tell him that Polish, like Ukrainian, was a Slavic language and that I could understand it. After Carp handed me his change, I promised to return with his newspaper.

With a quick skip, I headed straight toward *Poskonka*. I wanted to make a good impression on my elderly neighbor. Once in the store, I looked around for newspapers and found the *Dziennik związkowy* stacked neatly near the cash register. Mrs. P. greeted me and expressed disbelief that I was purchasing a copy of the *Dziennik związkowy* instead of a comic book. I told her that I was buying it for my neighbor. When I headed toward the door, she said, "Come back real soon. We just received a new stack of used comic books."

I marched back to Carp's home, gripping his *Dziennik związkowy* as if it were a prized possession. I ran up the stairs of his building and handed the waiting fisherman his paper and change. He took the newspaper, thanked me, and then handed me a quarter. It was a generous tip! He explained that reading the daily Polish newspaper was important to him. Carp was so pleased that he asked me to buy the *Dziennik związkowy* for him regularly. He held out his hand, and I held out mine. With a firm handshake, I became his official newspaper delivery girl. I now had a source of income more lucrative than collecting empty Coke bottles for pennies. Not only was I making more money, but my father was still handing me pennies, nickels, dimes, and quarters. I decided to use Tato's money for everyday purchases and save my "earned" money for unforeseen expenses.

I had another valuable possession: a diary where I could write down all of my secret thoughts, feelings, and experiences. The best part was that it could be opened only by the writer using a tiny key. I knew that my parents would never try to read my diary, but I wasn't so sure about my brother. So, I lectured him about how a diary is a private book written by and read only by its owner. Roman crossed his heart and tried to reassure me that he had no intention of ever touching my diary or showing it to any of his friends.

Throughout the summer, I continued writing in my diary except on days when the weather was so hot and sticky that all I could think about was staying cool. Ordinarily, Mama loved to open windows for *shvizhe povitre*, or fresh air, but whenever the air was very humid, she had to close them and use fans. Unfortunately, they merely moved the hot air around and shattered the serenity of the day or evening with their loud humming noises. On those sultry nights, I wished I were inside an air-conditioned movie theater.

The following day, I asked Mama if I could wear my bathing suit outdoors since my friends had been talking about looking for new ways to stay cool. Mama suggested that I wear a pair of shorts over the bathing suit. I took her advice, left the apartment, and knocked on Karolina's door. When no one answered, I assumed that she had gone out with her mother and brother. I headed over to Bobby's home, but didn't see him or his grandfather, Carp, who practically lived on his porch when he wasn't out fishing. Disappointed, I walked past Babusia's grand garden and noticed some robins making their way toward a water-filled container.

A neighbor's cat scampered across the street, reminding me of the neighborhood cat we called Midnight. He attracted attention because of his large size, penetrating green eyes, and thick black fur. Midnight's dauntless meanderings in and out of people's backyards and gardens were well-known. He would also show up unexpectedly and plop himself on someone's front steps or porch. I never minded when he appeared on our front steps and neither did any of my friends. Midnight may not have had an owner like some of the other cats in the neighborhood, but he had the affection and companionship of the boys and girls who befriended him. I wondered how Midnight was faring on such a hot day and hoped that he was safe in a cool and hospitable niche.

The sun's rays continued to beat down. I walked toward Gads Hill, hoping to run into Debbie or some other bicycle riders. But there were no bicycles in sight or any boys hitting softballs over the fence. Then I saw Mrs. Bennet coming out of the building. A Gads Hill counselor with stylish short hair, she wore fashionable eyeglasses with delicate side chains that allowed her to rest her glasses on her chest.

Children gravitated toward her because she was a kind lady who helped them develop their talents while encouraging new endeavors. She wasn't very tall, but her enthusiasm and resourcefulness made her stand out from the other counselors. Parents also recognized her dedication and sincerity. Mama became impressed with Mrs. Bennet after their first meeting at the elevated train station. Mrs. Bennet was on her way home and Mama was going to work. Mrs. Bennet mentioned that she worked with the children at Gads Hill Center. Mama proudly informed her that Roman and I spent a lot of time there. Mrs. Bennet readily replied she knew and liked us. After that initial conversation, Mama and Mrs. Bennet frequently stopped to chat like old friends. Mama confided that Mrs. Bennet was going to head a drama class at Gads Hill Center and wanted me to join it.

As I approached Mrs. Bennet, she greeted me with a smile, and I asked her, "Where is everybody?" Mrs. Bennet said she saw a group of boys with towels wrapped around their necks riding their bicycles toward the nearby park.

The park was close and I had never been there before

so I decided to go. Besides, I was already wearing a bathing suit. I crossed the street and walked past the ravine until I reached a sidewalk. A tall young man dressed in a dark suit and tie walked up and asked me where I was going. He looked respectable, so I replied that I was heading to the swimming pool at the park. He asked if any of my family members were waiting for me. I said no, but some of my friends were, and I was going to join them. Leaning over, the man asked if I liked ice cream. I nodded and told him I loved it. He immediately offered to take me to the store that was "over there." I looked and saw only trees and bushes. I said, "There is no store over there!" The man angrily insisted that the store was there and that I had to go with him. That stern demand triggered fear in me. My parents' warnings never to go anywhere with a stranger flashed through my mind. I started running. He tried to stop me, but I ran as fast as I could and got away.

When I finally made it back to my apartment, I started wailing and told Mama about the stranger and how he had tried to take me to a non-existent store for some ice cream. She appeared shaken but then hugged me with a sense of relief. Practically in tears herself, Mama thanked God that I was safe, though she let me know that she wasn't pleased that I had gone to the park without her knowledge or permission. She made me promise that I would never do that again. When Tato came home, Mama told him about the incident. Tato commended me for obeying their rules, but reiterated that Roman and I were never to go anywhere with a stranger and never accept candy, ice cream, or automobile rides. Though frightened by the afternoon's threatening encounter, I was relieved to be safe at home. I never returned to that park again.

After Patrick and his mother moved out of the basement apartment, Tato rented it to a Mexican lady with a young daughter. I met them when the mother anxiously asked me to take care of her daughter, Rosario, because she had to go to work. The young mother told me that she had spoken with the landlord about my dependability and had even observed my interacting with the other kids. Her plea to take care of her daughter for the entire day convinced me to help her. Grateful and relieved, the mother said something to her daughter in Spanish and then told me that she would be home in the evening. I turned to the quiet, dark-haired Spanish girl and tried to reassure her that we would have a good time together.

Rosario and I got along from the moment we started playing. I happened to have a paddle that had a small ball attached to it with a rubber string. I showed her how to hit the ball in rapid succession. At first, Rosario had some difficulty hitting the ball but eventually improved her game. I also showed her how to do a cartwheel. She really enjoyed watching me but admitted that she wasn't quite ready to do a cartwheel by herself. However, Rosario did enjoy taking turns jumping rope with me. After playing for a while, I heard Mama's voice calling me. I walked over to the gangway and told her I was taking care of the little girl who lived in the basement. Mama was surprised since Rosario's mother had informed Tato that her daughter stayed with an adult caretaker when she was at work. I told Mama that I had agreed to watch Rosario for the day.

A short time later, Mama carried down a plate of Oscar Meyer liver sausage sandwiches and two glasses of cherry Kool-Aid. She also mentioned that I should call her if I needed help with my young charge. When Rosario and I were finished eating, I brought down a few games, comic books,

183

and a Slinky toy.

Rosario had never seen a Slinky before, so I demonstrated how to make it "walk" down our stairs. She was quite captivated with the wiry coil and couldn't stop giggling when the Slinky escaped from her small hands. After playing with the Slinky, the two of us played hop-scotch. When I noticed that Rosario was tired, I read *Marge's Little Lulu* comic books to her. She rapidly became intrigued with Little Lulu's friends Tubby, Annie, Iggy, Alvin, and Ol' Witch Hazel.

Later that day, the two of us went for a long stroll toward the busy street near the gas station where we bumped into several boys I knew, along with a boy I had never seen before. The friendly boys said,"Hi," but the unknown boy stopped and abruptly asked, "What are you doing with that girl?" I realized that he was not accustomed to seeing Spanish children in our neighborhood, but that was no excuse to ask such a rude question. I was about to say that I was watching Rosario until her mother came home from work, but then changed my mind because I didn't owe him an explanation. I just kept walking straight ahead while he and the other boys continued walking in the opposite direction. I never talked about the incident to Rosario, because my main responsibility was to keep her happy and return her safely to her mother.

That evening, when Rosario's mother returned from work, her daughter was sitting on the front steps waiting for her. The mother called out "Rosario," and her *hija* ran over and embraced her. That ordinarily reserved child began to give her mother a full account of her day in Spanish. The mother patiently listened and then said they would continue their conversation at home. As they walked toward their apartment, the mother thanked me for watching her daughter.

About a month later, Tato told Mama that he needed to clean the basement apartment again so that he could rent it. I couldn't believe what I was hearing. I asked Tato if Rosario and her mother had moved out. The disappointed look on his face confirmed my fear. He said that his tenant had given him notice that she and her daughter would be moving. She didn't give Tato any reason for their departure. Mama commented that it was difficult for a mother to raise a child by herself. She also said that Mexicans were hard-working people who cared about their families. Rosario and her mother would be missed.

One day, Mama was standing outside speaking with Harriet when our mailman showed up. He pulled a package out of his bag and handed it to Mama. She thanked him, looked at it, and said it was addressed to me. I had never received a package in the mail before. When Mama handed it to me, I remembered that I had ordered a set of walkie-talkies from the bubble gum company. I ran back upstairs to open it.

I cut open the sealed envelope and pulled out two thin aluminum paddle-shaped objects. They had tiny holes on one side and were connected by a string. The peculiar looking toy didn't look anything like the walkie-talkie I thought I had ordered. I asked my brother what he thought of the paddles.

He glanced at them and said that Jimmy had real walkie-talkies, not paddles. I was disappointed but nevertheless asked Roman to place one of the paddles near his ear. He laughed and said it would be a waste of time. While Roman stood there with a paddle near his ear, I tried speaking into the other one. After we both had a good laugh, I told Roman that I would never, ever order any toys from a bubble gum company again. I had to admit, though, that I would continue buying bubble gum because I loved its flavor and blowing gigantic bubbles.

Chapter

25

It was the end of the month, and I still hadn't written out the rent receipts for Tato's tenants. Mama reminded me that I had to complete them before the tenants showed up with their monthly payments. She walked over to the kitchen drawer and pulled out the rent-receipt book and a couple of pens. As she handed the items to me, she asked that I not write a receipt for the couple who lived in the third-floor, rear apartment because they were moving. As soon as I began to write, Mama returned to the stove to finish preparing her mouth-watering *pyrohy* (pierogi). When I had completed writing the rent receipts, I handed them back to her. Mama put them away and then brought over her freshly made blueberry pyrohy. She suggested that I brush my bluish teeth before leaving the house.

As I headed downstairs, I could hear familiar sounds of rubber balls, or pinners, bouncing against Tato's brick building. Bobby, Nick, Mike, my brother, Frankie, and other boys would regularly throw pinners at the brick wall and catch them as quickly as they flew back. Sometimes, I would join the boys for a game because I was pretty good at throwing and catching. I usually followed their lead, except when the boys launched their pinners with such strength and speed that they would fly past the sidewalk and land on the street or bounce off a moving vehicle. It was the boys' way of competing to see who had the best throwing arm.

While pinners were flying into the street, John, who owned the local tavern, was bravely dodging them while hosing down his Pontiac. A young, blond-haired girl handed him a can of car polish. A short time later, she came over and told me that her name was Kathy. She mentioned that the man polishing the automobile was her father. I liked John, so I assumed that he was a good parent. We spoke for a while before she asked me if I wanted to meet her mother.

The two of us walked toward the tavern with the prominently displayed Schlitz sign that summoned thirsty patrons to come in for a drink, lively conversation, and Cubs baseball. As we entered, a Hamm's beer commercial showed a portly bear moving through the woods to a tune that would become familiar to Cubs fans. I heard that tune whenever I made my way toward the backroom where Kathy, her mother, and little brother resided while John waited on his patrons. He tended bar most of the time but also hired neighbors to help him. That corner tavern had a family-friendly atmosphere where a parent could walk in with children, ask for a bottle of pop and a bag of Yo-Ho potato chips, and never hear any inappropriate or coarse language. In fact, the patrons were always polite and courteous. During the baseball season, patrons could always count on watching a Chicago Cubs' game on the tavern's large television screen.

Mrs. Catherine, Kathy's mother, was a kind and lovely lady with short, bouncy blond hair. She made me feel welcome in her other "home" inside the back room of the tavern. Like any other nicely decorated kitchen, it had modern appliances and a table with chairs. Children's games and toys were piled neatly in the corner. Mrs. Catherine announced that she was going to make waffles for Kathy and her brother and asked if I would like one. I said, "Yes," because I had never eaten a waffle before. Mrs. Catherine cooked the waffles and slid them on separate plates for us. I watched Kathy put butter and syrup on top of her waffle, so I did the same. When I took my first bite, I knew that I had discovered yet another tasty American food. After Kathy and I finished our second helping, we played a board game and then went back outside to play outdoor games. When I saw John's meticulously polished four-door sedan, I had to tell Kathy that it was the shiniest-looking car on the block. That afternoon, she and I became friends.

My brother and I were used to having company on weekends because our parents had many friends. Mama loved to cook, and Tato loved to talk, so naturally when our guests arrived, there was always plenty of food to eat and stories to listen to. Pan Jaroslaw was one of our frequent visitors. When my family and I were living in Mississippi, he was the one who wrote Tato urging him to come to Chicago where a large community of Ukrainian immigrants had settled. Mama and Tato would always be grateful for his life-changing advice.

IT LOOKED LIKE FOREVER

My mother tried to make Pan Jaroslaw feel at home by preparing some of his favorite Ukrainian dishes such as *borscht* (beet soup) and *holubtsi* (cabbage rolls). He appreciated her efforts and always complimented her on her fine meals. Pan Jaroslaw would arrive on Saturday afternoons in an automobile called a Volkswagen Beetle that had an unusual design and looked really small compared to the large wing-tipped cars on the road. The Volkswagen drew many curious stares from the local residents because it starkly contrasted with their bird-like vehicles.

One day, when Pan Jaroslaw was sitting at the kitchen table and slowly sipping hot borscht with my family, a loud banging on our back door startled us. It was Mrs. Jeffries, screaming, "Fire! Fire! Joe, open the door! Fire!" Everyone stopped eating. Tato jumped up and raced to the back door.

"Joe, there's a fire in my basement apartment! Call the fire department!"

"I come down, Mrs. Jeffries." Then Tato turned to Mama and said, "Justyna, call fire department. Keep everyone in apartment and don't follow me!"

Mama pleaded with Tato, "Josyf, *proshu* (please) wait for the firemen to arrive," as she headed toward the telephone. Tato dashed down the stairs.

While Mama, Roman, and I were anxiously waiting to hear from Tato, Pan Jaroslaw was calmly eating his meal! I couldn't believe that a close friend of Tato's wouldn't help during an emergency. When I heard the loud sirens, I ran to the living room window. I could see firemen rushing toward the gangway.

After nervously pacing the floor, I saw the firemen leave. A short time later, an exhausted-looking Tato showed up at our back door. His face and clothing were covered with soot, and his thick eyebrows were singed.

"Tato, your *brovy* (eyebrows)!" I cried. My father saw the fear in my eyes.

"*Ne zhurysia* (don't worry), Nastya!"

I could tell that Mama was holding back tears when she asked him, "*Chomu* (why) didn't you wait for the fire department to put out the fire?"

Tato asked her to bring him some fish oil for his burns. When Mama returned with it, he explained, "*Ya musiv* (I had to) put out the fire in the kitchen because I was concerned that the flames would spread to the first-floor apartment. When the firemen arrived, I asked them not to use their water hoses because I had already put out the fire. I didn't want more water damage to the charred kitchen. But they told me they had to put out any flames that might still be smoldering in the apartment. They said that their job was to protect everyone in the building. They also suggested that I get immediate treatment for my burns."

Before the firemen left, they inspected the kitchen and determined that the fire had started on the stove. The tenant was frying something in a hot skillet, walked away, and returned to find shooting flames. When the firemen left, Tato checked the damage and the soaked stove, walls, floor, and ceiling. He knew that he would have a lot of cleaning and repair work to do before his tenants could return to their apartment.

The next day, my father and I were sitting at the kitchen table and talking about the basement fire. I told Tato that I couldn't understand why Pan Jaroslaw continued eating and never attempted to help him. Tato said that he understood how I felt. However, he wasn't going to judge Pan Jaroslaw.

He was a good man who respected Tato's request not to follow him downstairs and possibly get hurt. After our conversation, I still couldn't comprehend how a grown man could appear so apathetic when his friend was in danger. But after thinking about the incident, I realized Tato was right. My parents never again mentioned the basement fire to Pan Jaroslaw, nor did they ever criticize him for his inaction.

Chapter

26

It was a warm summer evening when Mrs. Catherine invited Kathy and me to go to a carnival with her. I had never been to a carnival before, so I was really excited. Mrs. Catherine suggested that I get my father's permission and not bring any money since she would pay for everything. I ran home and told Tato about Mrs. Catherine's kind offer. He said that I could go with her and then reached into his pocket and pulled out four dollar bills "just in case" I needed them. I ran back outside where Mrs. Catherine was waiting in front of the Pontiac with Kathy and her toddler son, Michael.

While Mrs. Catherine was driving, Kathy and I talked about the fun we would have at the carnival. She told me that her mother had a lucky streak that enabled her to win contests at numerous events. When we arrived at the carnival, Mrs. Catherine parked her car, took a stroller out of the trunk, and then headed toward the rides and booths. She stopped when she recognized a huge wheel with riders in suspended seats rotating high above the carnival grounds. Mrs. Catherine said that the Ferris Wheel was often the main attraction at summer carnivals because it offered riders the thrill of soaring high in the air while taking in the beauty of the brilliant sky. I loved seeing the Ferris Wheel up close but was intimidated by its size and height.

Mrs. Catherine must have sensed my apprehension because she said that we should head toward the concession stand. On the way there, we ran into groups of children, teenagers, and adults munching eagerly on popcorn, ice cream, and pink puffy cotton candy. When we located a concession stand, Mrs. Catherine asked me to pick out a treat. I looked at the short menu and said that I would like a cotton candy. The food vendor must have heard me, because he swiftly swirled my first sticky pink cotton candy around a stick. Kathy asked the vendor for a snow cone. He scooped some crushed ice into a paper cone and poured a syrupy red liquid all over it. While I was trying to figure out the best way to eat my sticky sugary treat, Kathy was slurping hers. Mrs. Catherine also bought an ice cream cone for herself and Michael.

We stood around enjoying our treats before making our way toward the Merry-Go-Round. On the way there, a swarm of carnival barkers tried to coax us into their booths to win one of their incredible prizes. Mrs. Catherine just kept moving. At the Merry-Go-Round, she purchased four tickets and then looked for a wooden horse for Michael. When she found a white stallion with robust teeth, she placed him on the horse's saddled back. By the time the wooden horses began to move up and down to the rhythm of calliope music, Kathy and I were already riding on our white stallions.

After our ride, I told Kathy I was ready for something more exhilarating. She felt the same way, so we asked Mrs. Catherine if we could ride the Tilt-A-Whirl. She agreed and handed us our tickets. We enjoyed that ride so much we asked her if we could do it again. She said yes, but reminded us it was getting late, and we still hadn't played any games.

A young carnival worker clutching a baseball in one hand walked up to us. He insisted that Kathy and I could easily "knock down a set of three bottles and win a prize." The fast-talking young man claimed it was easy as he placed the ball into my small hand. As hard as I tried, I couldn't knock down all of the bottles. I was disappointed because I really wanted to win the wide-eyed Kewpie doll with a curl on the top of her head. What I didn't know was that the bottles were heavy, difficult to topple, and that the third one was strategically placed over the other two making it a Herculean task for a player like me to knock them down.

Kathy and I moved on to a duck booth where small plastic ducks floated in a water-filled container. The carnival worker told us all we had to do was pick up a duck, turn it over, and then give it back to him. He would then check the numbers underneath the ducks against his list of prizes. After the worker inspected our ducks, he handed Kathy and me a flowered paper fan.

From there, we followed Mrs. Catherine to another booth. Once we made our way to the tent inside, the carnival worker pointed to a deep glass bowl filled with tickets. He said that we didn't have to play any games to win one of the oversized stuffed animals suspended from the ceiling and walls of the tent. Kathy pleaded with her mother to purchase tickets and win a big stuffed animal for her and her little brother. Mrs.

Catherine opened her purse and purchased four tickets. She reached into the immense bowl, pulled out four tickets, and handed them to the booth worker. He carefully scrutinized the numbers on the tickets and then walked over to the stuffed animals. The gum-chewing worker reluctantly took down a huge black-and-white furry panda and handed it to Mrs. Catherine.

Besides the panda, Mrs. Catherine won an oversized teddy bear for Michael and a doll for me. Kathy wasn't exaggerating when she said that her mother was lucky. Mrs. Catherine told me that she often won the most sought-after prizes at carnivals, bazaars, and church raffles. She was not only lucky, but kind and generous, bringing "gifts" of happiness to others.

Before we left the carnival grounds, Mrs. Catherine led us to a site where a crowd had gathered around an eight-foot structure with a bell mounted at the very top. A young man with a ducktail haircut and dressed in a black short-sleeved rock and roll shirt was standing in front of the structure. He took a deep breath, picked up the mallet, hoisted it over his right shoulder, and with a powerful thud slammed it down on the board or pivot. The bell did not ring. The men, women, and children standing around the challenger groaned in sympathy.

Immediately, a barker's booming voice invited other males to step up and "test your strength by ringing the bell." A couple of teenagers tried to do it but failed. The frustrated crowd began to disperse when a middle-aged man wearing a Da Vinci blue knit shirt with black stripes stepped up to the pivot. With sheer determination, he walloped that pivot with such force that the bell resoundingly clanged. Everyone cheered. I'll never forget the excitement that an average-looking man created on that warm summer evening. That carnival competition made me wonder if my own father could ring that bell. But then I thought, "Of course, Tato can do anything once he sets his mind to do it."

That evening, I told my father and brother about the carnival. I mentioned the rides, food, games, and colorful workers who made my amusement park visit so memorable. Happily, it would not be my last visit. Mrs. Catherine would invite me to yet another neighborhood carnival where Kathy and I would enjoy another fun-filled evening.

Chapter

27

During the summer months, I had more free time to write in my diary. Whenever I had an opportunity, I would jot down some of my ideas or describe my experiences. My brother knew that I kept a diary locked with a key, but couldn't understand why I wanted to conceal it from him, so he often teased me about finding the key. One time, he actually did find it but luckily never used it to open my diary.

After that incident, I decided to hide the key somewhere where no one would ever think of looking. I scanned the apartment, walked over to a rarely used lamp, took off the large white shade, unscrewed the light bulb, and removed it from the socket. When I slipped my tiny diary key in its place, I immediately heard a crackling sound and saw tiny sparks rapidly traveling around the wires in the room! When I smelled smoke, I really got scared! Had I damaged the wires?

Fortunately, the crackling sound disappeared, and the smell began to dissipate. I felt a sense of relief, but also knew that I was in trouble. Somehow, hiding my diary key didn't seem so important anymore. Now my biggest concern was explaining to my father why I had put my diary key in a place where it didn't belong.

I went back outside to play with my friends but couldn't forget about the incident. I kept thinking about the electrical damage and the consequences of my actions. I was especially concerned since Independence Day was around the corner. I didn't want to lose any privileges such as purchasing fireworks and participating in the traditional activities that the neighborhood kids enjoyed every Fourth of July.

When Tato finally returned from work, I cleared my conscience by telling him what had happened. He didn't seem fazed or upset by what I said. He merely walked over to our living room and checked the lamps, cords, and outlets. To my great relief, he said I hadn't caused any damage. But in the future, I shouldn't put any metal objects that conducted electricity into the socket. That day, I learned not only a practical science lesson about electricity but also realized I could look forward to the Fourth of July with all of its dazzling festivities.

The boys and girls in my neighborhood shopped for fireworks well in advance of the national holiday. They purchased red and roundish firecrackers called cherry bombs. When hurled against the sidewalk, cherry bombs would explode with a loud bang. Sparklers were always a favorite with the youngsters because they were inexpensive and exciting to watch when they were lit. They illuminated the darkness with a shower of sparkling flickers. I always had plenty of sparklers on hand and even saved a couple for my birthday.

On the Fourth of July, Americans showed their patriotism by displaying American flags in their homes, stores, and public places. Family members also enjoyed parades, picnics, and fireworks. They gobbled down hot dogs and hamburgers with all the trimmings and listened to stirring marches by John Phillip Sousa. In the evening, they watched James Cagney cavorting in the movie *Yankee Doodle Dandy*.

America's birthday was usually graced with sunshine and warmth. However, in 1956 the weather was cool, damp, and drizzly. Still, the patriotic spirit of Chicagoans never waned. They took part in various Independence Day celebrations throughout the city. My family participated because we felt blessed to be living in a country that valued freedom so much.

Another summer treat – daily visits from the Good Humor man. Easily recognizable by his white truck and "good guy" uniform, he wore a white and dark colored cap, white jacket, shirt, and trousers. Children would come dashing from all directions whenever the bell on his truck tinkled. Mothers would scramble outside so that their little ones didn't miss out on the Good Humor man's creamy cold treats. I often kept extra change in my pocket to buy myself a Good Humor strawberry bar.

Like the Good Humor man, Karolina and I sold a product that was cold and refreshing. Enterprising females, we opened up a lemonade stand and sold drinks to children and adults who wanted to quench their thirst. Every so often we switched from lemonade to a popular Kool-Aid flavor just to keep our refreshments distinct and unpredictable. For a nickel or a dime, our customers received a tasty, cold pick-me-up that brought smiles to their faces. Sometimes, a generous customer would hand Karolina and me a dollar bill and say, "Keep the change." Receiving a "George Washington" bill was an unexpected bonus that quickly made its way into our glass money holder. We not only made a profit selling ice-cold drinks on hot days but learned that running a successful business took time and effort.

Karolina and I usually worked as a team except once when she and I opened up separate stands. As two seasoned business owners, we were ready to compete for our own customers. Our mothers, Harriet and Mama, made the refreshments for us and even donated the cups. I realized that since I was no longer working with Karolina, I needed my own stand. I asked Tato if he had any old tables that I could borrow. Within a short time, he returned with a small cleaned and polished rectangular one. Meanwhile, Mama squeezed some fresh lemons into a pitcher of water, added sugar to sweeten the tart taste, and then put in some ice cubes for that cool lemony flavor. I thanked Mama as she placed the pitcher on my table and then ran back upstairs to bring down my hand-printed lemonade sign.

Karolina was already outside. She was holding paper cups in one hand and her neatly printed sign in the other. Within minutes, Harriet appeared carrying a small square stand. After placing it on the sidewalk, she went back inside and soon emerged with her large pitcher of lemonade.

When our first female customer arrived, we found ourselves scurrying to compete for her business. In the past, we would have casually approached her. But that day, we were no longer partners.

Karolina and I had to be more aggressive to vie for our customers' business. In our own youthful way, we became business rivals while living the American dream.

It was Saturday, a day when plenty of people were outside. Many adults and children strolled past our lemonade stands while others stopped to purchase a lemonade before walking to the local grocery stores. A few drivers stopped and parked their cars to buy a lemonade. If there were two customers, one would buy a drink from Karolina and the other from me. But if there were three thirsty individuals, they had to choose between Karolina and me.

Our lemonade business was going fairly well until I saw Harriet coming out with a handful of brown bags that still had that "just popped" aroma. Harriet placed them on Karolina's stand and told her that if she needed more to let her know. I was stunned to learn that my friend was going to give away bags of popcorn to her customers without telling me. At that moment, I realized that Karolina had changed the dynamics of how we were doing business. She was also in a better position to lure away my customers. Who would pass up a free bag of popcorn with their drink?

Needless to say, I had to take action. I ran over to the gangway and called Mama. When she stuck her head out the window, I told her that Karolina was giving away fresh popcorn and I needed to do the same. Mama replied that we had some popcorn but not enough for a lot of people. I asked her to make the popcorn and bring it out as quickly as possible.

Mama showed up with about half a dozen bags of popcorn. I knew that meant that Karolina would probably sell more lemonade. Business was brisk and customers kept coming to our stands. Most of them wanted a bag of popcorn with their lemonade. Harriet kept coming out with more popcorn for Karolina, while I ran out of my supply. That day, I realized that I would have to add popcorn or another treat to my future lemonade stands if Karolina and I continued to compete for customers. By the end of the day, we didn't brag about how much we made because we didn't want it to affect our friendship. We continued selling cold drinks during the hot weather and enjoyed every minute of it.

Chapter
28

A couple of weeks before Labor Day, Mama asked Roman to come with her to purchase school supplies. He was finally going into first grade. He never mentioned that fact to any of his playmates who assumed that he was already in school. I was happy to have a traveling companion on my long bus rides to and from school.

When we returned from our shopping expedition, Bobby came up to us, urging my brother and me to "pass the word around" that it was time to prepare for our annual Labor Day balloon fight. The kids on our block had an informal pact to meet on Labor Day for one last balloon fight. The contest allowed us not only to stay cool on a hot day but also helped us get rid of any pent-up frustrations lingering over the summer months. Roman and I bought a bunch of penny balloons at *Poskonka*.

On Labor Day, I prepared for our yearly skirmish by attaching balloons to a faucet's aerator, filling them with cold water, tying them, and then gently placing them in a bucket. Inevitably, a number of balloons popped, spilling water on the kitchen floor. After mopping up, Roman and I picked up our buckets and carried them outside.

Boys and girls were congregating in front of the designated meeting place with stockpiles of water-filled balloons. The watery arsenal was tricky to hold because the balloon's surface was wet, slippery, and stretched out so much that it jiggled like a bowl of Jell-O. Bobby let out an ear-splitting whistle to get everyone's attention. He said that all participants were free to throw water balloons as long as they didn't aim at their target's face or head. As Bobby was about to signal the start of the scrimmage, someone hurled a plump water balloon at him. That unexpected launch triggered a barrage of flying water balloons and a flurry of laughter and screaming. During the battle, I saw several balloons headed in my direction. I lunged to catch at least one but missed and got soaked. One frazzled girl tried to call time out, but nobody listened. Bobby finally blew his loud whistle to stop the hullabaloo. After a brief truce, the friendly battle resumed.

When the supply of water balloons ran out, the wet warriors groaned with disappointment but were thrilled that they had had such a sopping good time! Later that day, Mama brought out her broom and dust pan to sweep up the dozens of scattered pieces of popped rubber balloons.

After Labor Day, I was back to waiting on the street corner for the bus to take me to school. This time, my little brother, Roman, was with me since it was his first day as a first grader. He had never traveled without my parents before, so

I reassured him that I was a seasoned bus rider who knew my way to and from school.

As we headed to our separate classrooms, I reminded Roman to meet me after school by the St. Nicholas School's front door entrance. From there, we would make our way toward Damen Avenue and stop at a small grocery store to buy two bags of potato chips, Fritos, or shoestring potatoes along with two bottles of pop. If the weather was inclement, we would walk to Chicago Avenue, take a short bus trip to Damen Avenue, cross the intersection, and then double-back to the grocery store to buy our snacks before returning to Damen for our bus ride home.

I was happy to see my Ukrainian school friends again: Stephanie, Anna, Lydia, Oksana, Helen, and Vera along with the rest of my classmates. And I was especially pleased to meet my fifth-grade lay teacher, a cheerful, laid-back educator, the complete opposite of my sullen and demanding instructor the previous year. My classmates and I welcomed her with smiles, enthusiasm, and the resolve to do our best school work.

The faculty at my Ukrainian Catholic school not only educated boys and girls in reading, writing, and arithmetic but also encouraged them to participate in extracurricular activities. My brother Roman joined the school band and played the drums. That early training served him well. As a teenager, he played the drums in a band called *Yesterday's Children*. Roman also volunteered to be an altar boy. Altar boys assisted the priests during the solemn celebration of the Ukrainian Byzantine Rite Liturgy. The boys scheduled to serve the earliest liturgies had to wake up at the crack of dawn. Roman was not an early riser, so Mama became his "alarm clock," especially during cold, rainy, or snowy days when crawling out of a cozy bed seemed impossible.

Occasionally, our principal rewarded the pupils for their diligence by allowing them to watch comedies or movies on a large screen in the school's auditorium. One such movie was *The Song of Bernadette*. Directed by Henry King, it starred Jennifer Jones as Saint Bernadette Soubirous, a peasant girl from Lourdes, France, who purportedly had some eighteen visions of the Blessed Virgin Mary from February to July in 1858. Skeptics and non-believers mercilessly interrogated and berated the young Bernadette, inflicting much anguish and suffering. Watching a film about faith, love, and forgiveness enabled the viewers to appreciate the importance of living a virtuous life.

A spectacular biblical epic called *The Ten Commandments* filmed in CinemaScope premiered on October 5, 1956. Directed by Cecil B. DeMille, it starred Charlton Heston, Yul Brynner, Anne Baxter, Yvonne De Carlo, Edward G. Robinson, Debra Paget, and John Derek. Tato heard about the epic film from friends who had highly praised it. They told him it was playing at a theater on the north side of Chicago.

Tato wanted to see the movie. He asked Mama, Roman, and me to go with him. Mama and Roman had made other plans, but I agreed to go since I loved going to the movies.

We took two buses to the Marbro Theater on Madison and Pulaski. After Tato purchased our tickets, we searched the crowded theater for two empty seats. Minutes before the feature started, we found them.

When I heard the narrator's authoritative voice-over, I was immediately transported to the days of the Old Testament. I witnessed baby Moses floating down the Nile River in a basket, the Hebrews' flight from bondage, the parting of the Red Sea, and Yahweh's entrusting Moses with the Ten Commandments. After the almost four-hour movie, Tato commented that the Ten Commandments were just as relevant in 1956 as when Moses first revealed them to the chosen people. He emphasized that a nation that honors God's laws will thrive and be blessed.

That evening, Tato gave Mama and Roman rave reviews of Moses and the extraordinary challenges he overcame to fulfill his destiny. They were so inspired by his recommendation that they asked Tato to take them to the Marbro Theater to see the feature. The following weekend they saw *The Ten Commandments* and loved it just as we had.

Chapter

29

The warm days of early autumn gradually gave way to cooler fall weather as October arrived. Autumn leaves painted with vibrant hues, enormous pumpkins, chewy caramel and crunchy red-candied taffy apples were some of the seasonal sights and treats that prompted boys and girls to start thinking about Halloween. Since westerns were popular, many children chose to dress up as one of their favorite cowboy heroes or heroines. Because department stores did not carry Halloween costumes back then, we searched our closets and toy boxes for hats, boots, vests, holsters, and cap guns. However, if we still needed a mask, we could buy one at a local store. Older siblings created their own costumes by borrowing their parents' old hats, shirts, pants, blouses, dresses, and skirts. Meanwhile, mothers with Singer sewing machines would purchase patterns and fabrics to assemble their youngest children's costumes.

I asked Mama to check her clothes closet for garments that I could borrow. She found a pretty white ruffled blouse with extra long sleeves and a black skirt that kept slipping off my slender waist. Mama told me not to worry because she would alter them. She also found a flaming red sash, white shawl, and a rectangular box. Mama wrapped the sash several times around my waist and draped the shawl over my shoulders. I asked if I could borrow some of her jewelry to accessorize my grown-up attire. She picked out a necklace with strands of red beads, a pair of gold-hooped clip-on earrings, and a gold bracelet that kept slipping off my wrist. Lastly, Mama handed me the rectangular box. I opened it and discovered a burgundy babushka covered with a sprinkling of dainty yellow, brown, and greenish flowers. She placed it on my head, tied it behind my long brunette tresses, and declared that I looked like a real gypsy girl.

Harriet must have helped Karolina with her costume because she looked like the female lead from *Carmen*. Her gypsy attire consisted of a multi-colored headscarf that covered her short wavy hair and a vest that fit nicely over her bouncy skirt and petticoat. Karolina also wore her mother's huge earrings, bracelets, and makeup to complement her look.

While I was putting together my costume, my brother was making plans to go treat-or-treating as a hobo, a vagabond who hitched rides inside boxcars while toting his meager belongings in a red kerchief tied to a short stick. Roman asked Tato if he could borrow an old hat, work shirt, pants, and a red bandanna. Roman also put an apple and a few pieces of penny candies inside a red bandanna and tied it to a short pole. He was ready for trick-or-treating.

On Halloween Day, two gypsy girls carrying shopping

bags with handles went trick-or-treating. By evening, we returned with four bags stuffed with Chiclets, cinnamon candies, Jawbreakers, taffy in orange and black wrappers, Life Savers, Necco wafers, Red Hots, Smarties, Mars, Hershey, and Snicker bars. A candied taffy apple and scattered pennies were at the bottom of our bags.

In the evening, Tato checked my shopping bags and my brother's for sharp objects, hard taffy, and unwrapped candies. After the inspection, the three of us sat around the kitchen table nibbling on our favorite treats while retelling our Halloween adventures.

In the morning, I strolled into the kitchen pantry to retrieve my two shopping bags filled with Halloween candy. When I couldn't find them, I asked Mama if she had put them someplace else. She replied that she hadn't seen any bags of candy.

"How could they suddenly disappear?" I asked.

Mama laughed and said, "Someone who can eat a half-gallon of ice cream probably helped himself to your Halloween candy."

I wondered how Tato could eat so much at one sitting. Mama suggested that I check the pantry shelves because he probably saved some chocolate bars for Roman and me.

In November, 1956, after recuperating from a mild heart attack, President Dwight D. Eisenhower handily won re-election defeating Adlai Stevenson, a senator from Illinois. Millions of Americans including my parents were relieved to learn that President Eisenhower would continue as America's Commander-in-Chief and the leader of the free world. I really liked President Eisenhower but sometimes wondered if he did any work at the White House. Every time I watched the news, he was out on the golf course.

In January of 1957, our parents presented Roman and me with a brand-new, wood-framed American Flyer sled with steel rudders. We couldn't wait to do some advanced sledding with Bobby and the other kids. When Bobby learned about our new Flyer, he said it was time for us to break the sled in and have some fun.

Not long after, I told Mama that Roman and I were going sledding on our new American Flyer. She asked us to dress warmly and wear thick socks to keep our feet dry in the deep snow. When we were ready to leave, I picked up the front of our sled while Roman grabbed the back end. We carried it outside, placed it on the snow-covered sidewalk, and pulled it toward Carp's house. Carp was bundled up from head to toe clearing snow off the front steps of his house. When I said, "Hello," he didn't respond, but when I shouted the greeting, he turned around and waved before returning to his shoveling.

The sun peeked through the clouds as my brother and I crossed the street with our American Flyer and headed toward an empty lot we called the prairie. As we approached the modest snow-covered hills, we heard laughter and shrill voices crying out "Whew," "Look out. Here I come," and "Get out of the way!" Nick was screaming at Bobby for knocking him off his sled, and Bobby was shouting back that it was an accident. Roman couldn't wait to try out our new sled, but I reminded him that I was going to be the first one to use it.

As I glanced around the sparkly white grounds crowded with sleds, I heard a familiar voice shouting, "Come on over." I turned and saw Gerry motioning for me to take his place on the hill. Before he left, I asked him to give me a push on my Flyer. He gave me such a strong shove that I flew down, spun out of control, and landed on an over-sized mound of snow. "Are you all right?" he asked. I said that I was fine as I brushed the dirty snow off my clothing.

As I hiked back up the bumpy hill pulling my sled, out of nowhere, Jimmy showed up with his sled. He asked me if he could take a turn on my hill. Before I could reply, Jimmy plopped down and maneuvered his sled with such force that it veered off and almost collided with Mike, who had just barreled down from an adjoining hill. "Why don't you learn how to control your sled?" Jimmy yelled. "And you should watch where you're heading," replied Mike. The two boys briefly exchanged insults before Mike double-dared Jimmy to a sled race. While the boys were arguing, I walked back to the top of the hill for one more ride when I noticed fresh snowflakes tumbling from the sky. I was so intrigued by the hexagonal ice crystals that I opened my mouth to sample Mother Nature's version of snow cones without the flavored syrup! I was enjoying my new discovery when my brother showed up. He insisted that it was his turn to use the sled. I begrudgingly handed him the Flyer and looked for an empty space that didn't have sledders. I found a small patch of ground that looked like a fluffy oversized white rug. I plopped down, extended my arms and legs, and made a snow angel.

That afternoon, everyone at the prairie had a great time. The sledders even made a pact to meet more often during the winter months. When darkness began to set in, Roman and I left the prairie with our American Flyer. The snow-covered trees, bushes, and sidewalks glistened under the street lights as Roman and I trudged home.

Chapter

30

Tato's desire to be "American" sometimes clashed with his other needs. Blue-collar workers generally placed their thermoses and sandwiches in lunch boxes that they carried to work. Mama always packed Tato's lunch box with a huge sandwich. Unfortunately, it didn't satisfy his hearty appetite, so Tato asked her to pack some additional food. Mama squeezed in items such as large homemade pickles, sauerkraut, and fresh fruits. Before long, his lunch box was broken and had to be replaced. After several more replacements, Mama told Tato that if he wanted meat, potatoes, vegetables, and *rosil* (chicken soup) for lunch then he would have to keep them in small covered pots and transport them in a shopping bag.

Tato knew that carrying small pots of food in a shopping bag was not the American way; nevertheless, he did so because he was a hardworking man who needed to replenish his energy. During lunchtime at the railroad yard, Tato would take out his pots and heat them up. The aromas wafting from those pots attracted his coworkers, who gathered around him with their cold bologna and ham sandwiches. Always generous and thoughtful, Tato often shared his food with them.

My father also had a soft spot for animals. One evening, Tato brought home a cardboard box covered with orange cloths. When he removed them, I screamed, "a *kotyk* (kitten), a real kotyk." There huddled a little gray, black, and white kitten.

Mama heard the commotion and walked over to look at the frightened feline. She asked Tato why he had separated the kitten from its mother. Tato replied that he had found the kitten curled up in a ball. Lost and stray cats sometimes wandered through the railroad yard. I hugged and thanked Tato for bringing the kotyk into our home. He smiled and admitted that he was occasionally tempted to bring home a stray kotyk for me but didn't because Mama didn't want a pet in our apartment. He changed his mind when he heard the helpless kitten's whimpering. Tato found a cardboard box, placed him inside, and carried it to a box car. When his shift was over, he picked up the cardboard box and took it home.

Mama's heart must have softened because she asked Tato to gently lift the whimpering kitten out of the box and place it on a small covered cushion near the kitchen radiator. She heated up some warm diluted milk and fed the baby kitten. From that moment on, Keechka became a member of our family.

While I was in school, Mama kept Keechka active by tossing him items such as colored yarn so that he could run and fetch it with his little paws. Keechka became so accustomed to playing with Mama that every evening he would sit by the kitchen door and wait for her to return from work. When she walked in, he would stand on his little hind legs, run up, and nuzzle up to her. Mama would gently pat him on his furry head and lead him to his cozy bed. On the weekends, I would train my kitten to jump and retrieve objects such as rubber balls. Bright, playful, and affectionate, Keechka relished our games.

My father, a man with a great sense of humor, usually came home from work with a cheerful disposition. But then one Thursday afternoon, he stood in the doorway looking troubled and disheveled. I greeted him, but he seemed lost in thought. The last time I had seen my father looking so forlorn was the day he received a letter from a female relative living in Soviet-occupied Ukraine. Tato had asked her about his father's whereabouts. She related that he had passed away.

Mama asked Tato why he was home from work so early. Was he feeling all right? Tato nodded that "tak," he was fine. A few moments later, he asked Roman and me to leave the room. As I made my way toward the living room, I wondered if my father had lost his job. I was about to make myself comfortable on the couch when Roman asked me to look for a television program we both liked. I found it and turned around in time to see Mama wiping her eyes and Tato trying to console her.

The next day was grey and cloudy, which usually made it difficult to get out of bed. But that morning, I didn't mind because Mama said that Tato had gone to work. I was relieved to hear that he still had a job and that our family's morning schedule was still normal. Later that evening, I noticed that Tato was in a better mood, although he wasn't the same talkative and jovial person I knew and loved. I tried to cheer him up. "Tato, would you like to play a game of checkers with me?" He always enjoyed a challenge and was considered the best checkers player at the refugee camp in Germany.

Tato smiled halfheartedly and replied, "*Ni, Diakuyu*. Perhaps another time, Nastya."

It wasn't until Saturday afternoon that I finally discovered what had caused my parents so much anguish. I listened attentively as Tato told me that the savings and loan had unexpectedly closed. I was familiar with the savings and loan because my brother and I had often accompanied Mama whenever she made deposits there.

Tato was shocked when he first heard about the closing of the savings and loan. He and Mama had been saving their money there for a number of years. Now all their savings were in danger of being lost.

The day of the closure, Tato had asked his supervisor to be excused from work so that he could go to the savings and loan to check on their money. When Tato arrived at the savings and loan, he saw hundreds of frightened and infuriated men and women who had been prevented from entering the building. Tato was determined to get inside even if it meant squeezing and pushing his way through the crowd. During the melee, Tato bumped into his friend Stefan, who had waited in line for several hours. Stefan warned him not to enter the building because it was packed with outraged men and women who had been turned away when they had tried to withdraw money from their accounts. He said that several ladies had even fainted during the altercation.

After the crowd of hardworking customers had morphed into an agitated, screaming, and shoving mob, some twenty policemen arrived to restore order. As panic and anger escalated, the protesters were ordered to leave the premises.

Tato also revealed that the owner of the savings and loan had two other savings and loans uninsured by the Federal government. Mama hesitantly asked Tato if they would ever see their five thousand dollars again. *"Ya ne znayu,"* (I don't know) he reluctantly replied. Despite the disturbing closing of the savings and loan and the realization that their life savings were in jeopardy, my parents never gave up hope. They kept in touch with their fellow depositors, listened to the news, and checked the newspapers for articles about the savings and loan.

The savings and loan debacle had violated Mama and Tato's trust in financial institutions. Nevertheless, they realized they had to find a savings and loan insured by the Federal government and run by honest administrators. Tato consulted some of his trusted friends and identified some good financial choices. Eventually, he and Mama opened an account at a savings institution approved by the FDIC.

Chapter

31

Mama beamed when she looked at the church calendar and noticed that May was quickly approaching. A devoted admirer of the Blessed Virgin Mary, she looked forward to the yearly crowning of the Mother of Jesus at St. Nicholas Ukrainian Church. She wasn't the only one who loved and honored the Mother of God. On May 17, 1846, the bishops of the United States had proclaimed Mary, under the title of her Immaculate Conception, the principal patroness of America. My classmates and I were already rehearsing Marian hymns for the May Crowning. Mama seemed pleased, so I took the opportunity to ask her if she could buy me a new dress for the momentous occasion.

On the day of the May crowning, the St. Nicholas school girls arrived in their loveliest spring dresses while the second graders donned their white communion attire to honor Mary.

The boys looked impeccable in their neatly pressed shirts, dress trousers, sport coats, and ties. The solemn procession commenced when the Sisters signaled the participants to slowly walk toward St. Nicholas Church.

Inside the blossom-filled church, the parents and parishioners waited for the school children to praise and honor Mary with English and Ukrainian hymns such as "On This Day, O Beautiful Mother," "Immaculate Mary," "Serdechna Maty," (Tender-Hearted Mother) and "Radujsia Marije" (Rejoice, Mother Mary). At the culmination of the ceremony, an eighth-grade girl, attended by a court of her peers, placed a crown of woven spring flowers on the veiled head of the statue of Mary: "Oh Mary, We Crown Thee with Blossoms Today. / Queen of the Angels, Queen of the May."

Almost immediately, the joyful and heartfelt words "Ave, Ave, Ave, Maria, Ave, Ave, Ave Maria" resounded throughout the crowded church.

Given our reverence for Mother Mary, it was fitting that every year, on the second Sunday in May, Americans celebrated Mother's Day. Established in 1914 by President Woodrow Wilson, the popular holiday gave Americans an opportunity to tell their mothers how much they loved and respected them. Karolina and I took Mother's Day seriously. We saved our change and dollar bills so that we could purchase our mothers a lovely card, flowers, religious article, or candy. However, that year Karolina and I decided to simply ask our mothers what they wanted for Mother's Day.

The following day, Karolina excitedly told me that her mother, Harriet, needed a dust mop with a long handle. I told her that I had no idea what to get for Mama since she really didn't need anything. Karolina suggested that Mama might also like a dust mop. It was cleverly constructed, made dusting a whole lot easier, could work in difficult-to-reach places, and was easy to store. After mulling over the benefits of owning a dust mop, I decided that Mama needed one.

Karolina and I took a bus to a hardware store where we bought two long-handled dust mops. We doubled back to the bus stop. When the bus arrived, Karolina and I boarded it and looked for two empty seats. We couldn't find any, so we stood in the middle aisle holding our dust mops. In the meantime, a lady clutching a huge bouquet of mixed flowers and her companion, who was carrying a dozen flaming roses, boarded the bus. When they noticed our dust mops, the lady with the roses asked if we had bought them for our mothers. I proudly replied that we had. The lady smiled and smugly commented that her mom loved flowers. Karolina was about to say something back but the bus driver called out our stop. We excused ourselves, got off the bus, and walked home with our mops.

On Monday, Karolina told me that her Mom loved her Mother's Day gift. I wasn't so sure about my Mom. When I had handed the dust mop to her, she smiled and kissed me. She also looked a little puzzled as to how to use the mop so I gave her a demonstration. She thanked me and then placed it in a closet with her other cleaning tools: broom, floor mop, and vacuum cleaner.

When Tato entered the room, I took him aside and asked if Mama really liked her gift. "Of course, she liked it," Tato replied. "She's just never used one before." Tato also mentioned that some ladies liked practical gifts while others preferred personal gifts like flowers. Flowers with vibrant petals and distinctive scents often brightened a lady's day.

And then I recalled that Mama loved the pink-and-white carnation corsage that I had given her the previous year. I could still see her smiling as she kissed and thanked me for the *chudovi* (lovely) flowers before she pinned them on her jacket and proudly wore them to church.

I still wasn't sure. That evening, I asked Mama if she really liked her mop. She left the room and returned with a plastic figurine of the Blessed Mother that I had given her in first grade. Mama said that she appreciated every Mother's Day gift I had ever given her. She kept the dust mop and used it to dust hard-to-reach places for many years.

During the warmer months of the year, my brother and I spent more time outdoors, unlike our Keechka who was no longer a kitten but a frisky cat. He spent most of his time inside our apartment until the day he followed my brother and me down the stairs and out the partially opened front door. I was able to catch him, but when he started squirming and meowing, I knew that I had to let him go. He needed his outdoor freedom just as much as I did. And, because it was his first venture outdoors, I asked Roman to help me keep an eye on Keechka so that he wouldn't get hurt or lost. Our intentions were good, but we still lost track of him.

Luckily, Keechka didn't wander very far from our apartment building. He was standing near the front stairs meowing incessantly. About that same time, Tato walked outside, gingerly made his way toward Keechka, and then picked him up. He gently stroked Keechka's furry back and gradually turned the meowing cat into a purring one as the duo headed back to our apartment for supper. Later that evening, Tato said that I should keep an eye on my pet since he wasn't used to the outdoors.

While I kept an eye on Keechka, Tato continued to make improvements to the apartments. My parents always strived to have the best conditions for their tenants. Tato was especially relieved when the new family who had rented the third-floor rear apartment moved in. It was important to him that all his apartments were occupied mainly because of the loss of his money at the savings and loan.

Tato cheerfully told me that a family of six – two adults and four children – had just moved in. He didn't know their specific ages but said that the couple had an older son, a daughter around my age, another son about Roman's age, and a much younger daughter.

It didn't take long before I met them. Butchy, the oldest, was a tall, brown-haired, adventurous boy. His sister Nancee was a friendly, blond girl who wore glasses. Buddy, the younger brother, had an impish quality, and Rose was the youngest of the four children. She was blond like her older sister and rather quiet. The older children were eager to make friends and find their way around the neighborhood. I invited Nancee to join me and my friends for some of our outdoor activities. She seemed ready and eager to be part of the group. Roman and Buddy soon became friends. Our block was packed with kids of all ages on both sides of the street.

The block also had a few secrets the adults kept. It was a warm and sunny Saturday afternoon. Nancee and I were sitting on the front steps chomping on "Chunky, what a chunk of chocolate" bars, while discussing our summer plans. I even talked about starting a clubhouse for girls when a lady with neatly coiffured waves emerged from Harriet's apartment. Nancee didn't notice, but I knew that it was Saturday, the one day when ladies stepped into Harriet's apartment with straight hair and within an hour or so sashayed out with bouncy waves or curls. Whenever the neighborhood ladies wanted to look fashionably attractive, they would visit Harriet for a wash, set, and style. If they needed haircuts, they would choose either the fashionably short haircut that included some cropping near the ears or lots of waves to keep their longer tresses.

Harriet must have been a pretty good hairdresser because her regulars walked out feeling attractive and confident with every strand of hair in place. They smiled and said, "See you next week." There were many times that I was tempted to compliment Karolina's talented stay-at-home mother but then I remembered that Mama and Tato had asked me never to divulge to Harriet or any of her family members that I knew she was a hairdresser. As I watched the parade of housewives leaving, I kept quiet.

Nancee and I were ready to play a game when Roman returned from playing baseball at Gads Hill. He started chatting with us when Bobby showed up unexpectedly. Ordinarily, he would greet us with his boisterous voice, but that day he just said, "Hi," in a subdued tone. And then without any explanation, he walked over to John's parked Pontiac, stared at it briefly, and then circled it several times.

"Is something bothering you?" I asked him. He finally turned around, walked over to where we were sitting, and started complaining about his confrontation with John the previous day. "My older buddies and I were just sittin' on John's Pontiac, minding our own business and doin' nothin' wrong, when John showed up." Apparently, John didn't like what the boys were doing, so he let Bobby know about it. We never learned what John had said to him. All Bobby did say was that John had overreacted in front of his buddies.

Then Bobby got that "I'm-going-to-show-him-who's-boss" look in his eyes. He confided to us that he was going to let the air out of John's tires. I thought that Bobby was kidding until I saw him look around to check if any adults were in the vicinity. Then he went over to the front of the Pontiac, bent down, and unscrewed the small caps to let the air out of the tires. He walked toward the back and did the same thing.

His revenge was complete. Everyone laughed. Bobby convinced his audience that what they were witnessing was fair payback after John's unfair treatment of him the day before. I laughed along with everyone else, but deep inside I knew what Bobby did was wrong.

The next day, when Nancee and I were sitting outside, we saw John walking toward his Pontiac. He approached the driver's side and started to open the car door when he noticed something was wrong with his front tires. He checked them. They were noticeably deflated. John quickly turned around and made his way to the back of the vehicle to inspect the rear tires. They also were deflated. Since I'm not a tattletale, I just sat there hoping that John wouldn't ask me who had let the air out of his tires. Then he grumbled something under his breath, scratched his head in disbelief, and headed back toward the tavern. He had to inflate all his tires before he could drive anywhere.

I never mentioned the incident to my parents because they wouldn't have approved of Bobby's behavior. The next day, I was glad to see the Pontiac in its usual place with all four tires fully inflated.

A few days later, Debbie arrived on her bicycle. We hadn't seen each other in a while, so the two of us sat down on the top cement step and eagerly chatted for a while. During our conversation, she mentioned the teenage boy she had a crush on. His name was James.

"He's tall with dark hair and really cute! Would you like to meet him sometime?"

"I sure would!" I replied.

The following day, Debbie showed up on her bike just as Nancee and I were about to take our bags of play clothes and makeup to the back porch. "We're going to play dress-up. Do you want to join us?" I asked.

"Sure, but could we play someplace else today?" Debbie asked.

"What other place?" I asked.

"Behind Gads Hill."

"Behind Gads Hill? Everyone spends time in front of or inside Gads Hill but never behind it."

Debbie countered that "the harebrained boys who liked to tease us would never think of looking for us there." Debbie's suggestion seemed absurd; nevertheless, Nancee and I decided to give it a try. I picked up my bag and followed Debbie while she rode her bicycle. Nancee begrudgingly walked beside me holding her bag as the three of us headed toward the back of Gads Hill.

Our new play area was comprised of a flight of stairs, a landing, and a back door. "Is this the secret place that you wanted us to come to?" I asked Debbie. Before she could answer, Nancee plopped down on the lower step, mumbled something about the back porch, and then offered Debbie an outfit that she could wear.

"Thanks," replied Debbie, "but if you don't mind, I'd like to make a quick stop on my bike." Then she hopped on her bike without telling us where she was going. I assumed that she was going home to check in with her strict grandmother.

A short time later, Debbie returned with a good-looking teenaged boy, tall and dark-haired. She quickly slid off her bicycle, kicked the kickstand, and turned to me and Nancee. "This is James." James smiled and said, "Hi, girls." Then he threw his arms around Debbie. The two began kissing like two grown-ups in a romantic movie. Before they could unlock their lips, an elderly grey-haired woman wielding a long stick loomed out of nowhere. She screamed at Debbie. "What are you doing here, young lady?"

Debbie looked horrified as her grandmother waved her stick and headed toward James, ordering him to "get out and stay away from my granddaughter." James was so terrified that he split from the scene quickly, practically tripping over his feet. Debbie's grandmother also marched up to Nancee and me, shook her pointer finger at us, and scolded us for meeting up with teenaged boys in strange places. Fuming, she ordered Debbie to push her bicycle back home while she walked beside her. Debbie was in big trouble, but I still hoped that her grandmother would eventually forgive and let her play with us again. Sadly, that never happened. We never saw her again.

Chapter

32

During the summer months, the staff at Gads Hill Center presented complimentary outdoor movies for local residents. A large movie screen was positioned in front of the building, and by evening a 16mm reel was set up on a stand. When darkness descended, boys and girls along with family members started arriving with chairs and blankets to watch the movie. Occasionally, a staff member had to correct a problem with the reel's mechanism before the start of the film. The first time that I begged Tato to let Roman and me go to an outdoor movie, he said we could but only if he accompanied us. Tato emphasized that children should never attend an evening event without a parent or guardian.

Our first outdoor movie experience was so enjoyable that Tato agreed to accompany my brother and me to every movie night. He even volunteered to carry our chairs. Whenever we arrived, I looked for the best spots to view the feature.

Sometimes, they were already taken by kids who had "dibs" on them. During the feature, I nibbled on M&M's, Tootsie Pops, and other candies. Watching a good movie under the city stars on a warm summer night with family, friends, and neighbors was a memorable community experience.

The staff at Gads Hill also held dances in the middle of the street for teenagers, young adults, and the young at heart. Wooden horses or barriers strategically set around the dance floor protected the dancers from cars and trucks.

When the music started, the enthusiastic young crowd gyrated to the hypnotic beat. Some girls wore attractive blouses with colorful full-circle skirts while others sported pretty short-sleeved cotton circle-skirt dresses with belts or cummerbunds. My friends and I were too young to participate, but we relished watching the young men twirl their dates and step in perfect rhythm to the jitterbug.

When the beat of Frank Yankovich's "Beer Barrel Polka" erupted, spectators swarmed the dance floor along with locals who had been relaxing on their front porches. "Roll out the barrel. We'll have a barrel of fun. Roll out the barrel. We've got the blues on the run. Zing Boom Terrara. Join in a glass of good cheer. Now it's time to roll the barrel. For the gang's all here." As the crowd swelled and became noisier, melodic popular tunes filled the night air.

Some of the popular songs that year included Elvis Presley's "All Shook up" and "(Let Me Be) Your Teddy Bear," Pat Boone's "Love Letters in the Sand," the Everly Brothers' "Bye, Bye, Love," Johnny Mathis's "It's Not For Me to Say," Paul Anka's "Diana," and Nat King Cole's "Unforgettable." When I left, many of the young men and women were still dancing, though some boys just chatted with girls while puffing on cigarettes.

That summer, I joined Mrs. Bennet's drama class performing plays based on fairy tales. A talented instructor, she complemented me on my acting skills, noting that I had a natural ability to bring any fairy-tale character to life.

One afternoon, while reciting my lines, I felt as if someone were staring at me. At first, I thought that it was my imagination until I turned and noticed a really cute boy standing near the door. When I finished reading my lines, I glanced back. He smiled and waved.

When drama class was over, I left the room hoping that the mysterious boy was still in the building. He wasn't. A little disappointed, I headed toward the exit door, opened it, and there he was. He turned toward me and said, "You're really a good actress!"

"Oh, thank you. Are you also taking a class at Gads Hill?"

"No, I'm not. I'm here because my friends said Gads Hill is a popular place to go for all kinds of activities including baseball. By the way, I'm Danny."

As we began chatting, we heard a group of high-spirited baseball players rooting for a batter running the bases. When he reached home plate, everyone cheered, including Danny. That's when I realized that he probably spent a lot of time under the summer sun. His nose was sprinkled with tiny freckles, and his brown hair was interspersed with blond streaks. "Where do you live?" he asked me. "Down the street," I replied as we made our way toward my home.

The following day, I was sitting with Nancee on our front steps when a boy wearing a Cubs hat and holding a baseball bat over his shoulder stopped and said, "Hi." It was Danny again. This time he was with another boy. "This is my buddy, Johnny," he said. I then introduced Nancee to them. Johnny was an attractive, dark-haired boy, taller, and a bit older-looking than Danny. Johnny wore a catcher's mitt on his left hand and tossed a ball into it with his right hand. The two Cubs fans chatted for a while before continuing their trek to Gads Hill. Nancee was impressed with the new boys. "They are not only good-looking but also very nice," she said.

After that first meeting, Danny and Johnny often stopped by to talk. During one of those friendly meetings, they met Bobby, my brother, and some of the other boys. One time when Danny and I were chatting, he pointed to the corner building and confided that he would sometimes go with his dad to the tavern for a pop and a bag of Yo-Ho potato chips. His dad would order a beer for himself and then discuss with the other patrons the Cubs chances for the pennant and the World Series. His dad also spoke highly of John, the tavern owner. He said that John was a good family man, always polite and respectful of anyone who walked into his establishment. Children accompanied by their parents were always welcome. However, he never tolerated inappropriate language or behavior from any patron in the tavern.

One morning, staring out of my bedroom window, I spotted a man I had never seen before. He was carrying a large shaded lamp and walking with a woman who was holding several medium-sized boxes. I wondered if they were visiting someone or making a delivery when I heard Mama calling me for breakfast. "*Ya idu,*" (I'm coming) I replied.

That day, Nancee and I had made plans to go roller-skating on the sidewalk. What we hadn't planned on was skating while the boys were playing pinners. A challenging game, it required quick tossing and catching skills. Players hurled a rubber ball as fast as a "speeding bullet" onto a surface like Tato's

236

building and then caught it in midair after it ricocheted off the building. Ordinarily, I didn't mind when the boys played pinners because sometimes I played too.

However, that day Nancee and I just wanted to skate and not dodge flying balls. We were having fun until we inadvertently skated past Gerry, just as he was expecting his ball to come back to him. Instead, it flew right past him into the street. "Watch where you're skating," he shouted. Gerry ran toward the street, stopped, looked both ways, and was about to retrieve his ball when a stranger picked it up.

"Is this your ball?" he asked.

"Yes, thank you," replied Gerry.

"I noticed that the boys in this neighborhood are usually playing ball," remarked the stranger as he returned the ball to Gerry.

Gerry replied, "Around here, baseball is everyone's favorite sport."

The stranger laughed and recalled that recently he had walked past Gads Hill, when a sixteen-inch softball, or clincher, flew over the fence and narrowly missed hitting him.

Then he extended his hand and said, "My name is Chief Thundercloud. My wife and I just moved into the neighborhood with our little son." Gerry shook the Chief's hand and introduced the other boys as well as Nancee and me. I had watched enough cowboy movies to know that a chief was the leader of his entire tribe.

"Are you a real Indian Chief?" I asked.

Chief Thundercloud proudly nodded and said, "Yes, I am."

I was in awe of our new neighbor. I had never met a real Indian, let alone a chief. Chief Thundercloud didn't look like the chiefs on television. He didn't wear a headdress brimming with feathers. He had a thin build, was of average height, and wore casual clothing. His only distinctive feature was his dark hair. It was longer and neatly pulled back at the nape of the neck.

Just as we were getting acquainted, a thin young woman waved to get the Chief's attention. She had long, dark, braided hair, wore roundish glasses, and a dress embroidered with beads. As soon as the Chief spotted her, he waved back and shouted that he was on his way home. He excused himself and said that his wife was waiting for him. Just then, Bobby asked the Chief if he would like to join the boys in a game of baseball sometime at Gads Hill. Chief Thundercloud readily replied that he would really love to play ball during the day since he worked in the evenings.

That night, I told Tato about our new neighbor. He said that over the years, he had met many interesting people from different countries and backgrounds but never a real Indian chief. Tato looked forward to meeting him.

My brother, Roman, Bobby, and the rest of the boys brought their bats, balls, and gloves to Gads Hill for their first game with Chief Thundercloud. The Chief brought his enthusiasm and knowledge of the game. His suggestions helped the boys improve their catching, hitting, throwing, and running skills. "Play like winners," he told them. The Chief also was friendly to my friends and me. He listened, offered suggestions, and shared ideas about games, good manners, and topics that interested us. Eventually, my father met the Chief and liked him. Tato said that Chief Thundercloud was a good man who took pride in his family, heritage, and neighbors.

Chapter

33

By the time summer arrived, Keechka had matured into an adventurous feline ready to explore the great outdoors. One afternoon, when Mama wasn't watching, he snuck out of the opened kitchen door, dashed down the stairs and through the unlocked front door. Fortunately, he stayed close to home. Sometimes, Tato would find Keechka and bring him back to our apartment. It was during those warm months that Keechka modified his "waiting-for-Mama" routine. Instead of waiting inside our apartment, Keechka would wait outside. Mama would open the front door and lead him upstairs to our second-floor apartment.

One night, Keechka was missing when Mama arrived home from work. A creature of habit, he always waited for her except on rainy days when Tato would pick him up and carry him back to the apartment. When Mama couldn't find Keechka, she went upstairs, grabbed a flashlight from a kitchen drawer, and ran back outside. She checked the sidewalk and then walked to the curb. Mama heard some faint cries. She hesitantly scanned the space between two parked cars. Her worst fear was realized. Keechka was lying on the ground badly injured and meowing in pain. Practically in tears, Mama told him that she would be right back.

She ran back to our apartment to wake up Tato. Within minutes, they ran down the stairs carrying a jug of water, a large towel, and clean rags. Mama led Tato to the spot where poor Keechka lay meowing in pain. Tato could tell that Keechka had sustained some serious injuries. Half of his tail was missing, and one of his legs appeared to be broken. He gently leaned over and picked up Keechka, placed him on a large towel, and carried him upstairs to our apartment. Tato washed Keechka's wounds and poured some iodine on them. Then he wrapped Keechka's tail and legs in gauze. Mama gave Keechka some water and put him in his bed. Still in pain, Keechka whimpered like a little child. In the meantime, Tato went back outside and cleaned up the blood and debris.

It was painful for me to watch my once energetic and playful Keechka trying to drag himself across our kitchen floor. I wanted to hold him, but Mama had asked me not to because of his injuries. Instead, I gently stroked his furry head and told him how much I loved him. He must have understood because he whimpered and nuzzled up to me. Mama tried to make Keechka as comfortable as possible while Tato changed his bandages. I repeatedly asked Tato if Keechka would get better. He replied that we would have to wait and see if his condition improved.

Sadly, that didn't happen. Keechka was in constant pain and continued to limp. Tato realized that Keechka needed more help than he and Mama could give him. He decided to speak with a pet owner, who recommended that Tato take our beloved Keechka to an animal treatment facility. Tato wrapped Keechka in a warm blanket and headed toward the pet facility. In the meantime, I waited anxiously for Tato and my Keechka to come back home. When Tato finally walked in alone, I cried.

Years later, my younger daughter asked my husband and me for a kitten. At first, we had reservations about having a cat in our home. However, after further consideration, we decided it would be all right. Coincidentally, a family whose cat had just delivered a litter of five kittens offered to let us adopt one of them. We accepted their offer and then asked our older daughter to pick one of the kittens. She chose the "runt" of the litter. Meech Keech, as he was known, became like a family member. A smart and tidy kitten, he lived indoors with us. However, during the summer months when he matured into a cat, he occasionally dashed out the front door and hid behind the front bushes. Sometimes when it was dinner time, my son would scoop him up and carry him inside. Other times, when Meech Keech was hungry, he would scamper toward the front door and meow until we let him in. Fortunately, Meech Keech never strayed past our backyard, living contently with us for over twenty years.

Chapter

34

One day, Danny, Johnny, and I were standing outside Gads Hill. Ordinarily, the three of us would be talking and laughing, but that day Johnny was quiet. That surprised me because usually he was outgoing and talkative. Finally, he said he had an important question to ask me.

"Would you like to go to a movie with me?" he asked.

I was startled by his question. Going to a movie with a boy meant going out on a date, and I wasn't old enough to date. I was still in grammar school, unlike my teenaged friend, Patsy. The only other teenager I knew who was old enough to date lived across the hall from me. A kind and thoughtful young lady, Gayle baked the most delicious pies and shared them with my family. Mama often said that Gayle would easily win over any boy's heart with her baking skills.

I liked Johnny. I recalled a recent conversation in which Danny had mentioned that Johnny really liked me. When Johnny repeated his question, I replied, "It is very thoughtful of you to ask me, but I'd like to think about it." Johnny looked disappointed but agreed to wait. I had never gone out on a date before. I wanted to tell Mama about Johnny's invitation, but she was old-fashioned. She would tell me that I was too young to go out with a boy. I decided to share my dilemma with my brother. Roman quickly told me that Mama would never approve of my going to the movies with Johnny. In fact, Roman didn't even want her to know that he knew about the invitation. That evening, I decided not to say anything to either one of my parents. I went to bed in a quandary.

The next day, I still hadn't made a decision. Johnny and Danny were waiting at Gads Hill for my answer. I rode my bike there and when I got off, Johnny asked, "Have you thought about going to the movies with me?"

I nodded and said,"Yes, I'd like to go."

The expression on his face dispelled any awkwardness that may have existed between the three of us. Johnny turned to Danny and gave him that I-told-you-so look. That afternoon, Johnny and I made plans to go to the Illington on Cermak Road. We didn't know what was playing and didn't especially care. Johnny said that he preferred cowboy features, but whatever was playing was okay with him. We agreed to meet the next day and walk to the movie theater.

The following day after lunch, I went outside to meet Johnny. I was a little nervous until I saw the smile on his face. I smiled back. We strolled and chatted all the way to the Illington. In fact, we were having such a good time that I didn't even look at the movie marquee to see what was playing.

It wasn't until we approached the ticket window that I noticed the action-packed western posters. Tato would have approved.

Johnny paid for my ticket and bought me a large box of buttered popcorn with extra butter and a Coke. Later, he bought me a box of Junior Mints at the concession stand. The two of us sat in the middle of the theater, munching and quietly chatting. Occasionally, we glanced at the screen whenever we heard booming voices or gunfire. Luckily, it was a weekday, so there weren't many adults to tell us to stop talking and pay attention. When the feature was over, Johnny walked me home. A real gentleman, he thanked me for coming with him.

A few days later, I ran into Chief Thundercloud and confidentially told him about my movie date with Johnny. He didn't seem surprised. In fact, he said that he knew Johnny was going to ask me to go out with him. Apparently, Johnny had discussed the matter with the Chief before working up the courage to ask me. Chief Thundercloud was pleased that I had said yes. He said that Johnny was "a fine young man."

Not long after, the staff members at Gads Hill Center were preparing for their annual neighborhood carnival. They set up food stands, game booths, and rides for children, including a newly built two-seater automobile with a small motor constructed by my brother, Roman, and his fellow woodworking classmates. Their instructor, Mr. Charles, emphasized that teamwork, good instruction, and skillful use of tools and materials would enable them to create an amazing kid-sized version of the Model T. The boys put together the most popular ride at the carnival.

I was especially excited about the carnival because Mrs. Bennet had asked me to run the fishing booth. She informed me that an instructor, Miss Handler, would speak with me later that day about the fishing booth. Then she pointed to a tent near the fence and asked me to meet her there in about an hour.

I walked toward the tent and almost tripped when I spotted a woman wearing a flaming red babushka, a colorful puffy blouse, and a long dark skirt. When she waved, I did a double take. It was Mrs. Bennet. She had transformed herself from a drama teacher into a fortuneteller!

When I approached her, she said, "I am Madam Cosmina. Welcome to my fortune-telling booth. Would you like me to predict your fortune without charge?"

"Yes, I would," I replied.

Then Mrs. Bennet, or rather Madam Cosmina, asked me to sit on one of two chairs in the sparsely furnished tent. She walked up to a crystal ball in the center of a circular table, closed her eyes, took a deep breath, encircled the crystal ball with her hands as if it were a sacred object, muttered some peculiar words, and drifted off into another dimension. While I sat there in awe, she slowly reopened her eyes and like a clairvoyant predicted that stage acting would be in my future.

After that amazing experience, Madam Cosmina asked me if I could stay for a little while. She needed someone to collect tickets from carnival goers. Before long, I was taking tickets from a long line of curious children, young people, and adults eager to have their fortunes told.

When I was done collecting tickets, I made my way to the fishing booth where Miss Handler greeted me. A friendly lady with curly short hair, she said that Mrs. Bennet had highly recommended me. She also noted that the Gads Hill staff was expecting many boys and girls to visit the popular fishing booth and my responsibility was to collect a ticket from every player before handing him or her a fishing pole.

"The players will cast their fishing poles into a large tank of fish and try to pull one out," she explained.

To demonstrate, Miss Handler picked up a pole, pointed its long dangling rope inside the fish tank, and brought up a fish. She showed me the little magnet on the bottom of the rope that would enable a boy or girl to catch a fish. Miss Handler also cautioned me that if too many fishing lines were in the tank at the same time the magnets might get tangled. She reminded me that once someone caught a fish, I should check underneath it for a number that corresponded to a prize.

That evening, many children visited my booth to fish and win prizes. Most of them shrieked with delight when they caught their first fish. My friend Tommy showed up with two of his friends. When I asked them for tickets, he told me, "Good friends don't need tickets. They can play for free." I replied that Miss Handler had explicitly told me that everyone must have a ticket including friends and family. Eventually, Tommy and his buddies relented. They showed off their fishing skills and impressed the other players. By the end of that carnival night, I was tired but thrilled that I had had the opportunity to run my own booth at the Gads Hill Carnival.

In August, *American Bandstand* appeared for the first time. Hosted by an exuberant announcer named Dick Clark, the show featured teen dancers and singers. Many young viewers dreamed of dancing on *American Bandstand* and meeting one of their idols. Sometimes, while switching channels, I would stop and watch the couples whose hearts and feet moved to the beat of the music.

Summer vacation was quickly winding down. Those "lazy, hazy days" of fun and freedom would soon disappear.

I would really miss the kids and adults who had made it so unforgettable. "*Chas* (time) to think about returning to school," Mama reminded my brother and me. She also suggested that we go to bed on time since we would have to wake up early for school.

I was in sixth grade now. My new teacher warmly welcomed us, outlined our academic goals, and explained how she would help us achieve them throughout the year. I felt good about my new instructor and the upcoming school year.

One night, as I was preparing for bed, loud sirens pierced the air. At first, I didn't pay attention to the wailing because I was used to hearing fire trucks rushing down the streets. However, that night the fire truck's siren was so piercing that I covered my ears and stared out the window. The fire truck was parked right across the street. Fires were frightening, so I called Tato to see the flashing lights and the fire truck. Tato didn't see any smoke or flames, but he agreed to find out what was going on. He told me not to worry and that he would be back shortly. He made his way outside and ran into a neighbor, Steve, standing in front of our building. Steve told Tato that he tried but wasn't able to get any details about the fire. He hoped no one had been hurt.

In the morning, I headed straight toward my window. I didn't see any evidence of the fire that had occurred the previous night. A few weeks later, I spotted Susana, a friendly lady who lived across the street from our apartment building. I asked her if she knew anything about what had happened the night of the fire. Susana said a kitchen fire had ignited in Chief Thundercloud's apartment. She didn't know what had caused it, but the apartment was badly damaged and uninhabitable. I was very saddened to hear that Chief Thundercloud, his wife, and child had to endure such an ordeal but happy that they were safe. Susana also mentioned that they had moved away. I had been wondering why I hadn't seen the Chief lately. A good-natured person, he not only listened to our complaints and problems but took an interest in our activities. He even helped the boys become better ballplayers. Sadly, I never had a chance to say "thank you" or even "good bye."

Chapter

35

On October 4, 1957, the Soviet Union stunned Americans by launching an artificial satellite called *Sputnik I* to orbit the earth. Scientists, television newscasters, newspaper editors, and the American public were debating about how such an incredible event would affect America's standing as a world leader. My parents were dismayed that the Russians and not the Americans were the first to fire that rocket into space. The launching of *Sputnik I* inaugurated the space race between America and the Soviet Union.

On November 3, I had just entered the kitchen when I heard Tato informing Mama that the Russians had launched yet another satellite into space called *Sputnik II*. She couldn't believe it. America was not only the best country in the world but also the strongest and the most innovative. Tato added that the news about *Sputnik II* also increased our government's fear that Soviet missiles could attack America. To make matters worse, the second Russian satellite was much larger and even had a dog named Laika on board. The dog was presumably monitored by special machines to record the effects of space travel on living animals. Tato spoke to me about Laika because he knew that I was concerned about the dog. He forewarned me that the poor animal probably wouldn't survive the trip. Tato was right.

As if the news wasn't alarming enough, on November 26, President Dwight D. Eisenhower suffered a stroke. Fortunately, it was mild and merely impaired his speech for a while. My family was saddened but relieved to hear that the President would continue to serve the country during his recovery.

Everyone in our household was looking forward to the New Year, 1958. We were optimistic that it would be a good year for our family and the country. Our expectations were soon met when on January 31, the United States launched the *Jupiter-C* rocket into space from Cape Canaveral, Florida, along with the first earth satellite called *Explorer I*. President Eisenhower was overjoyed to hear the news while playing his first round of golf since his stroke in November. America had officially entered the space age.

All this exciting political news faded after a time, and the events in our neighborhood became more important. It was a bright sunny day when Nancee and I were playing a popular game that involved identifying the make and model of American automobiles. It was challenging because we had to recognize the cars while they zoomed past us.

Many cars in the 1950s were stylishly long, had huge tailfins, and were two-toned with contrasting colors. In fact, their large size earned them the moniker "road hogs." Some of the vehicles were Chevy Bel-Airs, Buick Centuries, Oldsmobile

Super 88s, Pontiac Bonnevilles, Packer Caribbeans, Ford Thunderbirds, and Studebaker Starlights. Supposedly, the 1957 Chryslers had the most excessive style line. I personally liked a luxury model called the Cadillac. I wanted to add it to my scorecard, but I rarely saw one since most of the motorists in our neighborhood drove more affordable models. The other automobile that I wished to see was the highly publicized Edsel, named after Mr. Edsel Ford. It had a unique shape, top, body, and grill design. However, I never saw anyone driving one in my neighborhood.

About half way through our game, Bobby showed up. He loved automobiles so he didn't mind spending some of his valuable time with girls who knew a little something about them. But when he questioned us about an automobile's engine size, acceleration, speed, and horsepower, we were stumped.

I had just correctly identified a Pontiac Bonneville when a Chevy pulled up in front of Bobby's home. Michael, his teenage brother, stepped out. Bobby waved to him and then told us that he had to leave.

Then Nancee's younger sister, Rose, came running up to us and said it was time for her to come home for supper. I was about to say "after while crocodile" when Nancee asked me to have supper with her. I reminded Nancee that her mother wasn't expecting me. "Mom won't mind," she replied. I remembered Mama's observation that Nancee's mother, Caroline, was a very gracious lady. I decided to accompany Nancee after checking in with Tato.

We made our way to the back porches and then walked up to the third-floor apartment. As we entered, Caroline, a tall, slender, blond-haired woman with glasses, welcomed me as if I were one of her daughters. I glanced around the modest living room that had a sofa, a television, and a couple of chairs.

Nancee's father, Fred, a tall slender man, walked in wearing what looked like a delivery man's uniform. Noticing my quizzical look, Fred proceeded to tell me that he worked for the beautiful *Chez Paree*. He emphasized that it was a well-known nightclub where movie stars like Frank Sinatra performed.

When Caroline announced that supper was ready, Fred headed toward the kitchen table. Butchie, Buddy, and Rose were already sitting in their chairs. Fred sat down next to them, praising his wife's fine meals. When I heard that compliment, I pictured a really tantalizing dish. Whenever I was introduced to a new mouth-watering American food, I would tell Mama about it and then ask her to make it for us.

Caroline walked over to the pots on the stove, took out the contents, and placed them on two separate large plates. Then she placed one of the plates on the table next to her husband. She asked us all to fold our hands as Fred said a prayer of thanksgiving for their food. After a few moments of silence, Fred picked up the dish filled with hot dogs and eagerly stuck his fork into several before passing the rest to us. I stared at the hot dogs, certain that another entree would be coming. Caroline returned with another plate filled with pork and beans. She placed it next to the hot dogs before sitting by her husband. I looked around the table. Everyone was eating and relishing their meal, so I stuck a fork into my hot dog and began to eat it.

Suddenly, I felt a twinge of sadness. It wasn't that there was anything wrong with hot dogs and pork and beans. Mama often made them for us. I just realized that Nancee's family probably couldn't often afford to buy chicken, pork chops, beef, or other meats. That evening when I came home, I told

Chapter 35

Tato that I had had a delicious meal with a wonderful family.

Our neighborhood was also a place where the latest crazes swept through the population of kids. One afternoon, I was pedaling my bicycle around the block when I noticed four girls moving their hips to keep oversized hoops twirling on their waists. I slammed on my brakes and shouted, "Hello!" Just then Judy's oversized plastic hoop started rolling down her legs and plopped on the sidewalk. Undaunted, she picked it up, yelled, "Hello!" and then told me the "hula-hoop" was a birthday gift. I told her that it was the "coolest" gift I had ever seen. She smiled and started twirling it around her waist again. Her playmates joyfully screamed that hula-hooping was so much fun.

The next morning, I told Mama about my latest discovery and how much I would enjoy having a hula-hoop of my own. The next day, we went to Woolworth's. Mama headed toward the aisle displaying kitchen towels and pot holders, while I made my way toward the toys and games. It didn't take me long to spot the brightly-colored hula-hoops. I was so excited I ran back to tell Mama the good news. She had no idea what "who la hoops" were but said she would look at them.

As soon as Mama paid for her purchases, I led her to the hula-hoops aisle. She picked one up, looked at it, and said that a "who la hoop" didn't look like anything she had ever seen before. She checked the price tag and said that it "cost one dollar and ninety-eight cents!" I told her that it was worth every penny and that I would practice whirling it around my waist as many times as I wanted to. I also told her that Karolina, Nancee, and the rest of the girls were talking about getting their own hula-hoops. Mama wouldn't buy me a hula-hoop that day but did promise to return the following week when she had to pick up a few more items. I didn't want to "wait another week," so I decided to speak with Tato.

I described the hula-hoop and told him how much fun I would have playing with a one dollar and ninety-eight cents hula-hoop. He replied that he couldn't understand why I wanted an oversized plastic tube but would give me the cash if Mama approved it.

The next day, walking to the elevated train station, Mama noticed several children twirling hula-hoops around their waists. Their laughter and excitement convinced Mama that children loved playing with hula-hoops. Within a week, I had a bright blue one. A bit wide for my small waist, it repeatedly slid down my legs. But that didn't stop me or my friends from spending countless hours practicing our twirling.

Before long, the hula-hoop frenzy spread to cities all over the country. Millions of children and even some adults were eager to learn a skill that was not only challenging and fun but physically beneficial. Some "hula-hoopers" became so adept at twirling their hula-hoops that they learned to twirl several at the same time. I was content to keep my single hula-hoop twirling around my waist.

Chapter

36

My brother and I had just finished eating our bacon, eggs, and Tang breakfast one morning when Mama suggested that Roman and I go shopping for brand-new winter coats. I told her that it was too warm to go shopping for winter clothing. Mama said that early shopping offered buyers a larger selection of coat styles and colors. With her busy schedule, it was an ideal day to go. Mama said that we would not be going to Marshall Field on State Street.

"What?" I said. "We love shopping at Marshall Field!"

Mama conceded that it was the best store in Chicago, but her friends had suggested another place with good quality clothing at much lower prices. She said that we would have to take two buses instead of the elevated train.

We arrived at a fascinating part of the city: an outdoor market where crowds swarmed around card tables, crates, and even blankets on the ground. Roman and I followed Mama to a large table displaying cooking and baking utensils. While she was examining them, we strolled over to a stand where a vendor was coaxing shoppers to "save money and prepare for Chicago's snowiest months with my sturdy snow shovels." While some men were inspecting the shovels, we heard Mama calling us.

As the three of us wound our way through the noisy market, we saw a man with a booming voice randomly stopping women and escorting them to his trinkets display. One woman with a fancy sunbonnet and pageboy haircut refused to go. As I watched, he grabbed her by the hand and escorted her to a table covered with earrings, necklaces, bracelets, and rings. He picked up a pearl necklace and told her that it would look beautiful on her. Then he suggested she also purchase a pair of matching pearl earrings and a bracelet to "complete her elegant look." When she told the peddler that "I can't afford all three pieces," he offered to "throw in the bracelet" if she purchased the pearl necklace and earrings. While the woman was examining the pearl collection, the peddler rolled up his shirtsleeves and revealed a row of men and women's wrist watches on each arm. "I also have the best time pieces in Chicago, and they make great gifts," he bragged. Such audacity!

We stopped at other stands with items that appealed to us. Mama was delighted when she spotted huge rolls of solid and print cotton fabrics along with boxes of bright and dark-colored spools of thread. A vendor offered her a handful of needles and crocheting yarn at an incredibly low price. Mama declined the offer, so we continued our search for children's coats. We passed by a large stand stacked with casual and dressy footwear for men, women, and children. An elderly gentleman had just tried on a pair of shiny black-laced shoes when he cheerfully asked the vendor if he could lower his price by a few more dollars. The vendor placed his hand on the man's shoulder and said that he was already getting the best price anywhere for his leather shoes. The gentleman appeared disappointed but then reached into his pocket, pulled out some bills, and paid for his new shoes.

A few pushcart vendors were heading in our direction when one of the men enthusiastically gestured to us to come see his merchandise. Mama heard him and ordered us to keep walking. That didn't stop the brazen peddler who continued to follow us until another family crossed his path. We kept moving quickly until we came upon racks of women's frocks flopping outdoors and even on the exterior wall of the store. About five or six young ladies were rummaging through dresses when a vendor wandered out and crowed that he carried the best selection of women's gowns. He claimed that they would cost three times as much at a downtown department store.

Finally, we came across a store sign that advertised a wide selection of clothing. We were greeted by a mustached vendor with a thick head of hair. I told him that we were looking for children's winter coats. He said his store carried women's casual and dressy clothing, such as brightly colored capri pants, pedal pushers, and black cigarette pants. Mama asked me to tell the overly zealous vendor that she was shopping not for herself but for her children. I relayed Mama's message as we headed out the front door. The vendor told us that a store with children's clothing was right down the street.

A middle-aged merchant was outside trying to cajole shoppers to enter his apparel store when he noticed us heading toward the entrance. He greeted us and then motioned to his young assistant to help us. I told the assistant that we were looking for children's winter coats. He said to follow him to the children's rack where he asked me to try some coats on for size. I had a slim frame and must have tried on a dozen coats when Mama asked me to pick one. I chose the red coat with a faux fur black collar. Mama said that it was a good choice but not practical to wear to school every day. She suggested that I take the darker one instead. It had a warmer lining and would look good with a warm scarf and furry winter hat.

Mama also asked the merchant to look for a winter parka for Roman. Before long he and Mama chose a blue parka. It was a little bigger than his current one, but Mama reminded him that it should be bigger so he could wear a warm sweater underneath it. She picked up my coat and Roman's parka and handed them to the young assistant. He carried them to the front counter.

The assistant totaled up the two purchases, turned to Mama, and told her that she was getting a great deal. Mama replied that she wanted a lower price for the coat and parka. The young man was taken aback by her request but nevertheless politely picked up the two items and showed Mama the price tags. She glanced at the price tags and said that the winter clothes were "too much money." Mama insisted that he come down in price, or she wasn't going to purchase them. The befuddled salesman replied that he would love to lower the prices but couldn't mark them down anymore. Mama turned around and told my brother and me that we were leaving. The young man tried to stop us. Near the open doors, Mama repeated that she was going someplace else for a better bargain.

The older merchant, still looking for possible shoppers, noticed that the three of us were leaving without making any purchases. He quickly approached Mama and said, "Please, Mrs., don't go. Let's go back inside the store and talk." He suddenly realized that he was staring at a stubborn woman who wouldn't back down. "Mrs.," he repeated, "you look like a reasonable woman. Please come back inside so we can talk."

Mama must have changed her mind because she turned around and headed back inside the store. Roman and I were right behind her. That merchant escorted Mama to the front counter where he put his young assistant on the spot by asking him to explain why she was leaving the store. The assistant picked up the coat and parka and said that Mama wanted a lower price for the winter clothing. Mama told the merchant in broken English, "Too much, too much money for coat and jacket."

The experienced merchant explained that he did not want her to leave his store empty-handed. He picked up the coat and parka and looked at the price tags. Then he took a pen out of his pocket, scratched out the numbers, and wrote in new ones. He showed them to Mama. She looked at the new prices, shook her head, and said, "No good," as she headed toward the door.

The merchant stopped her a second time and led her back to the counter. He took his pen out again, crossed out the second set of figures, and wrote in revised numbers. He told Mama that she could not get a better price anywhere else and that he was losing money on the sale. Mama looked at the numbers again and said, "Okay, I take coat and jacket."

She opened up her purse and took out her dollar bills and change. The merchant took the money, wrapped up the coat and parka, and handed them to Mama. As she left the store, she said, "Thank you," while he replied, "Mrs., please come back again and bring your husband." Mama left the store happily carrying her purchases while I wondered how a warm and kind lady could morph into such a tough yet clearly successful haggler.

Maxwell Street was an open-air market that intersected with Halsted Street just south of Roosevelt Road. The market offered a vast selection of goods that appealed to many people, particularly the poor and immigrants. Those shoppers came to this market looking for great discounts on everything from produce to clothing to hubcaps. Many people brought their children to give them a taste of a shopping experience that was not only eye-opening but rewarding. On Maxwell Street, men and women could haggle with the mostly Jewish merchants, who let their customers bargain for the lowest prices, something they could not do if they shopped elsewhere.

Visitors and shoppers were often serenaded by Black singers who loved playing and singing the blues. I was already familiar with rock-and-roll, thanks to Elvis Presley, but not with blues music. It was interesting to watch men and women of different ages and races crowd around the musicians and move to the beat of their music. Tipping was common and very much appreciated.

All the shopping made us hungry, so we approached the food stands. Was there anything better than a Chicago-style hot dog with all the trimmings? Mama must have read my mind because she asked the vendor for two Kosher hot dogs. He placed them in soft poppy seed buns and topped them with colorful condiments. Then he reached over to a basket full of hot French fries, took some out, and placed them at the bottom of a bag that quickly turned greasy. French fries and Chicago-style hot dogs were made for each other.

Roman and I weren't the only ones getting something new. Mama tried to convince Tato that her current washing machine could not handle her weekly laundry loads. It was time to replace it with a modern model. Mama emphasized that she had spoken with knowledgeable salespeople who recommended a Maytag washing machine. Tato replied that he appreciated all that she did for her family and then asked, "How much is this new washing machine going to cost me?"

Mama smiled and replied, "The Maytag washing machine will cost about one hundred and fifty dollars."

We all knew "Whatever Mama wants, Mama gets." By the time her birthday rolled around in October, she had a brand new Maytag automatic wringer-washer. Mama's new appliance could wash up to ten pounds of laundry at a time, and the instant-stop wringer protected her from accidents. Her weekly laundry task became more efficient and less arduous.

Chapter

37

On the fourth Thursday of every November, families gathered to give thanks to God and eat turkey with all the trimmings. They also looked forward to the upcoming Christmas shopping season, which traditionally began the Friday after Thanksgiving. But that cheerful anticipation quickly vanished on December 1st when flames engulfed Our Lady of the Angels School, turning it into a raging inferno. Overwhelming grief gripped the city when the fire claimed the lives of ninety-two children and three nuns. Seventy-seven seriously injured survivors endured unspeakable pain and prolonged suffering.

My family as well as millions of people across the country and worldwide were deeply shocked, saddened, and devastated by such an unimaginable tragedy. It was difficult to comprehend why such unbearable anguish would befall innocent boys and girls, their beloved and devoted teachers, and their families. Those horrifying news stories troubled me for quite some time. I just couldn't understand why such a ghastly event had occurred at a school.

As a result of that horrendous fire, all Chicago schools instituted safeguards. Sprinkler systems and fire alarm boxes were installed, and fire drills were routinely conducted throughout the school year. My classmates and I often saw firemen in the building and their fire trucks parked outside St. Nicholas School during our fire drills.

While Americans were preparing for the new year, 1959, a revolution occurred fewer than a hundred miles south of Florida. Fidel Castro and his band of rebels spearheaded a coup against Cuba's unpopular dictator, General Fulgencio Batista. On January 1, Batista fled to the Dominican Republic while Castro seized control of Cuba. The Cuban people jubilantly embraced their new leader, hoping that he would establish a just government and a better way of life. Only later would they discover that Castro was not a liberator but a communist dictator.

On January 3, President Dwight Eisenhower signed a proclamation officially recognizing Alaska as our forty-ninth State. A new flag was prepared with seven stars in seven staggered rows. We were now a nation of forty-nine states – one more state to learn about in school.

Events close to home were also intriguing. One morning, I was startled to see the billboard near my home displaying a mysterious message in bold letters: "I will bring a mountain to Chicago." I wondered who could possibly bring a mountain to any city let alone to Chicago. No one, except maybe a comic book superhero! I began to wonder what the people behind that outlandish message were trying to promote. Tato said that some of his friends and neighbors had found the claim absurd. A few, however, actually believed that it was possible to bring a mountain to Chicago. We both laughed and agreed that the statement was an ingenious device to stir public speculation about its true meaning.

Eventually, everyone would learn that the "mountain" was an advertisement for Folgers mountain-grown coffee. The marketing staff at Folgers were obviously clever, creative, and imaginative. They certainly captured our attention for all that time.

My brother, Roman, could be equally ingenious. He and his friends had been racing their bikes, until one of his friends, Jimmy, shouted that he was ready for a skate crate race. When Roman heard the word "skate crate," he exclaimed, "We should build our own skate crates!" That remark set off a flurry of excitement among the boys. All agreed it was time to show off their mechanical as well as racing skills.

My brother was ready for the challenge. He had helped construct a Model-T at Gads Hill and had worked with Tato on small repair jobs. Roman drew a design of his skate crate and listed all the materials he needed: a 24-count soda crate, wooden foot planks, and roller skates.

While the rest of the boys were planning their skate crates, Roman was searching our back alley for discarded odds and ends. When he couldn't find what he needed, he spoke with our local grocer and convinced that kind businessman to give him a soda crate. Tato donated wooden planks while I gave Roman my old pair of roller skates for wheels. He completed his skate crate by nailing two separate handles on an angle on top of the wooden vehicle so that he could easily maneuver and control it.

Before long, ear-splitting sounds erupted whenever the skate crates charged down the sidewalks as the boys raced. Bystanders and pedestrians had to jump out of the way. Inevitably, a rider's wheel would break off, eliminating him from the race. Despite the problems, the boys continued to maneuver their homemade skate crates while the girls loved watching and making fun of how competitive they were.

Roman was ready for a grander challenge after the success of his skate crate. He jotted down some notations, drew a sketch, and told Tato about his newest vehicle. He also asked for plywood, two-by-fours, tools, and a motor. Tato told Roman that he would give him the plywood and other items but not the motor. He said, "*Synok,* (Son) you need to use your imagination and come up with another idea!"

Roman took Tato's advice. With his own savings, he purchased horseshoe nails at the local hardware store and scoured the back alley for some six-inch wheels and a set of headlights. He found the wheels on an old baby carriage but couldn't find any headlights, so he asked Mama for a couple of empty cans. Roman was ready to begin construction of his motorless car.

Bobby and the rest of the boys were stunned when Roman brought out the Model-G, which coincidentally looked a lot like a soap box. They immediately tested the car's durability by aggressively kicking the wheels. Roman asked for a volunteer to push him down the street while he steered the car with his clothesline side ropes. Bobby, the strongest, quickly volunteered. Huffing and puffing, he pushed the car while Roman zigzagged at a fair clip. Some pedestrians stopped and cheered. After Roman's triumphant ride, every boy wanted a turn in the Model-G. Roman graciously gave everyone a turn.

However, the next day, the junior entrepreneur began charging the boys a penny to steer his Model-G. That motorless car gave Roman a sense of accomplishment and put some extra change in his pocket. It also brought him and his buddies hours of fun and a trove of priceless memories.

The boys and girls in our neighborhood were always looking for places to amuse themselves. One such place was the back alley. Paved with cinder block ash and glass instead of gravel or asphalt, it always posed a risk of bruising and scraping knees and legs. Nevertheless, that never stopped us from playing games like hide-and-seek or climbing into and jumping out of abandoned trucks. While scurrying around the alley, my friends and I also had to endure the loud screeching and grinding sounds from L-trains that roared along the overhead tracks. We simply covered our ears and continued playing. Ear-piercing sounds were just part of the backdrop of living in the city.

The alley had other attractions. Across from Tato's three-flat, several other back porches faced the alleyway. On weekdays, dozens of toddlers and young children were there amusing themselves with toys while their older brothers and sisters played with their friends. After a while, the restless tykes tried to crawl down the porch's stairs while their alarmed mothers hurried to stop them from falling onto the alley's surface.

On the far-left side of the alley was a ravine-like area overgrown with weeds and grass. Stumbled upon by exploring boys, it looked strikingly different from the hilly ravine where we went sledding during the winter. When word spread about the unexplored ground, both boys and girls excitedly agreed that it provided the ideal terrain for modern-day pirates to hunt for buried treasure. I offered to provide the treasure chest, booty, and copies of the map. Everyone gladly accepted my offer, when Bobby unexpectedly threw his arms into the air and shouted, "The boys will be the first to find the buried treasure!" As usual, Bobby turned our game into a boys-versus-girls competition. After several back-and-forth rebuttals, Jimmy yelled, "Quiet! Tomorrow we will discover who will be the first pirate to find the buried treasure."

I rushed home and found a medium-sized metal container with a goldish cover hidden behind a box of Cheerios. In the kitchen drawer, I found a pencil and sheets of paper. I also asked Mama if she had any jewelry that I could use as a prize. Mama replied that *chloptsi* (boys) weren't interested in women's jewelry. While I was thinking of another idea, I remembered that I still needed a shovel, so I dashed down to the basement where Tato kept his tools. I found a small shovel and placed it in my bag.

I wandered around the make-believe island at least a dozen times before finding the perfect hiding place. When I found it, I dug a hole, placed the treasure chest inside, and covered it with a layer of soil. Finally, I painstakingly drew a map that was easy to follow by using words, arrows, and pictures. Afterwards, I went home and took a few swigs of Coke and made copies of the map while the pirates' chorus from *Treasure Island* by Robert Louis Stevenson hummed in my mind. "Yo-ho-ho and a bottle of rum." I took another swig of Coke and sang, "Yo-ho-ho and a bottle of Coke."

My island map depicted the terrain and markers such as small slopes, vegetation, odd-shaped rocks, a misfit tree, and a miniature cave. The modern-day pirates counted their footsteps and followed directions imprinted inside two-crossed swords: north, south, east, and west. The first pirate to reach the spot marked with an X would find the treasure. To make the maps look authentic, I crinkled them and sprinkled droplets of water on them before rubbing them in dirt. The next day, I passed them out to the pirates. They faithfully followed the map's instructions and never complained despite the heat and challenging terrain.

At the top of his lungs, Tommy shouted that he had found the treasure chest hidden in a miniature cave! With his grimy hands, he lifted the treasure chest and held it as if it were his most prized possession. Everyone ran up and surrounded Tommy while he dusted off the treasure chest and opened it. His eyes grew wide, and a dazed expression on his face had everyone asking, "What is it?" Tommy picked up a neatly folded piece of paper with a black skull and crossbones that read: "Congratulations! You're the Winner." "That's it! That's all that I get! Where's my treasure?" he asked me. I told him that his prize was having the satisfaction of being the only pirate who found the well-hidden treasure chest. Bobby intervened and said, "Tommy, you should be proud of yourself. You proved that the boys are the best pirates!" The girls and I immediately surrounded Bobby, Tommy, and the rest of the boys and shouted, "We will win the next challenge."

Tired and disheveled, we pirates never complained as we trudged home. We'd had a great time searching for buried treasure on a make-believe island, just as Long John Silver and his band of pirates did in Walt Disney's movie version of *Treasure Island*.

And speaking of islands, on August 21st, 1959, Americans welcomed a real set of islands, Hawaii, as the fiftieth state in the Union. Hawaii was not only beautiful, but the only state completely comprised of islands. The flag had to be redone again, this time with nine rows. Five rows of six stars alternated with four rows of five stars – adding up to 50 stars.

Chapter

38

The girls needed a place to talk about their own topics such as the latest clothing, make-up, hair styles, jewelry, hobbies, music, movies, and movie stars without the boys teasing them. One summer day, I discovered such a place. Tato said that I could use the shed near his garage but only during daylight hours because it had no electric lights.

The next day, with pen and notebook in hand, I made my way toward my new clubhouse. When I arrived, I opened the slightly creaking door and gazed at the long narrow room. It was well-lit, clean, and large enough to accommodate the girls. We would finally have a space where the boys' annoying wisecracks would not disturb us.

When the weather was hot, the girls and I enjoyed our cool clubhouse. On rainy days, we would run toward it singing, "Rain, rain, go away. Come again some other day," or "It's raining, It's pouring. The old man is snoring. He went to bed like Uncle Ned (from Bozo's circus) and got up in the morning." Occasionally, after a rainfall, a beautiful rainbow dazzled the sky. One afternoon, after a downpour, a diminutive rainbow hovered over the barrel of rainwater near Mama's potted plants.

Unfortunately, it didn't take long for the boys to find out about our clubhouse. They showed up when I was conducting a meeting. I wondered how they had discovered it, since the girls were sworn to secrecy. And then it dawned on me. My brother, Roman, must have listened in on one of my private conversations with Mama or Tato. Eventually, the girls and I got so tired of the uninvited guests, that I put up a sign on the clubhouse door that read: "Only Girls Allowed." Needless to say, it didn't stop the pesky intruders.

During one of our meetings, I spoke about Walt Disney movies and how much fun it would be to put on a production of *Snow White and the Seven Dwarfs*. I would take charge and Nancee would be my assistant. She was very excited about helping me out and appearing in the play. While I was writing the dialogue, she worked on the costumes. When I finished my script, Nancee asked if she could have the role of Snow White. I told her that I had first dibs since I had written the play. But after careful consideration, I gave her the role of Snow White and took on the challenging role of the wicked Queen. I also planned to hold our performances in the circular part of the gangway and charge a small admission fee.

We practiced our lines every day and spent countless hours putting together the costumes. The play needed a prince, so Nancee suggested her older brother, Butchie. A tall and obliging boy, Butchie was flattered to play the part of the handsome prince. When he was informed that he would have to memorize lines, however, Butchie began making excuses why he was too busy to learn them. Several other boys expressed some interest in the play but later confided that they didn't want to learn lines or wear silly costumes. They just wanted to play baseball.

Without a boy to play the prince, Nancee and I knew that we would have to cancel our first performance. At first, we were disappointed but then realized that we had had a lot of fun preparing our kid version of *Snow White and the Seven Dwarfs*. It was a marvelous experience trying something different even if it didn't work out.

While we were eating supper, Tato mentioned that some of his coworkers at the railroad station were raving about an amusement park they had recently visited with their families. Their children loved it so much that they were already making plans to return. Tato was so impressed with his coworkers' recommendation that he decided to take the four of us on an excursion to that park.

I asked Tato to give me a little clue about where this amazing park was located. He said that he couldn't tell me. He wanted it to be a surprise.

On Saturday afternoon, my family and I visited the mysterious park located at Belmont and Western. After exiting the bus, my father, like a Ukrainian pied piper, escorted us through an unfamiliar neighborhood. Eventually, we ran into a group of people strolling and chatting when a young boy suddenly yanked off his Sox cap, pointed toward the sky, and shouted, "It's a parachute, a real parachute!" Everyone cheered as the parachute descended toward the ground. The group even picked up its pace when catching sight of the park's patriotic red, white, and blue arched entranceway adorned with two dome-shaped structures on each side of the arch flanking a smaller one in the middle. After Tato paid the entrance fee (less than a dollar per person), we proceeded toward the sign welcoming us to Riverview Park with its enormous grounds and attractions. I felt as if I had been transported from a working-class Chicago neighborhood into an enormous playground for kids from all walks of life.

We started our Riverview Park adventure at the Pair-O-Chutes, where brave teenagers lined up to take their seats in unopened parachutes and then were lifted to an observation tower where the parachutes opened before descending to the ground. I mentioned that some of the young parachutists probably had butterflies in their stomachs before their parachutes opened. Mama commented that experiencing fears on a daunting ride was natural but could be overcome by facing them. Tato agreed and then offered to take a parachute ride with me. I quickly replied, "*Ni diakuyu.*" (No, thank you)

After observing the parachutists, we made our way toward the mammoth Merry-Go-Round with its handsome, hand-carved prancing horses and four Lover's Chariots complete with wooden Cupids embraced in a kiss. Mama noticed that every horse had remarkable details and distinctive characteristics. She even picked a favorite: a horse with a full mane of forelocks and embellished with exquisitely carved roses. Before long, a swarm of excited parents, children, and the young-at-heart mounted the wooden stallions and waited for the musical chimes to bring them to life. The youngest riders held on tightly to the reins while their horses pranced up and down. Mama asked if I wanted to take a ride on the carousel. I was tempted because I had never seen such extraordinary horses but declined. "*Ni diakuyu.*" I was too old

276

to go on a little kid's ride.

After a tasty meal with plenty of soda pop, we headed toward a concession stand where a young woman was swirling out freshly made pinkish treats. I asked Tato for the fluffy cotton candy while Roman wanted a large box of popcorn. Tato asked for a taste of my cotton candy. Then he pulled off a piece, took a bite, winced, and said that it was too sticky for his fingers and teeth.

The four of us strolled over to the Tunnel of Love where families and especially couples traveled by boat through scenic canals before disappearing into long dark tunnels. Tato suggested that we take a ride in one of the boats, but the line was too long and he didn't feel like waiting.

We strolled until we came upon a crowd of bystanders gawking at screaming riders right before their boat plunged down a gigantic slide and veered into a muddy pond. Water-soaked ladies wiped their attire, face, and coiffures while a park employee approached their boat with a long pole to bring them back to the loading pier. The good-natured but waterlogged riders waved and giggled after their exciting ride on the Shoot-the-Chutes.

Riverview offered visitors incredible rides, concession stands, picnic areas, pavilions, concerts, games, shooting galleries, and sideshows at The Palace of Wonders. Carnival barkers shouted, "Come and see the world's tallest man, sword swallowers, magicians, contortionists," and other bizarre performers. Mama and Tato apparently weren't impressed with the Palace of Wonders, because they urged Roman and me to "keep moving."

I jumped up and down when I discovered the Penny Arcade. "*Proshu* (please) stop! It's the perfect place to win a prize." I led Mama and Tato toward the glass enclosure filled with lots of prizes including a pretty doll with wide eyes and a doleful expression. It appeared as if she was searching for someone to rescue her from the glass enclosure.

I quickly discovered that it wasn't easy to maneuver the claw attached to the crane. But that didn't stop me from trying. On my final attempt, the claw was so close to the doll that I was almost certain that it would pick it up. But it closed without the doll. In the meantime, my brother who had been waiting to take his turn discovered a stuffed animal. He insisted that he would capture it with two attempts. He slowly maneuvered the claw toward his prized puppy and managed to carry it toward the exit drop. And then it slipped out. That day, the crane wasn't going to allow any of its enticing treasures out of the glass enclosure. Mama suggested that we head toward a concession stand and console ourselves with ice cream cones. Roman and I happily accepted her offer.

It was getting late. Tato suggested that I pick a ride that I really wanted to go on. In broken English, he reminded me that the rides I had been considering – the Whip, Flying Scooter, Fire Ball, and some kind of Mouse – were good choices. "The Bobs! I want to ride The Bobs," I explained. "The Bobs?" Roman repeated. That response prompted Mama to ask me where it was located. I told her that it was straight ahead. As we made our way toward The Bobs, a chorus of riders screamed at the top of their lungs. "Are you *pevna* (sure) that you want to go on that ride?" Mama asked. Tato jumped in and asked why I chose what looked like the biggest ride at the park. I told him that Two Ton Baker, a TV personality, often shouted, "Laugh Your Troubles Away," while riding The Bobs at Riverview Park. Now it was my turn. Roman agreed and then begged Mama and Tato to let him ride with me.

The four of us were surprised to find a modest garden growing in front of The Bobs. The colorful summer blossoms in front of the mammoth coaster put Mama's mind at ease. Roman and I waved to our parents before we lined up, handed in our tickets, and took a seat with a thick lap bar. After the roller-coaster worker pulled it down to protect us, I felt a sense of excitement. I turned toward my brother and told him to hold on tight.

The roller coaster made a thumping sound as it started to move over the wooden tracks. At first, the speed seemed normal until the car gained enough traction to climb a hill. That's when I took a deep breath and hoped that the hot dog, cotton candy, and ice cream cone that I had devoured would stay inside my stomach. I put my clammy hands around the bulky lap bar and held on for dear life. When the roller coaster suddenly dipped, I lost control and joined the chorus of screaming riders. And just when I thought it couldn't get any worse, the roller coaster swerved with such force that I closed my eyes and held on tightly. I barely opened my eyes when the roller coaster swerved around a curve, flipping me and the other riders so intensely that all of my nickels and dimes flew out of my pants pocket.

I was shaken but grateful when the ride was finally over. When my lap bar was taken off, I could hardly wait to get off The Bobs. I ran up and embraced my parents when I saw them waving. They asked if I enjoyed riding the roller coaster. I replied that riding The Bobs was the most exhilarating experience and that I could hardly wait to go back!

Tato suggested that before we head home, we visit a unique castle. I was thrilled because I knew that castles were the domains of kings and queens. However, when we arrived, I saw an oversized Arabian Genie with a thin mustache and beard attached to the castle. He wore a turban, a striped shirt, and held a magic lamp. While I was staring at him, his eyes rolled back and forth. I wondered out loud if I were hallucinating after my wild ride on The Bobs. My parents laughed and said that I was not seeing things. Aladdin's eyes did move. Little did I know that those "moving eyes" foreshadowed creepier things to come.

Inside Aladdin's Castle was a labyrinth with countless screen doors. I suddenly realized that I couldn't get out of it! Tato reassured me that he would get us out in no time. After a number of futile attempts, he finally found a door that opened.

We continued our trek through the castle and came upon a room full of oversized mirrors. I laughed when I saw my reflection as a short, roly-poly girl with pudgy feet. I also made silly faces and struck several comical poses while standing in front of a distorting mirror. Roman looked pleased with his elongated head and magnified features. Mama and Tato just chuckled at all the exaggerated caricatures.

I led my family into a room with a tilted floor. "Who walks on tilted floors?" I wondered. Mama asked Roman and me to be very careful. Tato reminded her that we were agile kids who wouldn't have any problems crossing that sloping floor. He was right. We made our way out of that strange room without any mishaps.

We found ourselves in a hall that was so dark, I expected a creepy creature to jump out and scare me. When that didn't happen, I calmed down and resumed walking toward another room. When I entered it, I felt a strange sensation beneath my feet. I looked down and was amazed to see the floor covered with twirling circular discs. They were fascinating but difficult to cross over. After some careful maneuvering, we were able to make it across that spinning floor.

As we moved along, we wandered into a room with an oversized rolling barrel. My brother managed to crawl over it, while I almost lost my balance. Mama wasn't too happy when she had to make her way over the barrel wearing a skirt. The four of us eventually found our way to the outdoor corridor where a woman shrieked loudly as her pretty cotton skirt flew up from a blast of air in the floor. Bursts of laughter followed her as she frantically pushed her skirt down and hastily disappeared. When Mama came near that same crossing place, she held tightly onto her skirt. Tato laughed and so did she.

Twilight began to set in. Glimmering lights were turning on throughout the park as we left Aladdin's Castle. I couldn't stop talking about the fun we had had roaming through its weird halls. Mama and Tato promised we would return to Riverview Park soon.

Chapter

39

In late September, my teacher, a nun with a cheerful disposition, was discussing art supplies with me. Unexpectedly, she mentioned that the Chicago White Sox were going to play the Indians in Cleveland for the American League pennant that evening. I was flabbergasted to hear a nun express interest in baseball. Sister was obviously overjoyed. I didn't have the heart to tell her I was a Cubs fan who lived in a neighborhood where most of the residents cheered for the Cubs. Her enthusiasm won me over.

That evening, I talked to my father about the "Go-Go Sox." I told him that they had a great team with stars such as "Little Louie" Aparicio, Nellie Fox, Ted "Big Klu" Kluszewski, and many other outstanding players. I even tried to convince Tato that the Sox would bring glory to Chicago by winning the pennant. Looking me in the eye, Tato asserted that he didn't like baseball. He preferred soccer, a sport that he and his

European friends had grown up watching and playing. I tried to convince him that baseball was an all-American summer sport and that he would enjoy watching baseball games. I even mentioned that Roman regularly played ball with his friends. Tato said that he was glad that his son enjoyed playing baseball; however, soccer was the only sport for him.

After reciting my Guardian Angel prayer, I went to sleep. Suddenly, piercing sirens jolted me awake. Tato explained that the frightening sounds were air-raid sirens, warning people to hide from danger or attack. "Danger or attack!" I repeated. Tato quickly added that the sirens probably went off by accident. He hinted that if they continued, we would have to take shelter in the basement. He and Mama were familiar with air-raid sirens. They had lived through too many of them in Germany during World War II. Tato asked me if I would like to come to the kitchen for a glass of milk. I nodded gratefully and said I would. Then we heard agitated voices outside my bedroom window. Tato opened the window, stuck his head out, and saw some of our neighbors and tenants congregated outside. He wondered why they were out so late.

While Tato was pouring a glass of milk for me, Roman walked in rubbing his eyes. Tato asked him to go back to bed and not worry about anything. Then he quickly left the room and headed outside. I ran back to my bedroom window to find out what the adults were saying. Unfortunately, I couldn't make out very much since they were all talking at once. I did, however, pick up words like "red alert," "Cold War," and "Khrushchev." I had watched enough news programs to know that the United States and the Soviet Union were locked in a Cold War.

Tato looked upset when he walked into the kitchen.

I asked him if the Soviet Union was attacking us. Most people knew that Mr. Khrushchev had threatened to "bury America." Tato merely replied that the unidentified danger must have passed since there were no more blaring air-raid sirens. I reminded him that Nikita Khrushchev was currently visiting the United States and was probably still angry with President Eisenhower and our government for denying his request to visit Disneyland. Tato cracked a smile and said that he doubted Mr. Khrushchev would take that kind of revenge on his host.

"Go back to bed and get some sleep. I'll stay up to keep you and the tenants safe. I wish your mother was back from work."

The next day headlines in the Chicago newspapers proclaimed that Mayor Richard J. Daley had apologized to the citizens of Chicago for the sirens that had triggered hysteria in the city. Apparently, the Mayor had given his Fire Commissioner, Robert J. Quinn, permission to set off the sirens after the White Sox had won the American League pennant by defeating the Cleveland Indians 4 to 2 at Municipal Stadium. Mayor Richard J. Daley, a loyal White Sox fan, was thrilled that after forty years his team was finally going to the World Series.

Needless to say, Tato was not too happy about Mayor Daley's enthusiasm for the "Go-Go Sox." He and thousands of other people in the city did not appreciate the celebratory air-raid sirens. That incident made Tato more determined than ever to remain a soccer fan!

My father may not have watched baseball games on television, but like most Americans he watched westerns. In 1959, *Bonanza* with its rousing theme song, flaming Ponderosa map, and four fast-moving horsemen captivated television viewers. Lorne Green starred as Ben Cartwright along with his three grown sons: Adam played by Pernell Roberts, Eric or "Hoss" played by Dan Blocker, and Joseph or "Little Joe" played by Michael Landon. The Cartwrights were a western family whom Mama admired because they were good men who looked out for each other and their neighbors. Her two favorites were "Hoss," or "Hossey," as she called him, because of his gentle nature, and "Little Joe," who learned valuable life lessons from his father and brothers.

In October of that year, *The Untouchables* aired. Set during the Prohibition Era, it starred Robert Stack as Eliot Ness, a special FBI agent whose select team of G-men fought corruption and crime. Narrated by Walter Winchell, a well-known reporter, *The Untouchables* became one of Tato's "can't miss" shows because he had listened to Mr. Winchell's radio program and was curious about the Prohibition Era in America.

Movies were also a way to learn about history and valuable lessons about life. One day, our eighth-grade teacher announced that we would be taking a field trip to see an inspirational movie called *Ben-Hur* with Charlton Heston in the lead role. The movie was based on a novel by Lew Wallace, *Ben-Hur: A Tale of the Christ*, originally published on November 12, 1880. My best friend, Stephanie, and I were eager to see the movie and the tall and handsome star who portrayed Ben-Hur on the gigantic screen.

On the day of the trip, our class boarded a bus and headed downtown. When we arrived, we made our way inside the theater to watch the three-and-a-half-hour extravaganza. Charlton Heston played Judah Ben-Hur, a regal Jewish prince and merchant. Stephen Boyd played Messala, a Roman tribune and Ben-Hur's boyhood companion. Messala accused Judah Ben-Hur of a crime he did not commit, condemning him to a life as a galley slave. During Judah's journey to the galleys, a compassionate Jewish prophet offered him a gourd of water to save his life. Ultimately, Judah Ben-Hur returned to Jerusalem as a free man seeking revenge.

Judah Ben-Hur and Messala confronted each other in a spectacular chariot race. Unbeknownst to Judah, the ruthless Messala had attached a pointed saw to one of his wheels to sheer off Ben-Hur's chariot wheels. My classmates and I sat awestruck as Judah and Messala brilliantly maneuvered their speeding chariots during the brutal attacks, strikes, collisions, and turns.

Judah Ben-Hur also underwent a powerful conversion when he saw a condemned man carrying a cross and recognized him as the prophet who had once saved his life. Judah tried to reciprocate by offering him a sip of water, but the Roman soldiers pushed him away. Judah Ben-Hur realized that Jesus of Nazareth was the prophet who had preached love and forgiveness. A rainstorm during the day of the crucifixion washed the blood of Jesus to where Judah's mother and sister were living and cured their leprosy. It was a powerful ending to the movie!

Chapter

40

I was getting older and could take on more responsibility at home. On a cool Saturday afternoon, Mama announced that she and Tato would be leaving shortly for a business meeting. They would return around five o'clock. Mama put me in charge and asked if I would be willing to prepare my first batch of hamburgers for supper. "Tak," I replied. Mama enjoyed eating traditional American hamburgers but often prepared her own version of the popular meat. She called them *schnitzly*. She even made them with a gravy. Tato loved her schnitzly because they were not only *smachni* (delicious) but thicker and juicier than regular burgers. (Over the years, my brother, Roman, would call them "hockey pucks.") I reassured Mama that the burgers would be ready when she returned.

Around four o'clock, I washed, cut-up, and neatly arranged the lettuce, tomatoes, and other condiments on a serving plate before placing them back in the refrigerator. About four-thirty,

I took the meat out of the refrigerator, added some salt and pepper, rolled the ground beef into a ball, and sculpted my first patty. It looked a little lean so I added more ground beef to make it thicker and juicier. When the burger looked "just right," I proceeded to make the other burgers the same size and thickness. I dropped as many as I could into the sizzling pan, crossed my fingers, and hoped that they would come out looking just like Mama's – plump and mouth-watering.

My timing was just right because Mama, Tato, and an unexpected guest showed up at the door about the same time that my hamburgers were ready. Mama introduced me to Pan Boris, a prominent businessman in the Ukrainian community. He smiled and said that I must have made something really tasty because there was such a tantalizing aroma in the room. Mama proudly boasted that I had prepared hamburgers for everyone.

Then she walked over to the stove, picked up the lid on the frying pan, and discovered a number of perfectly-rounded thick hamburgers. She practically shouted with joy. "Nastya, these hamburgers look great!" I was so happy that my first batch had turned out so well. Mama asked our guest to join us for an American-style meal.

Then she strolled over to the kitchen drawer, picked up a knife, headed toward the frying pan, and cut into one of the burgers. It was raw on the inside. She did the same thing to a couple of other burgers. They were raw, too. My enthusiasm suddenly deflated. Mama told me not to worry. She would put the burgers in the oven until they were well-done. I apologized to Pan Boris for the delay. He was very understanding.

While we were eating, Pan Boris complimented Tato on his well-maintained brick building. He said that it looked splendid among the other well-kept brick buildings and single-family homes.

A few weeks later, a man named Pan Andrij paid us a visit on a Saturday afternoon. Apparently, he had been working with Pan Boris, a business man and Realtor. Pan Boris had recommended that Pan Andrij meet with Mama and Tato.

Mama offered Pan Andrij a cup of Sanka and a *kanapka* (Ukrainian sandwich). After several hot cups of coffee and two more *kanapky*, Tato asked Pan Andrij if he would like a tour of our apartment building. Pan Andrij smiled and replied, "*Tak,* I sure would."

The following week, Tato mentioned that Pan Andrij was planning to return for another visit. I wasn't exactly thrilled to hear the news, but then I trusted Tato. He and Mama had always tried to make the right decisions for our family.

Pan Andrij showed up on a late Sunday afternoon looking confident and relaxed. Tato showed him some of the various changes and additions he had made to his building over the years. Pan Andrij also chatted with me, asking about the neighborhood. I told him that I felt very comfortable living on a block with so many friendly children and adult neighbors who looked out for each other.

Tato interrupted our conversation when he mentioned that his tenants paid their rent on the first day of each month. He said that some of them would put a note and cash inside an envelope, seal it, and slip it under our middle kitchen door. Pan Andrij carefully checked the receipt copies and then complimented me on my accuracy and penmanship. "*Duzhe fajno.*" (very nice) He asked me if I would be willing to write out rent receipts for him. "*Tak,*" I politely replied.

Now, I was really confused. Tato was the landlord, yet a

man who didn't even live in our building was asking me to write out rent receipts for him. "What the heck is going on?" I asked myself.

That evening, Pan Andrij went home but promised to return soon. I cross-examined my father just as Joe Friday did to suspects on *Dragnet*. Tato patiently listened to my questions, paused, and then admitted that Pan Andrij had made him a fair offer to buy our apartment building.

I was stunned. The four of us had lived happily in an area populated with wonderful family-oriented people. So why were my parents talking about moving away? Tato said that he and Mama had some reservations about leaving a neighborhood where they knew their neighbors by their first names and had created many fond memories, especially during the summer months when he and Mama worked outdoors or sat outside and socialized. Mama commented that they never feared leaving their front door open.

Not long after, we heard a knock on our door. It was Pan Andrij. My parents spoke with him for a while, so I went to the living room to finish writing in my diary. I had just completed my final entry, when Pan Andrij asked me to write out the tenants' rent receipts without signing Tato's name. And then it dawned on me. My father had agreed to sell his building. Pan Andrij was the new landlord. I wondered where we would be living. My father assured me that Pan Andrij had promised him and Mama that we could continue residing in our apartment until we found a new home.

That weekend, my parents explained why we would be moving. First, they said there comes a time when people must make changes. We had been blessed to live in a safe and familiar neighborhood for several years. Now it was time to move on. Mama, "the heart," and Tato, "the head," of our family agreed that it was time to find another fine area in the city. Tato had accomplished what he had set out to do when we came to this country. He had found a good steady job and had worked diligently throughout the years. He also had a "good head" on his shoulders and a lot of common sense. Once Mama joined the work force, she and Tato were able to save enough money for a down payment on a solid brick apartment building. It needed some maintenance, but that was okay with Tato. He was willing to work and master new skills.

Mama and Tato were honest people who always treated others with respect and dignity. They never lied, overcharged, or took advantage of their tenants. In fact, they felt it was their duty to make sure that every new tenant moved into a clean and repainted apartment. After many years of dedication and toil, their apartment building was in pristine condition and ready for a new owner.

Mama and Tato's dream of purchasing a home near the Ukrainian Catholic Church was finally becoming a reality. Also, the realization that we would no longer have to take two buses during Chicago's harshest weather to get to church or school was indescribable. One year was especially challenging. The school administration had changed the traditional schedule, requiring pupils to start classes in shifts to alleviate overcrowding because of the influx of immigrant children. My classmates and I would start our regular class sessions later than usual, but remain in school until about four o'clock. I was disappointed with the decision but took it in stride. Boys and girls who lived near the school were not as adversely affected by the new schedule because they could walk home during the daylight hours. However, the ones who traveled a greater distance often arrived home in the dark.

During the autumn and winter months, as daylight hours decreased, our journey home at times became rather overcast and dusky. Sometimes clouds rolled in and we got drenched with rain. On those days, my brother and I would take the bus to Damen Avenue, cross the street, and make our way to the Italian restaurant on the corner. We would wait inside the foyer, watching out the window for our bus.

As soon as one of us spotted the bus, we would dash out, hop on it, find seats together, and sometimes nibble on our special treats. Those treats helped take our minds off the fact that twilight was settling in. Sometimes during those trips, we wished we could return to the school's traditional three o'clock dismissal time. Eventually, we got our wish when the school went back to its regular schedule.

I had mixed feelings about moving. My brother and I loved living in an area where so many girls and boys knew how to appreciate each of the four seasons: flying kites in spring, getting sopping wet under fire hydrants during the summer, hauling bags of candy after endless hours of trick-or-treating in the fall, and sledding down coarse prairie hills in the wintertime.

Living near Gads Hill, a social and recreational institution, was an extra blessing. We could check out library books, sign up for enrichment activities, attend plays and outdoor movies, participate in carnivals, and meet friends to go bike riding or play baseball. And what child wouldn't love living near a family-owned candy store where he or she could buy comic books, candies, gum, pop, ice cream, and kites?

But most of all, my brother and I would miss the camaraderie among the neighborhood kids. But now, it was time to say "so long" and as the well-known comedian, Bob Hope, would say, "Thanks for the memories."

After some discussion and reflection, my brother and I acknowledged that maybe Mama and Tato were right. It was time for a change. After all, we had many cherished Ukrainian friends who lived in or near the Ukrainian community. Now we would have the opportunity to see them more often. Also, in September of 1960, I would be entering high school. I was no longer the little immigrant girl who had moved into a new American community. The fifties were racing to an end, and the sixties would soon be upon us, a time of transformation for my family and the entire country.

Mama sensed our apprehension. We were about to sell our apartment building but still live there as tenants. She told me that Tato was actively searching for a building in the Ukrainian community. Mama emphasized that the search might take some time since Tato was looking for property bigger and better than our current building.

It took a while, but ultimately my parents announced that they had found a new home for us! Mama happily predicted that we would enjoy living there. I was glad to hear that I would finally be living near my Ukrainian school and good friends.

During that transition, I realized that I lived in two worlds. As a Ukrainian immigrant, I was comfortable interacting with other Ukrainian boys and girls who spoke Ukrainian, learned English, prayed to the same God, shared the same traditions, and lived by the same morals and values instilled by parents, priests, and nuns. Our parents, on the other hand, had limited English language skills and worked blue-collar jobs. But they continued to express their gratitude to be living in a free country where a positive attitude and hard work would eventually enable them to assimilate into American culture while still maintaining their Ukrainian identity.

Every school day, my Ukrainian friends and I honored the American flag by placing our right hands on our hearts and reciting the "Pledge of Allegiance." We also memorized and sang *The Star-Spangled Banner,* studied American history, the Constitution, presidents, heroes, and culture. We also learned about our Ukrainian heroes, poets, and writers. Often, we gathered in the school auditorium to honor and remember them. At the end of the tributes, we sang our national Ukrainian anthem, *Shche ne vmerla Ukraina* (Ukraine has not yet perished), to show our solidarity with Ukrainians still living under Soviet rule: "Ukraine has not yet perished, nor her glory, nor her freedom." As we stood together singing the powerful lyrics, our eyes and hearts turned toward the horizontal blue and yellow Ukrainian flag: blue representing the sky; yellow, the golden wheat. Across from that banner stood an American flag with its white stars, blue background, and red-and-white stripes: a powerful symbol of freedom and hope for the suffering Ukrainian brethren who believed that someday "fate shall smile once more" while their "enemies will vanish like the dew in the sun." And then they "too shall rule…a free land" of their own.

My American friends were just as important to me as my Ukrainian ones. However, unlike my Ukrainian friends, they were born and raised in the United States and fully embraced American culture. When I first met them, they were somewhat apprehensive about socializing with a displaced kid. But once they got to know me, they recognized that immigrants could be just as personable, fun-loving, and successful as they were. Their parents' trepidation and biases ultimately vanished when they discovered that immigrant families were much like their own American families. They worked hard for a living, sent their children to good schools to get an education, took pride in their property, and respected their neighbors. It took a while, but eventually, my family and I lost our Displaced Persons label and successfully assimilated into American life.

Chapter
41

In the spring of 1960, our family would be moving from our apartment into a new home. Tato said that our new home was located in a very good neighborhood and had a lot of living space. He also mentioned that he would have to do some painting and remodeling on weekends with the help of his friends. Mama eagerly added that we would finally be living near St. Nicholas Catholic Church.

Back at our apartment, my brother and I had just walked into the kitchen. Mama said that Tato had called and informed her that he had finally secured a truck for our move on Saturday morning. Mama was so excited that she immediately began to pack. She started on the china cabinet, which looked stark without the beautiful dishes, cups, and saucers. While I was eating, Mama disappeared into the pantry. A few minutes later, she returned with a handful of jellies, popcorn, Tang, and other nonperishable canned goods. She packed them in a cardboard box. I asked her if I could help, but Mama replied that my job was to finish my homework. She reminded me that I was an eighth grader getting closer to graduation. While I worked on my assignments, Mama carefully folded, wrapped, and placed her window curtains in large containers.

I was excited about the upcoming weekend and didn't have any homework, so I asked Mama if I could say "goodbye" to my friends. She said that I could go out but only for a short time. I still had to finish packing my clothing and other items. As I made my way down the hallway stairs, I thought about the umpteenth times I had either walked or run up those stairs. I opened the front door and glanced across the street. To my surprise, no one was playing outside. I strolled toward Carp's and Bobby's home. Neither was around, nor was my teenaged friend, Patsy. Even Carp's green-thumbed wife wasn't working in her Garden of Babusia. I wanted to tell her that I would miss her gorgeous flowers, bushes, trees, and the little critters who lived there. I also wanted to thank her for her patience over the years. I continued walking past a number of attractive single-family homes whose occupants always greeted me with a smile and kind words.

As I made my way closer to Gads Hill, I spotted boys playing baseball; sadly, I didn't recognize any of them. I wondered why the boys I knew were not playing ball. And then I remembered. Many of them were now teenagers. They were probably participating in high-school activities. I entered the Gads Hill building one more time and headed toward the library. I looked around and found a librarian helping a young girl. Once, I was like that little girl looking for exciting books to read. A gracious librarian had taken me over to the children's section and had introduced me to Nancy Drew mystery books.

It all seemed like such a long time ago. I looked down at my watch. It was getting late. I had promised Mama that I would be back in time to finish packing. I left the building and turned around one last time to gaze at the simple yet extraordinary place where I had spent so much happy time over the years. I looked over at the baseball field and smiled when I heard one of the young boys screaming, "You're out!"

I was still hoping to run into someone I knew as I walked toward my home. I even stopped and surveyed the other side of the street, searching for familiar faces of children playing or riding bicycles. I just couldn't understand why there was so little activity on a block with so many families. As I approached the apartment building that I had called home for many years, I realized that in less than twenty-four hours, I would move into a building I had never seen before.

Tato was removing lamp shades from our two table lamps and wrapping them when I walked into the living room. He said that everything had to be properly packed and sealed for our move in the morning. I told him that I still had to finish packing my clothing, school books, jewelry, diary, and other incidentals. I also mentioned that I hadn't had a chance to say good-bye to any of my friends. Tato replied that I shouldn't feel sad because over the years, I had had many memorable experiences that I shared with them, including ones that weren't so good. Then he gave me a hug and said that it was time for our family to move on with our lives. Tato revealed that over the years, he and Mama had had the good fortune of knowing fine men and women from all walks of life who helped, inspired, or enriched their lives. But Mama and he had avoided people who urged them to compromise their code of ethics.

On the morning of our move, my father and his old friend Pan Petro loaded up a borrowed truck with our furniture and headed to our new home. When they returned, Mama greeted them with coffee and Italian sausage sandwiches. After a hearty lunch, the two men reloaded the empty truck with the remaining furniture and made their second trip to our new home.

A few hours later, our chauffeur and good family friend Pan Ivan arrived in his automobile to drive Mama, Roman, and me to our new residence. In the meantime, Tato and Pan Petro returned to pick up the remaining packed odds and ends in our apartment. I asked Mama if I could run back to my bedroom to take one last look out of my bedroom window. She said that I could, but it had to be quick.

My window was like a looking glass to the outside world as well as a weather gauge. I would wake up alert and energetic on sunny days, linger under the covers on cloudy ones, fall asleep listening to soothing raindrops, and hide under the covers during a blustery storm. And, of course, that gigantic billboard had introduced all sorts of products to the public throughout the years.

I had just taken a final glance at the family-owned grocery store where the friendly owner knew his customers by their first names when Mama walked into my room. She said that it was time for us to leave and head home. It was strange to hear that because for some eight years this had been my home. I walked into the empty living room. I could picture our very first black-and-white, 21-inch television console. I stepped into the kitchen and stared at the window where my brother and I often heard one or more of our friends shouting from the gangway for us to come out and play. Mama also communicated with us by sticking her head out of that window thousands of times to inform us that it was time for us to come home for lunch, supper, or to simply relay a message.

I walked out the kitchen door and down the flight of stairs, grateful that God had blessed our family with more joyous experiences than unhappy ones. I walked out the front door still hoping to see someone I knew. Instead, I saw my mother and brother talking with Pan Ivan, the driver. Tato, already inside the vehicle, motioned for me to come inside. I asked him if he could "*proshu*" (please) give me a few more minutes. Tato didn't look pleased, but replied that he would be waiting.

I sat down on the top stair of the small concrete staircase and recalled that I was only a first grader when we had moved into our apartment. I remembered sitting there to get a better view of our new block and hoping that I would be happy living there. Little did I know that those stairs would become a meeting place for so many boys and girls. They would show up with their bicycles, games, marbles, comic books, hula-hoops, bats, balls, skates, dress-up clothing, Popsicles, and just about anything else that they could think of. My parents, their tenants, and next-door neighbors would also sit on those stairs, chatting endlessly during the spring and summer months.

My reverie was interrupted by Tato's voice calling me again. "Nastya, *teper pora ity* (time to go)." Just then, I noticed a little girl and a young woman heading in my direction. I was about to stand up and make my way down the stairs when the girl smiled at me. I smiled back and wanted to say something to her, but she and the young woman continued walking toward the corner and then disappeared. I headed toward the automobile, got in, and slammed the door shut.

I suddenly realized there was something familiar about that little girl. And then I remembered. She was the same child whom I had seen at the library the other evening. I hoped that her childhood would be as blessed as mine had been. As we drove away, I turned my head and looked one last time at our former home. It was certainly not the most beautiful one on the block. It didn't have a garden or a back yard, but it had a kind of welcoming presence that made children feel comfortable congregating or playing there all those years.

Pan Ivan drove us to the neighborhood where we would be living. He turned onto a boulevard, slowed down, and parked in front of a large imposing beige-brick apartment building with a small garden in front. Tato asked me what I thought of the building. Before I could reply, he pointed out that it was not only bigger on the outside but had more living space on the inside. I liked what I saw. The bricks looked clean and bright under the sun's rays. The building was definitely more attractive than our former one, which had a much darker hue. After I exited the automobile, I took a short stroll. Instead of a back yard, I found back porches.

I didn't realize how large our new apartment building was until Tato took me to the side entrance. He opened the door, showed me the foyer, and then walked up the carpeted stairs that led to the middle and rear apartments. Soon after, Tato and I returned to the front side of the building where Mama and Roman met us. Once again, Tato opened the entrance door that led to a foyer. We made our way up the carpeted stairs to the first floor. Tato took out his keys, opened the apartment door, and gave Roman and me a tour of our new home, which included sizable living and dining rooms.

When I strolled into the kitchen, I could feel fresh air streaming through the kitchen window and see an opened screened door adjacent to a small back porch. Tato asked me if I liked what I saw. I replied that *tak*, I did. There was definitely more open space in our new home, and I really liked the long hallway. Despite all of the improvements, I still felt a bit disheartened. I had hoped that my parents would have purchased a single-family home. I didn't want to dampen their spirits, so I didn't say anything. I just followed them into the spacious sunlit living room with a large white fireplace.

Mama and Tato had finally found a home for us only blocks away from St. Nicholas Church, school, and the Ukrainian Youth organizations SUMA (American Ukrainian Youth Association) and PLAST (Ukrainian Scouting Organization). Roman and I would become active members of SUMA.

Chapter

42

I wondered what the 1960s would hold in store for my family. Would the new decade be stable and prosperous like the 1950s or chaotic and unpredictable? Would the Cold War between the United States and the Soviet Union subside or escalate? Predicting the future is intriguing but impossible.

However, one predictable event occurred every four years: the election of a new president. Popular Republican President Dwight D. Eisenhower's second term was quickly coming to an end. His Vice President, Richard M. Nixon, would become the Republican presidential candidate. On the Democratic side, Senator John Fitzgerald Kennedy was seeking to become the first Irish-American Catholic President. Kennedy was young, good looking, and projected a kind of optimism, enthusiasm, and energy that attracted young people. However, his prospects weren't promising, mostly because many Americans weren't ready for a Catholic president.

Ultimately, Kennedy's chances of winning would improve on September 26, 1960, after the first televised face-to-face Presidential debate. The Catholic Senator projected the image of a robust and confident candidate while his opponent, Vice President Richard M. Nixon, appeared fatigued, haggard, and ill-at-ease. Also, Chicago's Mayor, Richard J. Daley – a Democrat, an Irishman, and a Catholic – would exert his powerful political muscle to help Senator Kennedy become our next president.

When entering high school, I never dreamed that the 1960s would be a watershed era for my peers and the rest of the country. Assassinations, demonstrations, marches, and protests would tear America apart. A controversial war in the jungles of Vietnam would kill thousands of young men drafted to fight in a God-forsaken place. The Vietnam years would be long, excruciating, and nightmarish for parents of draft-age sons. Among the draftees were the sons of many Ukrainian immigrants. They would risk their lives because they felt duty bound to serve a country that had once accepted their parents as refugees.

My own St. Nicholas Ukrainian Catholic Church would become embroiled in a bitter conflict when its leaders decided to change its centuries-old tradition of observing the Julian calendar. That unprecedented decree would shock the parishioners during Sunday Mass anticipating only a thought-provoking homily from the pulpit. Instead, the priest proclaimed that their Ukrainian Catholic Church would henceforth celebrate Christmas, Easter, and other holy days according to the Gregorian calendar. While the priest was speaking, I wondered what my parents were thinking. I couldn't read their minds, but in my heart, I knew that Mama and Tato would never accept the change. That jarring announcement would unleash a firestorm of dissension among Ukrainian Catholics, dividing families and alienating lifelong friends.

The arrival of a group of young, mop-top musicians from England would spark a different kind of revolution. The Beatles would provide a welcome relief for the young people who had witnessed the loss of their country's innocence after the assassination of their President, John F. Kennedy. Dressed in Edwardian suits, Paul McCartney, Ringo Starr, John Lennon, and George Harrison debuted before the American public on the *Ed Sullivan Show* on February 9, 1964. I would be one of the millions who witnessed a female audience screaming hysterically when the Beatles opened their show with *All My Loving*. I would grow to love the Beatles, especially Paul and Ringo, along with the other English rock groups that would invade our country with their long hair and sometimes iconoclastic music.

In 1965, my brother and I would be thunderstruck by Mama's announcement that she was expecting a baby! After our beautiful baby sister's birth, Roman and I would immediately recognize that despite the difference in our ages, our sister, Katyrina, was a special blessing from God. She would not only bring abundant joy to our family but enhance it with her love, intelligence, devotion, and numerous talents. Coincidentally, the month she was born, one of my favorite songs *Turn! Turn! Turn! (To Everything There Is A Season)* recorded by the Byrds and based on *Ecclesiastes* 3:1-8, topped the music charts.

Yes, the 1960s would be turbulent and challenging for America and its citizens, but fortunately toward the end of that decade, an astonishing feat would unite the American people.

On July 21, 1969, they would put away their differences to watch as Neil Armstrong, the commander of the lunar landing craft *Eagle*, stepped onto the surface of the moon and uttered these monumental words: "That's one small step for a man, one giant leap for mankind." His courageous fellow astronaut, Edwin E. Aldrin, Jr., known as "Buzz," would join him twenty minutes later.

These two extraordinary men would spend two hours and eleven minutes exploring the surface of the moon before returning to their spacecraft where pilot Michael Collins, the third courageous crew member, anxiously waited inside the command module to hear from them. America would once again reveal to the world that its people were visionaries who, like their forefathers, embraced tough times, challenges, and impossible dreams. The United States would once again take its place as the strongest and greatest nation in the world.

The astronauts and their spacecraft's successful landing on the moon demonstrated how far America had progressed since the end of World War II. My parents reminded me that we had traveled to the United States as refugees on a troopship that had once transported American soldiers who fought for liberty. Their sacrifices enabled us to proudly watch the moon landing as naturalized American citizens. God Bless America. My Home Sweet Home.

"It is impossible to rightly govern a nation without God and the Bible."
– George Washington

Bibliography

Chicago Daily News. *100 Years Of Famous Front Pages*. Chicago: Chicago Daily News, 1975.

Conquest, Robert. *The Harvest Of Sorrow: Soviet Collectivization and the Terror-Famine.* New York: Oxford University Press, 1986.

Gee, Dereck & Lopez, Ralph. *Laugh Your Troubles Away: The Complete History of Riverview Park Chicago, Illinois.* Livonia, MI: Sharpshooters Productions, Inc., 2000.

Wlodarczyk, Chuck. *Riverview: Gone But Not Forgotten 1904–1967.* Chicago: Riverview Publications, 1977.

Wyman, Mark. *Dps: Europe's Displaced Persons, 1945–1951.* Ithaca and London: Cornell University Press, 1998.

http://www.nasa.gov/mission_pages/apollo/apollo11.html

http:///www.uuarc.org